THE PHILOSOPHY OF RELIGION

A Buddhist Perspective

Arvind Sharma

DELHI
OXFORD UNIVERSITY PRESS
CALCUTTA CHENNAI MUMBAI
1997

Oxford University Press, Great Clarendon Street, Oxford OX2 6DP

Oxford New York
Athens Auckland Bangkok Calcutta
Cape Town Chennai Dar es Salaam Delhi
Florence Hong Kong Istanbul Karachi
Kuala Lumpur Madrid Melbourne Mexico City
Mumbai Nairobi Paris Singapore
Taipei Tokyo Toronto

and associates in

Berlin Ibadan

ISBN 0 19 564272 4

Printed in India at Rekha Printers Pvt. Ltd., New Delhi 110020
and published by Manzar Khan, Oxford University Press
YMCA Library Building, Jai Singh Road, New Delhi 110001

For

His Holiness

THE DALAI LAMA

Preface

The origin of this book lies in the fact that the study of Buddhist philosophy and the philosophy of religion both led me to ask the same question: *is nothing sacred*?

At the time I was teaching at the University of Sydney in Australia, and en route to the annual meeting of the American Academy of Religion, I stopped at Chicago to meet Mary MacDonald, a former student, who had apparently survived that fate in excellent shape. She was now enrolled in a doctoral program at the Chicago Divinity School and invited me for dinner. It was in the course of the conversation over dinner with her and her friends that I heard the word "deconstruction" intellectually for the first time. When I asked what the creature was, the question provoked much merriment and the attempts to answer it even more. After she finished I simply remarked, amidst even more merriment: "It sounds like Buddhism to me."

This book is about the philosophy of religion and not postmodernism as such. However, the remark does help to indicate that the world may be standing at the same multicultural and multireligious crossroads today where India once stood when Buddhism first appeared, sustaining many of the hopes of Hinduism without retaining any of its crucial props, with which it came in close contact at so many points that it ended up holding it in a tight, self-effacing embrace.

I began by saying that in both the philosophy of religion and Buddhism nothing is sacred. Now we must prepare ourselves for an even more sensational disclosure. According to Buddhism *nothing* (read No-Thing) *is*. But there are events. It will be pretentious of me to hope that this book might be welcomed as one but perhaps it might qualify as a *non*-event in a Zen kind of way, as when 'the moon is reflected deep inside the lake but the water shows no sign of penetration.' In a worldview in which plenty is the flip side of empty one would perhaps prefer to be accused of hollowness rather than shallowness.

Contents

Contents

Introduction

WHAT IS PHILOSOPHY OF RELIGION?

In his well-known book, *Philosophy of Religion*, John Hick distinguishes between three usages of the term: (1) as "the philosophical defence of religious convictions", (2) as "continuing the work of 'natural' as distinguished from 'revealed' theology" and preparing the ground for the latter and (3) as *"philosophical thinking about religion"*.[1] Hick goes on to suggest that the first sense is properly called "apologetics" and the second "natural theology", so that the expression "philosophy of religion" should properly mean only the third, namely, *"philosophical thinking about religion"*. Thus understood:

Philosophy of religion, then, is not an organ of religious teaching. Indeed, it need not be undertaken from a religious standpoint at all. The theist, the agnostic, and the person of faith all can and do philosophize about religion. Philosophy of religion is, accordingly, not a branch of theology (meaning by "theology" the systematic formulation of religious beliefs), but a branch of philosophy. It studies the concepts and belief systems of religion as well as the prior phenomena of religious experience and the activities of worship and contemplation on which these belief systems rest and out of which they have arisen.[2]

These remarks, emphasizing the distinction between *theology* and *philosophy*, are obviously germane to the "philosophy of religion" as understood within the Western intellectual tradition[3] which is characterized by this polarization, as also by an even more extended version of it, to wit, the polarization between religion and philosophy.[4] Indeed, if one is to define philosophy of religion as "philosophical thinking about religion" and wishes to move such a discussion in the direction of

Buddhism then it might be worth examining, at the very outset, how the intellectual enterprises denoted by the terms "philosophy" and "religion" are understood in a Buddhist context.

IS BUDDHISM A RELIGION?

The word religion has multiple meanings and its semantic boundary is at least porous if not fluid.[5] If, however, we use the word religion to refer to religions based on revelation such as those of Judaism, Christianity and Islam (as well as some formulations of Hinduism), then the Buddhist approach can be presented in bold relief. Buddhism is opposed to such a conception of religion. Of course it could be argued that the revealed religions are also opposed to each other[6] — but this misses the point, for Buddhism is opposed to revelation *per se* as the valid basis of religion. Thus the Buddha is known to have addressed a people called Kālāmas thus, who were perplexed by the rival truth-claims made by the followers of different doctrines.

Yes, Kālāmas, it is proper that you have doubt, that you have perplexity, for a doubt has arisen in a matter which is doubtful. Now, look you Kālāmas, do not be led by reports, or hearsay. Be not led by the authority of religious texts, not by mere logic or inference, nor by considering appearances, nor by the delight in speculative opinions, nor by seeming possibilities, nor by the idea: "this is our teacher". But, O Kālāmas, when you know for yourselves that certain things are unwholesome (*akusala*), and wrong, and bad, then give them up.... And when you know for yourselves that certain things are wholesome (*kusala*) and good, then accept them and follow them.[7]

Thus, inasmuch as religion is based on dogma, it labours under a serious shortcoming. Nor can it be alleged[8] that in opposing dogma in religion, Buddhism, in its own turn, becomes liable to the same charge by its own criterion on this issue, for "even during the lifetime of the Buddha there was no 'absolute Buddhism', no dogmatical form of truth, but only an indication of the direction by which truth could be realized individually".[9]

It is this feature of Buddhism which has led to the suggestion that it should be called a philosophy or a psychology rather than a religion. Thus Walpola Sri Rahula remarks:

The question has often been asked: Is Buddhism a religion or a philosophy? It does not matter what you call it. Buddhism remains what it is whatever label you may put on it. The label is immaterial. Even the label "Buddhism" which we give to the teaching of the Buddha is of little importance. The name one gives it is inessential.[10]

From a certain point of view, of course, truth is truth whether it be called religion or philosophy, but from the standpoint of the philosophy of religion, which is concerned with the ways in which religions arrive at their truths and the claims they make about it, the point involved does possess some and perhaps even considerable significance, for it then forces one to ask the following question:

IS BUDDHISM A PHILOSOPHY?

If the absence of belief in revelation in Buddhism prevents it from being called a religion, by which we here mean revealed religion, then its reliance on reason is also not so thoroughgoing as to allow us to satisfactorily describe it only as a philosophy, especially if philosophy is defined in terms of its reliance on reason. K.N. Jayatilleke's threefold typology of pre-Buddhist thinkers "according to the stress they laid on a particular way of knowing"[11] is useful in the present context. He distinguishes:

(1) The Traditionalists, who derived their knowledge wholly from a scriptural tradition and interpretations based on it. Prominent in this class were the brahmins who upheld the sacred authority of the Vedas.
(2) The Rationalists, who derived their knowledge from reasoning and speculation without any claims to extrasensory perception. The metaphysicians of the Early Upaniṣads, the Sceptics, the Materialists and most of the Ājīvikas fell into this class.
(3) The "Experimentalists", who depended on direct personal knowledge and experience, including extrasensory perception on the basis of which their theories were founded. Many of the thinkers of the Middle and Late Upaniṣads, some of the Ājīvikas and Jains are classifiable in this group. The Materialists, as empiricists, would also fall under this category if not for the fact that they denied the validity of claims to extrasensory perception.[12]

As the Buddha "identifies himself with members of the third group",[13] it is clear that Buddhism — the religion which he founded — cannot be described merely as a philosophy, no more than it can be described as a religion when the term is associated with revelation.

IS BUDDHISM A PSYCHOLOGY?

If Buddhism may not be characterized either as a religion (when the word religion is used to mean revealed religion) or philosophy (when philosophy is understood to be epistemologically restricted to reason), then may it not properly be called a psychology?

Just as it made *more* sense to describe Buddhism as a philosophy (= rationalism) rather than as a religion (= revealed religion), it makes more sense to describe Buddhism as a psychology rather than as a philosophy. But here again problems arise, especially if we use the word psychology to mean "scientific psychology". Thus: "Psychology can be studied and dealt with in two ways, either for its own sake ... or else for the sake of some definite object". Now in the "former case we get a description of all perceptible and logically deducible ("thinkable") phenomena of the inner life of human beings and their relationship with the outer world",[14] while in the "latter case it is a question of a selection out of the wealth of inner experiences in view of their application in a given direction".[15] Both — psychology as pure science and practical psychology — employ logic, which, in practical psychology "remains within the boundary lines of the given" and serves "for the shaping and arrangement of the material".[16] Thus, as Lama Anagarika Govinda points out:

From this it is clear that in Buddhism psychology and philosophy, as the process of knowing (cognition) and the formulation of the known, are indivisibly bound up with each other. The training of consciousness is the indispensable antecedent condition of higher knowledge, because consciousness is the vessel upon whose capacity depends the *extent* of what is to be received. Knowledge on the other hand is the antecedent condition required for the *selection* of the material to be received, and for the *direction* of the course to be pursued for its mastery. Without the presence of a tradition, in which the experiences and knowledge of former generations are formulated (philosophy), every individual would be compelled to master the entire domain of the psychic, and only a few favoured ones would attain the goal of knowledge. Just as little adequate, however, would be the mere acceptance or intellectual recognition of the results laid down as philosophy to the pioneer truth-seeker. Every individual must himself tread the path of realization, for only the knowledge that is won by experience has living, i.e. life-giving, value. It is here that the philosophy of Buddhism is distinguished from the intellectual philosophies of our times, which exhaust themselves in abstract thinking without exercising any influence on man. The same is the case with the purely scientific systems of psychology, especially when they have lost their spiritual background. It is the close interweaving of philosophy and psychology which protects Buddhism from stagnation.[17]

BUDDHISM AND THE PHILOSOPHY OF RELIGION

It was necessary to introduce these points at the very outset to alert the reader that in Buddhism one is dealing with a religion whose fundamental orientation is rather different from that of, say, the Judeo-Christian religious tradition. Once this fact is recognized and borne in mind it is indeed possible to bring Buddhism in relation to the Western philosophy of religion. But our preceding discussion does indicate that (1) in order to find the material from Buddhism relevant to the Western philosophy of religion we may have to look at segments of Buddhism which Buddhists as such may not regard as of great significance to them in terms of their own system but which may acquire new significance for us when juxtaposed with the Western philosophy of religion and (2) while this makes the task of locating the material relevant for the Western philosophy of religion more difficult and challenging it simultaneously holds the promise that when such material is identified its implication for the Western philosophy of religion is likely, on account of the contrasting natures of the systems, to be more exciting and provocative than might otherwise be the case.

The fundamental distinction between types of religions alluded to in the paragraph above is perhaps best described in terms of a dichotomy developed by Erich Fromm. Erich Fromm distinguishes "between *authoritarian* and *humanistic* religions".[18] The former are characterized by a belief in a higher unseen power who controls human beings and who is entitled to worship, while humanistic religions are centred around human beings and their own strength. According to Fromm "one of the best examples of humanistic religions is early Buddhism".[19] This distinction even goes beyond theistic and non-theistic religions, as some forms of humanistic religions could be theistic but in them "God is a symbol of *man's own powers* which he tries to realize in his life".[20] In this sense this book may be looked upon as a humanistic enterprise in the study of religion. At this point one may be tempted to ask:

WHAT IS RELIGION?

In the study of religion in the West many definitions of religion have been proposed along phenomenological, psychological, sociological, and ethical lines, etc.[21] As early as 1912 forty-eight different definitions of religion had been catalogued by James Leuba.[22] But as John H. Hick has pointed out, the trouble with most definitions of religion is that they are "stipulative: they decide what the term is to mean and impose this in the form of a definition. Perhaps a more realistic view is that the word 'religion' does not have a single correct meaning but that the many different phenomena subsumed under it are related in the way that the philosopher Ludwig Wittgenstein has characterized as family resemblance".[23] The classic illustration here is that of a "game". No one single characteristic seems to be definitive of a game of which cricket, football, tennis, solitaire, etc., and "the games people play" are various forms, yet "all these different kinds of game overlap in character with some other kinds, which in turn overlap in different ways with yet other kinds, so that the whole ramifying collection hangs together in a complex network of similarities and differences which Wittgenstein likened to resemblances and differences appearing within a family".[24]

If the search for a unique definition of religion is abandoned as the equivalent of the search for the Holy Grail in religious studies and a family resemblance approach to the meaning of religion is adopted, then it becomes possible to treat Buddhism as a religion, for it "retains those fundamentals ...

which philosophy could never have found out for itself".[25] As Edward J. Thomas explains:

Buddhism, in accordance with this distinction, began by being a religion. It is needless to dispute about the term religion. If it necessarily implies an intelligent and almighty entity as the ultimate explanation and the ultimate goal of things, then Buddhism is not a religion. We may prefer to say that the fundamental dogmas of Buddhism differ so much from the dogmas of religious systems that they cannot be brought under one definition. But Buddhism in one respect was at first rather on the side of religion than of philosophy in that it started with fundamental convictions, which only became a philosophical system when they had to be made consistent and defended against rival laws.[26]

THE SOTERIOLOGICAL CONTEXT OF WORLD RELIGIONS

John H. Hick argues that one feature which "is extremely widespread, even though it is not universal"[27] among the religions is the idea of salvation and liberation. Hick feels that this is not as marked a feature of "primitive religions as of the so-called world religions". This point could be debated[28] but there is little doubt that the major world religions,

all the great developed world faiths have a soteriological (from the Greek *soteria*, salvation) structure. They offer a transition from a radically unsatisfactory state to a limitlessly better one. They each speak in their different ways of the wrong or distorted or deluded character of our present human existence in its ordinary, unchanged condition. It is a 'fallen' life, lived in alienation from God; or it is caught in the world-illusion of *maya*; or it is pervaded throughout by *dukkha* (radical unsatisfactoriness). They also proclaim, as the basis for their gospel, that the Ultimate, the Real, the Divine, with which our present existence is out of joint, is good, or gracious, or otherwise to be sought and responded to; the ultimately real is also the ultimately valuable. Completing the soteriological structure, they each offer their own way to the Ultimate — through faith in response to divine grace; or through total self-giving to God; or through the spiritual discipline and maturing which leads to enlightenment and liberation.[29]

The point to note here is that although all the world faiths possess a soteriological content, Buddhism is characterized by it *par excellence.* Its soteriological structure constitutes, in its own perception, its very core. That is what it is all about — everything in it, including the *tradition itself* is ancillary to it — something to be discarded like a raft once the shore has been reached.[30]

CHAPTER 1

The Concept of God

MONOTHEISM

The Judaic-Christian concept of God is monotheistic. It consists of

the belief that there is but one supreme Being, who is personal and moral and who seeks a total and unqualified response from human creatures. This idea first came to fully effective human consciousness in the words, 'Hear, O Israel: The Lord our God is one Lord; and you shall love the Lord your God with all your heart, and with all your soul, and with all your might.' As these historic words indicate, the Hebraic understanding of God, continued in Christianity, is emphatically monotheistic.[1]

The same spirit finds expression in the description of God as a "jealous God",

And God spake all these words, saying,
[2] I am the Lord thy God, which have brought thee out of the land of Egypt, out of the house of bondage.
[3] Thou shalt have no other gods before me.
[4] Thou shalt not make unto thee any graven image, or any likeness of any thing that is in heaven above, or that is in the earth beneath, or that is in the water under the earth:
[5] Thou shalt not bow down thyself to them, nor serve them: for I the Lord thy God am a jealous God, visiting the iniquity of the fathers upon the children unto the third and fourth generation of them that hate me.[2]

The key point to bear in mind in this context is that "monotheism has never appealed to the Buddhist mind".[3] Several important consequences flow from this temper within Buddhism. One consequence of monotheism is what H. Richard Niebuhr called "the sanctification of all things". As John H. Hick explains:

It is a corollary of the prophets' teaching concerning the lordship of God over all of human life that there is no religious sphere set apart from the secular world but that the whole sweep of a person's existence stands in relation to God. Thus religion is secularized, or — putting it the other way about — ordinary life takes on a religious meaning.[4]

This does not quite happen in Buddhism in the same way. The point is perhaps best clarified with the help of a statement by William James that "philosophic theism has always shown a tendency ... to consider the world as one unit of absolute fact; and this has been at variance with popular or practical theism, which latter has ever been more or less frankly pluralistic, not to say polytheistic".[5] In the light of this statement one might say that while Christianity has been philosophically monotheistic and has at the practical level ever tried to control or at worst condone practical "polytheism", Buddhism has been free from any such tension:

The Buddhists would find no objection whatsoever in the cult of many Gods because the idea of a jealous God is quite alien to them; and also because they are imbued with the conviction that everyone's intellectual insight is very limited, so that it is very difficult for us to know when we are right, but practically impossible to be sure that someone else is wrong. Like the Catholics, the Buddhists believe that a Faith can be kept alive only if it can be adapted to the mental habits of the average person. In consequence, we find that, in the earlier Scriptures, the deities of Brahmanism are taken for granted and that, later on, the Buddhists adopted the local Gods of any district to which they came.[6]

This difference in values has led to a natural difference in the evaluation of "practical polytheism" by scholars whose main affiliation lies with one tradition or the other. For instance, John H. Hick notices the discontinuity between pure monotheism and practical polytheism. He writes:

The difficulty involved in maintaining such a faith in practice, even within a culture that has been permeated for centuries by monotheistic teaching, is evidenced by the polytheistic and henotheistic elements in our own life. A religiously sensitive visitor from another planet would doubtless report that we divide our energies in the service of many deities — the god of money, of a business corporation, of success, and of power, the status gods, and (for a brief period once a week) the God of Judaic-Christian faith. When we rise above this practical polytheism, it is generally into a henotheistic devotion to the nation, or to the American way of life, in order to enjoy our solidarity with an in-group against the out-groups. In this combination of elements there is no continuity with the pure monotheism of the prophets and of the New Testament, with its vivid awareness of God as the Lord of history whose gracious purpose embracing all life renders needless the frantic struggle to amass wealth, power, and prestige at the expense of others.[7]

Edward Conze, the famous British scholar of Buddhism, notes the same facts more casually and non-judgementally when he comments:

In order to appreciate the Buddhists' toleration of Polytheism, we must first of all understand that Polytheism is very much alive even among us. But where formerly Athene, Baal, Astarte, Isis, Sarasvati, Kwan Yin, etc., excited the popular imagination, it is nowadays inflamed by such words as *Democracy, Progress, Civilisation, Equality, Liberty, Reason, Science*, etc. A multitude of personal beings has given way to a multitude of abstract nouns. In Europe the turning point came when the French deposed the Virgin Mary and transferred their affections to the Goddess of Reason. The reason for this change is not far to seek. Personal deities grow on the soil of a rural culture in which the majority of the population are illiterate, while abstract nouns find favour with the literate populations of modern towns. Medieval men went to war for Jesus Christ, Saint George and San Jose. Modern crusades are in aid of such abstractions as Christianity, The Christian Way of Life, Democracy and The Rights of Man.[8]

It must be pointed out here that there is in Buddhism a philosophically explicit acceptance of polytheism which matches its explicit denial in the Judaic-Christian tradition. The following dialogue between the Buddha and a Brahmin youth, Saṅgārava by name, is not without interest.

SAṄGĀRAVA: Tell me, Gotama, are there gods (*devā*)?
BUDDHA: I know on good grounds (*thānaso*) that there are gods.
SAṄGĀRAVA: Why do you say when asked "whether there are gods" that you know on good grounds that there are gods. Does this not imply that your statement is utterly false?
BUDDHA: When one is questioned as to whether there are gods,

whether one replies that "there are gods" or that "one knows on good grounds that there are gods", then surely the deduction to be made by an intelligent person is indubitable, namely that there are gods.

SAṄGĀRAVA: Then, why did not the venerable Gotama plainly say so from the very start?

BUDDHA: Because it is commonly taken for granted in the world that there are gods.[9]

Thus with respect to belief in gods there is a clear divergence between Judaism and Christianity on the one hand and Buddhism on the other. However, curiously enough, Buddhism seems to allow for the existence of "prophets", albeit indirectly. It should be noted carefully in this context that the

Buddhist criticism of revelation does not imply that revelations are impossible. According to the Buddhist conception of things, it is possible for beings more developed than us to exist in the cosmos and communicate their views about the nature and destiny of man in the universe through human beings. All that is said is that the fact that something is deemed to be a revelation is no criterion of its truth and revelation, therefore, cannot be considered an independent and valid means of knowledge....[10]

According to

Buddhist conceptions, revelations may come from different grades of higher beings with varying degrees of goodness and intelligence. They cannot all be true. This does not mean that they are all necessarily false. For they may contain aspects of truth although we cannot say what these are by merely giving ear to them. This is why Buddhism classifies religions based on revelation as unsatisfactory though not necessarily false.[11]

INFINITE, SELF-EXISTENT

If no God is accepted in Buddhism, it is not surprising that God's infinity will be out of the question. The result is that while some Upaniṣads hold that "the world is enveloped by God" (*īśā-vāsyam idam sarvaṃ*), Buddhism held that "the world was without a refuge and without God (*attāṇo loko anabhissaro*)".[12]

It is an interesting fact that qualities attributed to God in the monotheistic traditions are attributed, as it were, to the universe in Buddhism. The early Buddhist texts tend to leave the question of whether the world is finite or infinite unanswered, as it was considered one of the questions not conducive to salvation and hence to be left unexplained. The later commentarial tradition of around the fifth century, however, pronounces the Buddhist astronomical counterpart of galaxies as infinite in number.

This is certainly going beyond the standpoint of the early Buddhist texts, which is uncommitted on the question of the origin or extent of the universe. While the later traditions of the Sarvāstivāda and Theravāda suggest that the number of galaxies or world-systems is infinite in extent, the Mahāyāna texts hold that the universe is infinite in time, stating that 'the universe is without beginning or end' (*anavarāgra*).[13]

The question of *self*-existence is more problematical. It is one of the cardinal Buddhist principles that there is no "self", both in the sense of there being no permanent substratum underlying the individual such as a soul and in the sense of there being any permanent substratum underlying the universe. The former view was advanced in early Buddhism and is known as the doctrine of *pudgala-śūnyatā*. The term literally means "emptiness of the person" and connotes the absence of any permanent "self" underlying the individual. It was further developed into the doctrine of *dharma-śūnyatā*. The term literally means "emptiness of *Dharmas*". The word *dharma* here does not possess its usual connotation of normative behaviour or doctrine but the more technical Buddhist sense of "element of being" or "constituent of existence". According to this doctrine no permanent entity underlies the objective universe as well, just as no permanent entity undergirds the subjective person. The word *nairātmya* or absence of "self" is sometimes substituted for *śūnyatā* or emptiness and helps link this idea with that of the 'self-existent'. Evidently, according to Buddhism, neither the individual nor the universe nor any entity in it like God is self-existent. A.L. Basham puts it succinctly: "Buddhism knows no being, but only becoming".[14] Buddhism is emphatic on this point: *sabbe dhammā anattā* (*Dhammapada*, verse 279). That is to say: All *dhammās* or *dharmas* are without self, that is, lacking in any permanent substratum.

This oracular pronouncement of the Buddhist position squarely challenges the very concept of self-existence. "There is no term in Buddhist terminology wider than *dhamma*. It includes not only the conditioned things and states, but also the non-conditioned, the Absolute, *Nirvāṇa*. There is nothing in the universe or outside, good or bad, conditioned or non-conditioned, relative or absolute, which is not included in this term".[15] Lest one be tempted into regarding the *dharmakāya* of the Buddha, sometimes equated with the God of theism, as an exception it must be pointedly stated that such is not the case, that it is precisely as a consequence of having no self-subsistence that "the Buddha becomes identical either with the Absolute, or with the sum total of existence, with the totality of all things at all times".[16] Alternatively, one can say that "it is only because he has merged with everything that the Buddha has cast off all traces of a separate self, and has attained complete and total self-extinction"[17] in contrast to the self-subsistence of the Christian God.

Thus of the two attributes — infinity, self-existence — one is transferred to the universe and the second denied both of the universe and God. The idea of self-existence or self-subsistence is formally designated by the term *aseity* which carries the twofold connotation that "(1) God is not dependent either for existence or for characteristics upon any other reality" and (2) that "God is eternal, without beginning or end". Buddhism turns this entire concept on its head, by maintaining the mutual interdependence of everything through its doctrine of *pratītya-samutpāda* or dependent co-origination so far as the first point goes, and postulating no beginning for the universe characterized by this process so far as the second point is concerned. A beginning is denied with respect to the universe rather than God.

Everything is process, one is to see conditionality in all things because if you "take away the causes and conditions", the elements of *dharmas* "no longer exist", and this is the basic feature of life itself.

Now a question may be raised whether life has a beginning. According to the Buddha's teaching the beginning of the lifestream of living beings is unthinkable. *The believer in the creation of life by God may be astonished at this reply. But if you were to ask him 'What is the beginning of God?' he would answer without hesitation 'God has no beginning', and he is not astonished at his own reply.* The Buddha says: O bhikkhus, this cycle of continuity (*saṃsāra*) is without a visible end, and the first beginning of beings wandering and running round, enveloped in ignorance (*avijjā*) and bound down by the fetters of thirst (desire, *taṇhā*) is not to be perceived.' And further, referring to ignorance which is the main cause of the continuity of life the Buddha states: 'The first beginning of ignorance (*avijjā*) is not to be perceived in such a way as to postulate that there was no ignorance beyond a certain point.' Thus it is not possible to say that there was no life beyond a certain definite point.[18]

CREATOR

Two versions of the Buddhist position on God as creator may be identified — a weak one and a strong one. Edward Conze presents a weak version of the position when he writes:

Buddhist tradition does not exactly deny the existence of a creator, but it is not really interested to know who created the Universe. The purpose of Buddhist doctrine is to release beings from suffering, and speculations concerning the origin of the Universe are held to be immaterial to that task. They are not merely a waste of time but they may also postpone deliverance from suffering by engendering ill-will in oneself and in others. While thus the Buddhists adopt an attitude of agnosticism to the question of a personal creator, they have not hesitated to stress the superiority of the Buddha over Brahma, the God who, according to Brahminic theology, created the Universe. They represent the God Brahma as seized by pride when he thought to himself: '*I am Brahma, I am the great Brahma, the King of the Gods; I am uncreated, I have created the world, I am the sovereign of the world, I can create, alter, and give birth; I am the Father of all things.*' The Scriptures are not slow in pointing out that the Tathagata is free from such childish conceit. If indifference to a personal creator of the Universe is Atheism, then Buddhism is indeed atheistic.[19]

Conze also identifies one possible exception to his position. After asserting that "monotheism never appealed to the Buddhist mind" and that "there has never been any interest in the origin of the Universe" he notes one exception:

About 1000 AD Buddhists in the North-West of India came into contact with the victorious forces of Islam. In their desire to be all things to all men, some Buddhists in that district rounded off their theology with the notion of an *Adibuddha*, a kind of omnipotent and omniscient primeval Buddha, who through his meditation originated the Universe. This notion was adopted by a few sects in Nepal and Tibet.[20]

The strong version of the Buddhist position is presented by K.N. Jayatilleke. He points out that when the word God is used in the sense of "a personal creator God" then "the Buddha is an atheist and Buddhism in both its Theravāda and Mahāyāna forms is atheism", as in Theravāda and "in none of the Mahāyāna schools is the Buddha conceived of as a creator God".[21]

A distinction may be drawn at this point between (a) a Buddhist belief in a creator God other than the Buddha; and (b) a Buddhist belief in the Buddha himself being a creator God. It is quite clear from the foregoing that — apart from the historical exception noted by Edward Conze — the Buddhists did not look upon the Buddha as a creator God.

However, the Buddhist texts do speak of a God who looked upon *himself* as the creator God. This is obvious from the citation by Conze and from the following description of the Mighty God or Mahā Brahmā who was considered "omnipotent (*abhibhū anabhibhūto*), omniscient (*aññadatthudaso*), the Mighty Lord (*vasavatti issaro*), Maker (*kattā*), Creator (*nimmātā*), the Most Perfect (*seṭṭho*), the Designer (*sañjitā*) ... [of] the creatures we are".[22]

The point of interest here is that "the Buddha does not deny the existence of such a being; he is morally perfect but not omniscient and omnipotent. He is the chief of the hierarchy of Brahmās who rule over galactic systems and clusters of galactic systems"[23] but the Buddha does not accept the claim that such a Mighty God is eternal, as claimed, nor is he *really* a creator. "Although Brahmā is believed to be the creator of the cosmos, he is none other than a temporary regent of the cosmos, an office to which any being within the cosmos could aspire".[24]

PERSONAL

The question of God being personal can be moved in two directions: (1) given the acceptance of a God in Buddhism who is morally perfect but not a creator nor omniscient and omnipotent, could one enter into a personal relationship with him? (2) Is it possible to treat the Buddha as a personal God in some sense?

Although it is obvious that one could regard the Mighty God (Mahā Brahmā) in personal terms, in the New Testament the "conviction as to the personal character of God is embodied in the figure of fatherhood that was constantly used by Jesus as the most adequate earthly image with which to think of God".[25] The Mighty God does declare that he is the "Father of all things".[26] The difficulty, however, arises from the fact that the way to gain companionship with him is not "by petitionary prayers but by cultivating the divine life".[27]

As for the Buddha himself, it was of course possible for his followers to relate to him in personal terms rather than as "a person" — a concept he denied. And he is known to have favoured monks and nuns with expressions of both physical and spiritual solicitude. But to go beyond this point and carry personal consultation to the point of personal adulation was problematical. He declared to the monk Vakkali, who was overly fond of keeping his company: "What is there, Vakkali, in seeing this vile body of mine? Who sees the spiritual Dharma, he sees me; who sees me, sees the spiritual Dharma. Seeing Dharma, Vakkali, he sees me; seeing me, he sees Dharma".[28] One can see here a difference which cuts deeper; the disciples of Jesus could relate to Jesus as a living historical prophet and even incarnation but a rather different ambience surrounds the Buddha. "Unlike official Christianity Buddhism is not a historical religion, and its message is valid independently of the historicity of the event of the life of the 'Founder', who did not found anything, but merely transmitted a dharma pre-existing him since eternity".[29]

Attempts were made to "personalize" even the *dharmakāya* of the Buddha. But as Edward Conze points out:

We can well believe in the selflessness of a Buddha conceived in this way. But when the Mahāyāna goes on to say that this Buddha — all-knowing, all-wise, all there is — is also all-compassionate, we remain slightly unconvinced. In an effort to humanize the Buddha the Mahāyānists called him a 'father' of all those who are helpless and afflicted, but this attribute never quite comes to life.[30]

This personal aspect of theism, however, stands out more clearly in relation to the Bodhisattvas rather than the Buddhas. Early Buddhism acknowledges one Bodhisattva or Buddha-to-be, Maitreya by name. Richard H. Robinson points out that,

Maitreya, unlike the Buddhas before him, is alive, so he can respond to the prayers of worshippers. Being compassionate, as his name indicates, he willingly grants help, and being a high god in his present birth, he has the power to do so. *His cult thus offers its devotees the advantages of theism and Buddhism combined.*[31]

The proliferation of Bodhisattvas in Mahāyāna Buddhism could also be attributed in part to this factor. Numerous inscriptions on rocks in Central Asia express the personal hope of messianic redemption with the succinctly worded importunity: "Come, Maitreya, come!".

LOVING, GOOD, WRATH

In dealing with the question of love in Buddhism it is best to begin by recognizing that the Buddhists "have never stated that God is *love* but that may be due to their preoccupation with intellectual precision, which must have perceived that the word 'love' is one of the most unsatisfactory and ambiguous terms one could possibly use".[32] The Buddhists prefer the less ambiguous word compassion or *karuṇā*, just as Christians like to distinguish *agape* from *eros*. The fact that in general there is more emphasis on wisdom or *prajñā* in Buddhism along with *karuṇā*[33] or compassionate love rather than love *per se* may have to do with the manner in which the two traditions, Buddhism and Christianity, evolved. Edward Conze has astutely observed:

There has existed throughout Buddhist history a tension between the Bhaktic and the Gnostic approach to religion, such as we find also in Christianity. There is, however, the difference that in Buddhism the Gnostic vision has always been regarded as the more true one, while the Bhaktic, devotional, type was regarded more or less as a concession to the common people. It is generally found in philosophical thought that even philosophical abstractions are clothed with some kind of emotional warmth when they concern the Absolute. We have only to think of Aristotle's description of the Prime Mover. In Buddhism, however, in addition, a whole system of ritual, and of religious elevation is associated with an intellectually conceived Absolute in a manner which is not logically very plausible, but which stood the test of life for a long time.[34]

The theistic parallel to this example would be the love of God despite the existence of evil representing a "manner which is not logically very plausible but which has stood the test for a long time".

Compassion and *agape* represent interesting points of comparison between Buddhism and Christianity. It is said that the New Testament writers took the word *agape* from the Greek language and "through their own use of the word, imprinted upon it the meaning of 'giving love' ".[35] This is a love not given out of any consideration but simply because "that person is *there* as a person. The nature of *agape* is to value a person in such a way as to actively seek his or her deepest welfare and fulfilment".[36]

The Buddhist use of the word *karuṇā* or compassion, it seems, underwent a similar development. The following verse of *Mātṛceṭa*, a Mahāyāna poet of the second century, is interesting in this respect:

Which shall I praise first, you or the great compassion, which held
You for so long in *saṃsāra*, though well its faults you knew?
Your compassion, given free rein, made you pass your time
Among the crowds, when the bliss of seclusion was so much more to
your taste.[37]

The two verses refer to two halves of the Buddha's life. The first "refers to the Buddha when he was a Bodhisattva, the second to the forty-five years of his ministry on earth after his enlightenment".[38] Two points need to be clearly recognized here: that the enlightenment experience does not of itself carry the obligation of leading others to it. That is to say, the decision to preach the *dharma* is by itself a *moral* choice, hence the significance of the Bodhisattva. Secondly, once a Buddha has passed away into final enlightenment, the way he can guide and help others becomes obscure because he is no longer a person in our usual sense. It can be argued that in some mysterious way help continues to flow from him but to many on this side this "has always seemed barely credible".[39] Hence the significance of the compassion of the Bodhisattva, who puts off his own passage into *Nirvāṇa* in order to be of use to others, "one who would bide his time until even the smallest insect has reached the highest goal".[40]

It is clear then that *agape* and compassion spring from the same source, the depths of the heart.[41] The Buddhist views about the conditional and therefore "illusory" nature of the universe and of personality mediate this in their own way, just as the Christian ideas of God make it flow in another direction.

Given these differences, it is rather interesting that the idea of goodness in both Buddhism and Christianity seemed to lead to a similar idea — the kingdom of God. The Christian concept is too well known to require elaboration, it is the Buddhist material on the point which is striking:

It is said that the cultivation of compassion in its purest form is 'called the divine life in this world' (*Brahman etaṃ vihāraṃ idhamāhu*). It is also said that when one lives the moral and spiritual life with faith in the Buddha, then 'one dwells with God' (*Brahmunā saddhiṃ saṃvasati*). The Buddha came to establish 'the rule of righteousness' or 'the kingdom of righteousness' (*Dhamma-cakkaṃ pavattetuṃ*) in this world, which is elsewhere called 'the kingdom of God' (*Brahma-cakkaṃ*).[42]

In this context one encounters the astonishing statement that in Buddhism "one who has attained Nirvana", it is said, "may justifiably employ theological terminology (*dhammena so Brahma-vādaṃ vadeyya*)".[43]

The fact that belief in God, unlike the Buddha, enables God to be in loving relationship with his creation may appear as an advantage, to which even the Buddhists may not have been insensitive. For in the *Lotus Sūtra* Buddha's earthly manifestation is considered merely an exercise in compassion, with which the eternal Buddha continues to shower the world like rain, which bestows on diverse plants moisture proportionate to their needs.

By mythologizing the life of the historical Buddha, the problem of post-mortem efficacy of the Buddha is solved. Now

not only is the teaching of the Buddha declared by this text to comprise a series of skilfully devised expedients, but the very appearance of the Buddha in this world is declared (chap. 15; chap. 16 in the Chinese) to be a mere stratagem to draw beings to the Dharma. The actual Enlightenment is an event that took place, if it occurred in history at all, aeons ago. The Buddha's apparent *parinirvāṇa* at age eighty is a mere simulacrum, comparable to that of a physician who feigns death in order to induce his wilful sons to take an essential medicine. Chapter 7 tells of a guide who leads his charges to a magic city he has conjured up as a resting place for the weary. Only when they have rested do the travellers learn that the city is a mirage, not the ultimate goal of their journey after all.[44]

The relationship between God and goodness has been considered problematic when the question is posed in the following manner: given the belief that God is good, "Does that belief imply a moral standard external to God, in relation to which God can be said to be good? Or alternatively, does it mean that God is good by definition? Is the Creator offered as the final standard of goodness, so that God's nature, whatever it may be, is the norm of goodness?"[45] The problem lands one in the following philosophical predicament:

Either position involves difficulties. If God is good in relation to some independent standard of judgment, God is no longer the sole ultimate reality. God exists in a moral universe whose character is not divinely ordained. If, however, God is good by definition, and it is a tautology that whatever God commands is right, certain other implications arise which are hard to accept. Suppose that, beginning tomorrow, God wills that human beings should do all the things that God has formerly willed they should not do. Now hatred, cruelty, selfishness, envy, and malice are virtues. God commands them; and since God is good, whatever God wills is right. This possibility is entailed by the view we are considering; yet it conflicts with the assumption that our present moral principles and intuitions are generally sound, or at least that they do not point us in a completely wrong direction.[46]

The predicament may be Christian in content but is structurally shared by Buddhism. It was pointed out earlier how the Bodhisattva, or the Buddha, for that matter, can be seen as exercising one's compassion in an 'illusory' universe — a universe consisting entirely of a nexus of dependent relationships and hence illusory in the sense of having no self-existence or truly independent existence, at least in Mahāyāna Buddhism. This raises its own predicament. Does it not leave us in the end with the world as "a kind of phantasmagoria, in which magically created beings are saved from magically created suffering by a magically created saviour, who shows them the unsubstantiality of all that comes into being"?[47]

In both Christianity and Buddhism the resolution of the predicament is circular and relational, and emotive rather than logical. John H. Hick proposes the following resolution in the Christian case:

Perhaps the most promising resolution of the dilemma is a frankly circular one. Good is a relational concept, referring to the fulfilment of a being's nature and basic desires. When humans call God good, they mean that God's existence and activity constitute the condition of humanity's highest good. The presupposition of such a belief is that God has made human nature in such a way that our highest fulfilment is to be found in relation to God. Ethics and value theory in general are independent of religion in that their principles can be formulated without any mention of God; yet they ultimately rest upon the character of God, who has endowed us with the nature whose fulfilment defines our good.[48]

It may be noted that here too ethics is seen as independent of a theology in theory but not in practice. In the case of Buddhism ethics is independent of enlightenment but only after it had been achieved, for proper moral conduct (*śīla*) is an element in the Noble Eightfold Path which leads to it. It was the post-enlightenment decision to preach which represents a free moral choice. Thus even though from the point of view of enlightenment — given the doctrine of emptiness as mentioned earlier — humanity must "appear as a mass of non-entities constantly worrying about no-things", yet those types of enlightened beings who tarry in the world are regarded "as superior to the others"; of course, from the point of view of the world!

We have talked of God's goodness, but what of his wrath? Here it must be recognized that God's wrath in the New Testament is quite different from vengeful anger.

C.H. Dodd, in his study of Saint Paul, pointed out that Paul never describes God as being wrathful, but always speaks of the Wrath of God in a curiously impersonal way to refer to the inevitable reaction of the divinely appointed moral order of the Universe upon wrongdoing. The conditions of human life are such that for an individual or a group to infringe upon the structure of the personal order is to court disaster. This disaster Paul calls, in traditional language, 'The Wrath,' or much more rarely, 'The Wrath of God'. ... 'The Wrath', then, is revealed before our eyes as the increasing horror of sin working out its hideous law of cause and effect.[49]

Such an interpretation of God's wrath is too close to the

Buddhist idea of evil *karma* to require more comment than this, that according to one view, the whole paraphernalia of hell is set up by our own bad *karma* for its expurgation, rather than the other way around.

HOLY

Holiness is closely associated with the concept of God in the Judaic-Christian tradition. Such sentiments are reserved for *Nirvāṇa* in Buddhism. The holiness of God derives from the fact of being "overwhelmingly aware of the divine reality as infinitely other and greater".[50] The same point is reached in Buddhism in relation to *Nirvāṇa*, a conclusion which,

emerges from three sets of questions and answers forming a topic of conversation between three different pairs of people. Although the wording differs to some extent in all these passages, the main points are the same: 'What is the counterpart of knowledge?' (or, What is knowledge for?). 'Freedom is the counterpart of knowledge.' 'And what is the counterpart of freedom?' 'Nirvāṇa is the counterpart of freedom.' The accent of the Teaching is on what is positive rather than on what is negative.' It is on happiness, mental development, freedom and the winning of *Nirvāṇa*. When it is asked: 'What is the counterpart of *Nirvāṇa*?' or, 'What is *Nirvāṇa* for?' this is a question that goes too far and is beyond the compass of an answer, a commentary saying (*Majjhima Com.* ii. 370) that *Nirvāṇa* is without a counterpart. All that can be said in reply to such a question is that 'the Brahma-faring is lived for the plunge into *Nirvāṇa*, for going beyond to *Nirvāṇa*, and for culminating in *Nirvāṇa*.'[51]

That *Nirvāṇa* represents the ultimate value in Buddhism, the holiest of the holies, may be gathered from the following consolidated and compact statement about it:

Just as it is impossible to tell the measure of the water in the sea or the number of creatures dwelling therein, though, after all, the sea exists, so it is impossible to tell the form or figure or duration or measure of *Nirvāṇa*, though, after all, it is a condition that does exist. These are some of its characteristics. It is untarnished by evil dispositions. It does allay the thirst of the craving after lusts, the craving after future life, and the craving after worldly prosperity. It is the refuge of beings tormented with the poison of evil dispositions. It does put an end to grief. It is ambrosia. It is mighty and boundless, and fills not with all beings who enter into it. It is the abode of all 'good men' — the *Arahats*. It is all in blossom, as it were, with the innumerable and various and fine flowers of purity, of knowledge, and of emancipation. It is the support of life, for it puts an end to old age and death. It does increase the power of *siddhi* or supernormal powers. It puts a stop in all beings to the suffering arising from evil disposition. It overcomes in all beings the weakness which arises from hunger and every sort of pain. It is not born, neither does it grow old, it does not pass away, it has no rebirth, it is unconquerable, thieves cannot carry it, it is not attached to anything, it is the sphere in which *arahats* move, nothing can obstruct it, and it is infinite. It satisfies every desire. It causes delight. It is full of lustre. It is hard to attain to. It is unequalled in the beauty of its perfume. It is praised by all the Noble ones. It is beautiful in righteousness. It has the pleasant perfume of righteousness. It has a pleasant taste. It is very exalted. It is immovable. It is inaccessible to sinners. It is a condition in which no evil dispositions can grow. It is free from desire to please and from resentment.[52]

CHAPTER 2

Grounds for Belief in God

It was indicated earlier that Buddhism is an atheistic religion. It should be recognized clearly, however, that in order to properly call Buddhism atheistic, the sense of the word theism must be clearly defined. The need for such clarity will become apparent towards the end of the chapter. The position is stated with admirable clarity by K.N. Jayatilleke:

Using the word in the above sense of a Personal Creator God, who is a Supreme being possessed of the characteristics of omniscience, omnipotence and infinite goodness, if we ask the question, "Does God exist?", there are four possible answers. They are: (1) those theists who say "yes" and affirm God's existence, (2) those atheists who say "no" and deny God's existence, (3) those sceptics or agnostics who say "we do not know" or "we cannot know" and (4) those positivists who say that the question is meaningless since the meaning of the term "God" is not clear.

What is the Buddhist answer to this question? Was the Buddha a Theist, an Atheist, an Agnostic or a Positivist? The answer is fairly clear. Given the above definition of God in its usual interpretation, the Buddha is an atheist and Buddhism in both its Theravāda and Mahāyāna forms is atheism.[1]

How do Buddhists arrive at such a conclusion and, equally importantly, how far are they prepared to go with their conclusion? The answer to this question is best obtained by identifying their responses to the various grounds offered for the existence of God in the Western philosophy of religion.

THE ONTOLOGICAL ARGUMENT

The ontological argument for the existence of God is associated with the name of Anselm (*c.* 1033–1109) and is found in two versions.[2] According to one version, if God is defined as "that-than-which-a-greater-cannot-be-thought" then God must obviously exist for the thought that God has various attributes *and* exists is certainly greater than the thought that he has all these attributes and does not exist. According to the second version, God possesses *aseity*, or necessary being so it is impossible to conceive of God as not existing.

One must begin by pointing out that Buddhism is basically unsympathetic to this form of reasoning, which makes ideas or concepts into things. It dislikes the fallacy of 'nominalism', which may be roughly described as the idea that something actually exists just because it has a name or is an idea. Thus K.N. Jayatilleke dismisses the argument with the remark: "Even when we take the arguments for theism in a modern context we find that the ontological argument was a mere definition, which mistakenly regarded existence as an attribute".[3] Actually, the Buddha offers a much more trenchant critique of the second version of the ontological argument if it makes God's existence unique as compared to the existence of the world, inasmuch as it is taken out of the realm of time. The Buddha asks: "The whole universe, as we know it, is a system of relations: we know nothing that is, or can be, unrelated. How can that which depends on nothing and is related to nothing produce things which are related to one another and depend on their existence upon one another?"[4]

However, the Buddhist position may not be as unsympathetic to the argument as may appear at first sight. One is led to this softer position through the following assessment of the argument by John H. Hick:

If existence is ... an attribute or predicate that can be included in a definition and that, as a desirable attribute, must be included in the definition of God, then the ontological argument is valid. For it would be self-contradictory to say that the most perfect conceivable being lacks the attribute of existence. But, if existence, although it appears grammatically in the role of a predicate, has the quite different logical function of asserting that a description applies to something in reality, then the ontological argument, considered as a proof of God's existence, fails. For if existence is not a predicate, it cannot be a defining predicate of God, and the question whether anything in reality corresponds to the concept of the most perfect conceivable being remains open to inquiry.[5]

It was noted earlier that the Buddha does not deny the existence of such a being as has some but not all of the attributes of the Christian monotheistic God, although he would be reluctant to establish it on the basis of the argument adduced above. On *purely* logical grounds he would leave the matter "open to inquiry" or oddly enough "closed to inquiry" as not really helpful in the search for salvation, *if it involved only metaphysical speculation.* Curiously enough, the existence of God is not one of the questions the Buddha ruled out of discussion as 'unexplained'.[6]

However, Buddha did accept the fact that the existence of God was a *desirable* conception not in a logical or linguistic but in a *practical* sense. One should also note that there is one Buddhist critique of God which at first blush might appear to apply to the ontological argument but perhaps is not really applicable. This is its critique of the idea that God may be described as 'inconceivable', but the ontological argument doesn't quite say that. It only mentions God as that-than-which-a-greater-cannot-be-thought of, not as inconceivable but that than which nothing greater can be conceived.[7]

COSMOLOGICAL ARGUMENTS

To the question, whether God exists, Thomas Aquinas (1224/5–74) says, "the existence of God can be proved in five ways".[8] These may be summarized as follows:

Aquinas's proofs start from some general feature of the world around us and argue that there could not be a world with this particular characteristic unless there were also the ultimate reality which we call God. The first Way argues from the fact of motion to a Prime Mover; the second from causation to a First Cause; the third from contingent beings to a Necessary Being; the fourth from degrees of value to Absolute Value; and the fifth from evidences of purposiveness in nature to a Divine Designer.[9]

The Buddhists do not find these arguments convincing. They rebut them as follows.

(1) The Buddhists find the concept of a prime mover inconsistent with that of an eternal God.

Dharmakirti says that an eternal God cannot be regarded as the cause of this world. To Chaitra, [or say Tom] a weapon causes a wound and a medicine heals that up. Both the weapon and the medicine are regarded as causes because they are momentary and capable of successful activity. God is neither momentary nor is He efficient. If the opponent is so fond of taking an inactive and inefficient entity like God to be the cause of this world, he should better hold a dry trunk of a tree as the cause of this universe. God is eternal and so He cannot change. And unless He changes, He cannot be a cause.[10]

(2) More attention in general is paid to the second argument. As his "first proof, which infers a first mover from the fact of motion, is basically similar",[11] the more comprehensive second argument may be summarized thus: "... everything that happens has a cause, and this cause in turn has a cause, and so on in a series that must either be infinite or have its starting point in a first cause. Aquinas excludes the possibility of an infinite regress of causes and so concludes that there must be a First Cause, which we call God."[12]

The main initial criticism of this argument, of which Aquinas himself seems to have been aware, is: why should an endless regress of events, requiring no beginning, be excluded as impossible?[13]

Although Buddha does not say it in direct refutation of the argument by first cause, he clearly states:

The first beginning of beings wandering and running round, enveloped in ignorance (*avijjā*) and bound down by the fetters of thirst (desire, *taṇhā*) is not to be perceived.[14]

This is tantamount to the position mentioned earlier: why should a beginningless series be dismissed as illogical? It is the standard Buddhist doctrine that *saṁsāra* is *anādi* (beginningless). And even if the subtle point is made that *saṁsāra* involves the beings and not the universe, yet although the position has to be stated now by implication it is not essentially altered.[15] It could possibly be argued that according to the text there *is* a beginning but too remote to be identifiable, but this seems a rather forced reading.[16] Buddha does not "imagine a world-maker far back in the ages, beginning the series of saṁsāra".[17]

But while an infinite regress of events is feasible, that of God, if defined as the First Cause is obviously not, as the Buddhists were quick to note. For now one has to search for the cause of God himself, *ad infinitum*.[18]

Can the argument be saved by being reformulated? John H. Hick recapitulates the efforts made in this direction by modern Thomists as follows:

They interpret the endless series that it excludes, not as a regress of events back in time, but as an endless and therefore eternally inconclusive regress of explanations. If fact A is made intelligible by its relation to facts B, C, and D (which may be antecedent to or contemporary with A), and if each of these is in turn rendered intelligible by other facts, at the back of the complex there must be a reality which is self-explanatory, whose existence constitutes the ultimate explanation of the whole. If no such reality exists, the universe is a mere unintelligible brute fact.[19]

In other words an ontological approach may rescue one from the chronological abyss. Hick finds the effort unsatisfactory for two reasons:

First, how do we know that the universe is not 'a mere unintelligible brute fact'? Apart from the emotional coloring suggested by the phrase, this is precisely what the skeptic believes it to be; and to exclude this possibility at the outset is merely to beg the question at issue. The argument in effect presents the dilemma: either there is a First Cause or the universe is ultimately unintelligible; but it does not compel us to accept one horn of the dilemma rather than the other ..[20].. Second (although there is only space to suggest this difficulty, leaving the reader to develop it), the argument still depends upon a view of causality that can be, and has been, questioned. The assumption of the reformulated argument is that to indicate the causal conditions of an event is thereby to render that event intelligible. Although this assumption is true on the basis of some theories of the nature of causality, it is not true on the basis of others. If, for example, as much contemporary science assumes, causal laws state statistical probabilities, or if (as Hume argued) *causal connections represent mere observed sequences*, or are (as Kant suggested) projections of the structure of the human mind, the Thomist argument fails.[21]

All of these points are extremely significant from the point of view of Buddhist thought. First of all, Buddhist thought is very sensitive to the fact that "a combination of causes and conditions" are responsible for an event, as suggested by neo-Thomists. But it uses this fact that an event is a combination of interdependent causes and conditions to *deny* that any ens could exist on the following grounds. For it to exist, it must self-exist, that is, possess independent existence. But if everything is directly or indirectly related to *other* causes and conditions, all things precisely lack this quality of independent reality. Hence, the Buddhists reach a conclusion opposite to that reached by the neo-Thomists from the same premiss.

On the point whether the universe is meaningless, the Buddhists would demur, for if by 'meaningless' moral responsibility and free will are denied, then such is not the case with Buddhism.[22] Similarly, the Buddhists would be closer to Hume in their views on causation so that the neo-Thomist view would not carry much conviction with them. One Buddhist critique of the first cause deserves special mention. Buddhists take such reasoning to imply determinism and therefore to be morally deleterious. According to them, the "idea of a first cause does not help us in moral progress. It leads to inaction and irresponsibility. If God exists, he must be the sole cause of all that happens, good as well as evil, and man can have no freedom of his own."[23] Modern Christian theology does not take this tack and allows for the fact that God, consistently with his omnipotence, endows human beings with free will. But modern Buddhists remain unconvinced. K.N. Jayatilleke writes:

Theists who do not take a predestinarian stand (which is logically consistent) try to evade this conclusion by saying that God has endowed man with free-will. But it can be shown that the concept of divine providence is not compatible with a notion of human freedom. To be consistent, one has either to give up the belief in theism or the belief in freedom or confess that this is a mystery that one cannot understand, which is a departure from reason.[24]

It is arguments (1) and (2) of Aquinas's Five Ways which K.N. Jayatilleke has in mind when he says that "the cosmological argument contradicted its own premises by speaking of an uncaused cause or using the word 'cause' in a non-significant sense".[25] Some ambiguity surrounds the use of the term cosmological argument. Sometimes it is used to cover all of the five arguments of Aquinas; sometimes the first two and sometimes mainly the third — to which we now turn.

(3) This third way of Aquinas, often monopolizing the name *the cosmological argument*, runs as follows:

Everything in the world about us is contingent — that is, it is true of each item that it might not have existed at all or might have existed differently. The proof of this is that there was a time when it did not exist. The existence of this printed page is contingent upon the prior activities of lumberjacks, transport worker, paper manufacturers, publishers, printers, author, and others, as well as upon the contemporary operation of a great number of chemical and physical laws; and each of these in turn depends upon other factors. Everything points beyond itself to other things. Saint Thomas argues that if everything were contingent, there would have been a time when nothing existed. In this case, nothing could ever have come to exist, for there would have been no causal agency. Since there are things in existence, there must be something that is not contingent, and this we call God.[26]

As John H. Hick rightly points out, "Aquinas's reference to a hypothetical time when nothing existed seems to weaken rather than strengthen his argument, for there might be an infinite series of finite contingent events overlapping in the time sequence so that no moment occurs that is not occupied by any of them".[27] This is a view fully in accord with the famous Middle Way of Buddhism in which the preceding gives rise to the succeeding so that nothing is annihilated nor does anything persist as it is.

Another version of the argument removes the reference to time and runs thus on the analogy of a watch:

The movement of each separate wheel and cog is accounted for by the way in which it meshes with an adjacent wheel. Nevertheless, the operation of the whole system remains inexplicable until we refer to something else outside it, namely, the spring. In order for there to be a set of interlocking wheels in movement, there must be a spring; and in order for there to be a world of contingent realities, there must be a noncontingent ground of their existence. Only a self-existent reality, containing in itself the source of its own being, can constitute an ultimate ground of the existence of anything else. Therefore, if there is an ultimate ground of anything, there must be a 'necessary being', and this being we call God.[28]

The Buddhist response to this line of reasoning is refreshing. For one thing, this is often the type of argument used precisely to justify the existence of a soul, which Buddhism denies. It should not be overlooked that according to Buddhism the ideas of soul and God are closely related.[29]

The statement has been sometimes made that although the Buddha has denied self as belonging to visible form (*rūpa*) or to mind (*nāma*) he has not said that there is no self at all, anywhere, of any kind at all. It is objected that to infer the absence of self altogether from the denial of self in either body or mind, is unjustified, because to do so would be to assume that the self, if it is to be found at all, must be entirely comprised under and within body and mind. "If I pull my typewriter to pieces", so runs the argument, "I shall find in it no typist; would it be correct, therefore, to say that there is no typist at all?"

The argument is evidently due to a confusion of thought. In Buddhism it is not only the typewriter that has been analysed; the typist has been analysed as well, and both man and machine have been discovered to be 'bundles' of *khandhas*, the typewriter having only *rūpa* (matter) in it while the typist has *nāma* (mind) as well. From the point of view of Buddhism, typist and machine agree in this, that they are both *anatta*, without self of any kind. If it is suggested, however, that there is an *atta*, outside and apart from body and mind, which uses body and mind for its expression and manifestation, in the same way as a typist uses a typewriter, it must be asserted that such a supposition finds no support in any of the records of the Buddha.[30]

The relevance of this argument in the present context will not be lost to the reader. The Buddhists also use an allied argument against the *mono*theistic assumption of the cosmological argument, for they point out that "though an effect presupposes a cause, yet all effects do not presuppose the same cause, otherwise from a fog we shall infer fire and even an ant-hill will be regarded as the work of a potter".[31] This argument of Dharmakīrtī may be developed further in the light of the remarks made by Sāntarakṣita and Kamalaśīla:

Even objects like houses, stair-cases, gates, towers etc. are made by persons who are many and who have fleeting ideas. If the opponent means only this that all effects presuppose an intelligent cause, we have no quarrel with him because we also maintain that this diverse universe is the result of intelligent actions. We only refute his one Intelligent and Eternal Creator.[32]

Let us now refer to John H. Hick's assessment of the cogency of the argument. He states:

The force of the cosmological form of reasoning resides in the dilemma: *either* there is a necessary being *or* the universe is ultimately unintelligible. Clearly such an argument is cogent only if the second alternative has been ruled out. Far from being ruled out, however, this second alternative represents the skeptic's position. This inability to exclude the possibility of an unintelligible universe prevents the cosmological argument from operating for the skeptic as a proof of God's existence — and the skeptic is, after all, the only person who needs such a proof.[33]

Here once again the Buddhist will have to demur. For him the choice is *not* between their being a God or being faced with a universe which is ultimately unintelligible. Rather for him, God is a red herring which comes in the way of the universe becoming intelligible to us on its own terms.

(4) Thomas Aquinas explains his fourth way as follows:

The fourth way is taken from the gradation to be found in things. Among beings there are some more and some less good, true, noble, and the like. But *more* and *less* are predicated of different things according as they resemble in their different ways something which is the maximum, as a thing is said to be hotter according as it more nearly resembles that which is hottest, so that there is something which is truest, something best, something noblest, and consequently, something which is most being, for those things that are greatest in truth are greatest in being, as it is written in *Metaph.* ii. Now the maximum of heat, is the cause of all hot things, as is said in the same book. Therefore there must also be something which is to all being the cause of their being, goodness, and every other perfection; and this we call God.[34]

Buddhism counters this argument. It argues that if we go by gradation then the grade of a Buddha is *higher* than that of God. K.N. Jayatilleke explains:

The idea that the Buddha was a 'mere human being' is also mistaken. For when the Buddha was asked whether he was a human being, a Brahmā (God) or Māra (Satan), he denied that he was any of them and claimed that he was Buddha, i.e. an Enlightened Being who had attained the Transcendent. This does not, however, make the Buddha unique for it is a status that any human being can aspire to attain. The significance of this claim is brought out in the *Brāhmaṇimantanika Sutta,* where it is shown that even a Brahmā eventually passes away while the Buddha, being one with the Transcendent Reality beyond space, time and causation, is not subject to such vicissitudes.[35]

Perhaps the point is more philosophically appealing if couched in different terms — that the transtheistic nature of the *Nirvāṇa* of the Buddha places him in a class above the theistic. It may be pointed out that according to the Buddha himself one "who has attained *Nirvāṇa*, may justifiably employ theological terminology (*dhammena so Brahm-vādam vadeyya*)". But the actual employment of such terminology by the Buddha, at least in the *Devadaha Sutta* is rather mischievous for therein,

the Buddha uses the arguments of the theists against them, saying that if theists are suffering psychologically, then according to their own theories it must be because God has withheld his grace from them whereas in his own case (if theism were true), 'he must have been created by a good God' (*bhaddakena issarena nimmito*) (M. II. 227).[36]

(5) The argument by design is the last of Aquinas's arguments and a very popular one. It is often developed with the example of a watch found in a desert, an analogy used by William Paley (1825). Unlike the wind, rain, etc. around, it is "utterly implausible to attribute the formation and assembling of the metal parts" which constitute the machine to "the chance operations of such factors as wind and rain". One must "postulate an intelligent mind which is responsible for the phenomenon"[37] even if we were seeing the watch for the first time and even if it did not function perfectly.

David Hume offered three main criticisms[38] of this argument, often referred to as the teleological argument: (1) order can come about other than by conscious planning, given the dimensions of time and space involving the universe; (2) even inert objects have inherent design, like crustaceans; and (3) "from a given effect we can only infer a cause sufficient to produce the effect, therefore from a finite world we can never infer an infinite creator".[39]

All of these criticisms of the design argument are encountered in Buddhist literature. But the first one undergoes a modification in Buddhism. The basic Buddhist argument is not that the universe may have become a viable entity by the factor of *chance* but that its order is to be explained by *antecedent* factors. The universe is viewed as an ordered whole *within* itself and since it never *first* came into being, a supposition implied in Hume's argument, the line of reasoning developed in Buddhism is somewhat different. Primacy here is accorded neither to God nor chance but to the self-regulating working of *karma*, or more broadly, the process of dependent co-origination according to which the preceding, in ceasing to be, gives rise to the succeeding. In more special terms,

the view of the orthodox that there is a supreme personal creator, Īśvara, and the view of the materialists (*svabhāvavāda*) that the development of the world is due to the innate independent power of things, are both repudiated by the Buddhists. The diversity of the world comes from acts. Actions bear a fruit of mastery. They create and organise the material things necessary to their reward. If a man is destined to be born a sun god, then not only is he born, but he gets an abode, a celestial palace, a moving chariot, etc., as the fruit of mastery. Even so at the beginning of the cosmic period the whole material universe is created by the mastering energy of the acts to be enjoyed by the future inhabitants. The receptacle of the world (*bhājanaloka*) is the fruit of the master of the acts of all living beings (*sattvaloka*).[40]

The second argument may now be considered. The Buddhist thinkers, Śāntarakṣita and Kamalaśīla (eighth century), ask, like Hume: if we suppose an intelligent being is necessary to produce objects which are not *consciously* composite — like a watch — and yet are useful objects, such as trees, what are we to presume in such a case? "It is like proving that an ant-hill is the creation of a potter."[41] If instinct is included as a form of consciousness, as instinctive consciousness, other instances can be given. "The proof that as a watch implies a watchmaker even so the world implies a God is offensive" to the Buddhists. "We need not have a conscious cause. Even as the seed develops into the germ and the germ into the branch, we can have production without a thinking cause or a ruling providence."[42]

The third argument used by Buddhists is in a way very similar to Hume's. They argue: we cannot conclude from the fact that the very object *in* the world is created the further fact that the *world itself* is created, for that violates logical consistency. Similarly, just as Hume could infer a 'God' but not a Judeo-Christian 'God' from argument by design, K.N. Jayatilleke argues:

The argument from Design, which is superficially the most appealing flounders when we consider the waste and cruelty of evolution, with nature 'red in tooth and claw'. It is impossible to contemplate that a loving God could have created and watched the spectacle of dinosaurs tearing each other to pieces for millions of years on earth.[43]

This is an old argument couched here in an evolutionary idiom. The general Buddhist position may be stated thus:

The teleological argument is untenable in view of the obvious imperfection of the world. The world seems to be an ingenious contrivance for inflicting suffering. Nothing could be more elaborate and masterly in its perfection than this scheme of pain. A perfect Creator cannot be the author of this imperfect world. Neither a benevolent God nor caprice, but a law which works with a fatal logic, is the truth of things. Buddha would agree with Spinoza in the view that the world is neither good nor bad, neither heartless nor irrational, neither perfect nor beautiful. It is man's anthropomorphism that makes him look upon the cosmic process as a sort of human activity. Nature obeys no laws imposed from without. We have only necessities in nature.[44]

MORAL ARGUMENTS

The moral argument for belief in God rests on the premiss that the sense of moral obligation felt by human beings testifies to the presence and therefore the existence of God. It is usually presented in two forms: (1) that the moral obligation possesses a supernatural source and (2) "that anyone seriously committed to respect moral values as exercising a sovereign claim upon his or her life must thereby implicitly believe in the reality of a trans-human source and basis for these values which religion calls God".[45]

John H. Hick makes short shrift of both these arguments. The first begs the question and the second "is not strictly a proof at all".[46]

The Buddhist places considerable emphasis on morality on the one hand and does not believe in the existence of God on the other, and one would therefore expect the Buddhist to endorse the arguments readily. The situation, however, turns out to be more complex on account of the Buddhist doctrine of "skill in means", whereby one may resort to a useful fiction if its moral effects are salutary. Thus to the extent that belief in God, even if it be philosophically a false belief, helps people lead a morally useful life it could be considered justifiable. The criterion has no doubt shifted from one of truth to that of value but it is useful to bear in mind that such a shift is acceptable within Buddhism.

However, even when veridical rather than pragmatic criteria are used, Buddha makes the interesting statement that a Mighty God (Mahā Brahmā) does exist and that God is "morally perfect but not omniscient and omnipotent".[47] However, the fact of his moral perfection cannot be used as an argument for his existence as is attempted in the Judeo-Christian case. Rather, the conclusion to be drawn is that one achieves companionship with him by cultivating moral perfection. Morality then is a means of approaching God, not a proof of his existence. One must recognize that when one deals with Buddhist atheism. "Buddhist atheism has at the same time to be distinguished from materialistic atheism. Buddhism asserted the falsity of a materialistic philosophy which denied survival, recompense and responsibility as well as moral and spiritual value and obligations, no less than certain forms of theistic beliefs".[48]

ARGUMENTS FROM SPECIAL EVENTS AND EXPERIENCES

An argument sometimes adduced in support of belief in God is the claim that people have actually experienced God, either directly or through signs such as miracles, answered prayers, etc. The basic response to this line of argument in the Western philosophy of religion has been that "any special event of experience that can be construed as manifesting the divine can also be construed in other ways, and accordingly cannot carry the weight of a proof of God's existence".[49]

Although the Buddhists would concur with the conclusion, they have their own explanation to offer of 'the other ways' in which these events and experiences can be explained. One of the 'other ways' in which such experiences can be explained is identified by John H. Hick as the growth of the "relatively new but potentially highly significant science of parapsychology which has already greatly enlarged the range of naturalistic explanations of the 'supernatural' "[50] which was used to bolster the case for belief in God. Parapsychology, however, has been taken seriously in Buddhist thought, indeed in Indian thought for a long time, if it has also been accepted rather credulously at the popular level as well. And strikingly, one of Buddha's arguments against the Judeo-Christian type of theism is that he knows of God first hand, as it were. It is claimed that, inasmuch as Mahā Brahmā corresponds to the Judeo-Christian idea of God, "the Buddha has held this office in the past *and has verified in the light of his extrasensory powers of perception* the conditions required for attaining fellowship with God or Brahmā".[51]

Buddha also asked those who believed in God to indicate any special event when they or their ancestors encountered him and predictably draws a blank. Buddha points out in his conversation with Vaseṭṭha that no one could even claim the privilege of having encountered God — not even in the burning bush.

"But yet, Vaseṭṭha, is there a single one of the Brahmans versed in the Three Vedas who has ever seen Brahmā face to face?"

"No, indeed, Gotama."

"Or is there then, Vaseṭṭha, a single one of the pupils of the teachers of the Brahmans versed in the Three Vedas who has seen Brahmā face to face?"

"No, indeed, Gotama!"

"Or is there then, Baseṭṭha, a single one of the Brahmans up to the seventh generation who has seen Brahmā face to face?"

"No, indeed, Gotama!"

"Well then, Vaseṭṭha, those ancient *Rishis* of the Brahmans versed in the Three Vedas, the authors of the verses, the utterers of the verses, whose ancient form of words so chanted, uttered, or composed, the Brahmans of to-day chant over again or repeat; intoning or reciting exactly as has been intoned or recited — to wit, Aṭṭhaka, Vāmaka, Vāmadeva, Vessāmitta, Yamataggi, Angirasa, Bhāradvāja, Vāseṭṭha, Kassapa, and Bhagu — did even they speak thus, saying: 'We know it, we have seen it, where Brahmā is, whence Brahmā is, whither Brahmā is?' "

"Not so, Gotama!"[52]

The Buddhist attitude to special events is very different from the Christian. Not only are 'miraculous' powers accepted as a matter of course, they are also viewed as paranormal abilities which the seeker attains as a matter of course. These are called the six-fold higher knowledges (*abhiññā*) and include: (1) psychokinesis (levitation, etc); (2) clairaudience; (3) telepathy; (4) retrocognition; (5) clairvoyance and (6) "the knowledge of the destruction of defiling impulses". This last one has a characteristically Buddhist flavour. It is known as *āsavakkhayañāṇa* and means that the aspirant has attained *Nirvāṇa* and knows that he has attained it as it is not possible without the destruction of defilements. It is clear then that special events are interpreted humanistically rather than theistically in Buddhism.

The Buddhist attitude to miracles also reflects a similar difference in attitude. In Christianity miracles are viewed as objective proofs of the existence of a divine power and are meant to *induce* faith. In Buddhism they are the *result*, not the cause but the consequence of the faith in which the object of faith becomes virtually inconsequential before the fact of faith.[53]

CHAPTER 3

Grounds for Disbelief in God

The Buddhist shares with the atheist or the agnostic the view that God either does not exist or that a determination in this matter is not possible. Actually, in this respect the Buddhist belief may properly be called atheistic rather than agnostic, though some tend to consider Buddha's position as agnostic rather than atheistic. This may result from the misperception that the question of the existence of God belongs to the category of the "unanswered questions" but, as was pointed out earlier, this does not seem to be the case. K.N. Jayatilleke clearly and it seems correctly asserts that considering the constellation of ideas associated with God in the western philosophy of religion, "Buddhism is a form of atheism".[1]

John H. Hick has pointed out that:

The responsible skeptic, whether agnostic or atheist, is not concerned to deny that religious people have had certain experiences as a result of which they have become convinced of the reality of God. The skeptic believes, however, that these experiences can be adequately accounted for without postulating a God, and by adopting instead a naturalistic interpretation of religion.[2]

Some of these approaches may now be examined in the light of Buddhism.

THE SOCIOLOGICAL THEORY OF RELIGION

The sociological theory of religion is associated with the name of Emile Durkheim (1858–1917) and his theory has been so influential that "few anthropologists" or sociologists for that matter "since his time have been able entirely to ignore his perspective".[3] His theory may be summarized as follows:

Durkheim wished to lay bare the fundamental basis of religion, to find religion in its purest form unobscured by 'popular mythologies and subtle theologies'. He found this elementary form of the religious life in the totemism of Australian aborigines, members of a society which, he felt, was surpassed by no other in its simplicity. He assumed that among these clans it was possible to explain their religion without reference to any other form of religion. Here, Durkheim argued, rituals and ritual attitudes were directed towards the totem, a representative of some species ascribed to all members of a given clan and the source of that clan's identity. This was not a case of animal-worship; animals and plants derived their sacredness from the fact that they were used as totemic objects rather than totems deriving their sacred character from the totemic species. The totem was a representative of something else, a power greater than itself which Durkheim calls the totemic principle or god. This principle was, in its turn, society itself. In worshipping the totem and observing taboos concerning the totemic object, the clansmen were re-affirming their collective sense of belonging. Society, Durkheim stressed here as elsewhere, is essentially a moral force; it is external to us and instils in each a sense of obligation. To Durkheim, society, morality and religion were three major elements of a closed and interacting system. The circularity in Durkheim's analysis was not seen as a weakness in his argument; rather, it emphasized that religion was not being 'reduced' to the 'merely social', for 'the social' was the most fundamental reality of all.[4]

In the context of Buddhism Durkheim's views can be examined either in relation to the Buddhist view of the emergence of society as a whole or in the context of the formation of the *Saṅgha*, or the Buddhist order of first monks and then nuns.

Buddhist thought does not see society as a religious phenomenon in the sense Durkheim does, though it does show traces of perceiving elements of religious life as a social phenomenon. Buddhism broadly subscribes, at least in its early forms, to a version of the theory of social contract. As distinguished from the Hindus, the Buddhists had "their own legend of the origin of kingship" which took the following form:

In the early days of the cosmic cycle mankind lived on an immaterial plane, dancing on air in a sort of fairyland, where there was no need of food or clothing, and no private property, family, government or laws. Then gradually the process of cosmic decay began its work, and mankind became earthbound, and felt the need of food and shelter. As men lost their primeval glory distinctions of class (*varṇa*) arose, and they entered into agreements one with another, accepting the institutions of private property and the family. With this theft, murder, adultery, and other crime began, and so the people met together and decided to appoint one man among them to maintain order in return for a share of the produce of their fields and herds. He was called 'the Great Chosen One' (*Mahāsammata*), and he received the title of *rājā* because he pleased the people. The etymology of the word *rājā* from the verb *rañjayati* ('he pleases') is certainly a false one, but it was widely maintained and is found even in non-Buddhist sources.[5]

A.L. Basham then puts this theory in the following perspective:

The story of the Mahāsammata gives, in the form of a myth worthy of Plato, one of the world's earliest versions of the widespread contractual theory of the state, which in Europe is specially connected with the names of Locke and Rousseau. It implies that the main purpose of government is to establish order, and that the king, as head of the government, is the first social servant, and ultimately dependent on the suffrage of his subjects. Thus in ancient Indian thought on the question of the origin of monarchy two strands are evident, the mystical and the contractual, often rather incongruously combined.[6]

One might protest that the point of interest here is not whether the Buddhists anticipated the sociological theory of religion but rather whether Buddhism itself can be explained in terms of the theory. The point is well taken but this exercise was necessary because the Buddhists do, in fact, anticipate elements of the Freudian theory of religion.

Can Buddhism itself be explained in Durkheimian terms? This does not seem to be the case. For while Durkheim explains religion in terms of tribal solidarity, the rise of Buddhism has been associated with the "break-up of old tribes and their replacement by kingdoms".[7] Besides, to the extent that Buddhism as a movement rose in opposition to Hinduism, Durkheim's basic thesis becomes vulnerable. In general his theory is difficult to apply in a conflictual situation.[8]

Would the Durkheimian approach explain the emergence of the Buddhist *Saṅgha* any better, with its emphasis on internal cohesion? By joining the *Saṅgha* one actually abandoned society.

The application of Durkheim's theory is seriously limited by this factor, though it must be noted that while members of orders such as the Buddhist "lived outside social and communal organizations, they constituted by themselves a well-defined community".[9] However, the Buddhist order hardly conforms to the Durkheimian model. Membership was not by birth but voluntary, the decision-making process was surprisingly democratic and monks could join or leave the order more or less at will.[10]

THE FREUDIAN THEORY OF RELIGION

One may begin by noting the following key elements in the Freudian theory of Religion. Sigmund Freud (1856–1939) (1) "regarded religious beliefs as 'illusions, fulfilments or the oldest, strongest, and most insistent wishes of mankind' ",[11] (2) he regarded the personalization of the impersonal forces of nature as a way of dealing with them in human terms;[12] (3) the projection of God as a father-figure was a key development in this respect;[13] (4) religion was "the universal obsessional neurosis of mankind";[14] (5) Freud associated religion with the Oedipus complex, namely, the "child's unconscious jealousy of his father and desire for his mother", a complex he regarded as universal;[15] (6) this had led the sons into killing their father (who was hoarding all the desirable females) and eating his body, which filled them with remorse, while on the other hand the inability of all to replace the one father gave rise to the tabu of incest.[16] Religion was thus the "return of the repressed". (7) Religion was closely related to childhood in two ways: (i) at a societal level religion represented a development which corresponded to the childhood of humankind and (ii) at an individual level, in a crisis, one regressed to an experience of childhood when one felt protected.[17]

Thus religion, according to Freud, is a repetition of the experience of the child. Man copes with threatening forces in the same manner in which, as a child, he learned to cope with his own insecurity by relying on and admiring and fearing his father. Freud compares religion with the obsessional neuroses we find in children. And, according to him, religion is a collective neurosis, caused by conditions similar to those producing childhood neurosis.

Freud's analysis of the psychological roots of religion attempts to show why people formulated the idea of a god. But it claims to do more than to get at these psychological roots. It claims that the unreality of the theistic concept is demonstrated by exposing it as an illusion based on man's wishes.[18]

Buddhist thought strikes a responsive chord with many of Freud's ideas.

Two ideas are psychologically deep-rooted in man: self-protection and self-preservation. For self-protection man has created God, on whom he depends for his own protection, safety and security, just as a child depends on its parent. For self-preservation man has conceived the idea of an immortal Soul or Ātman, which will live eternally. In his ignorance, weakness, fear, and desire, man needs these two things to console himself. Hence he clings to them deeply and fanatically.[19]

It should be added, however, that according to the Buddhists, it is easier to rid oneself of the idea of God than of the 'self'. In the journey of the Bodhisattva a point comes when,

A Bodhisattva can reach his goal. And yet — and this is somewhat of a paradox — only one single little obstacle separates him and us from Buddhahood, and that is the belief in a self, the belief that he is a separate individual, the inveterate tendency to indulge in what the texts call 'I-making and Mine-making'. To get rid of himself is a Bodhisattva's supreme task, and he finds that this is not an easy thing to do. He takes two kinds of measures to remove this one obstacle to Buddhahood — actively by self-sacrifice and selfless service, cognitively by insight into the non-existence of a self. The latter is due to wisdom, defined as the ability to penetrate to true reality, to the 'own-being' of things, to what they are in and by themselves, and held necessary to disclose the ultimate inanity of a separate self. And in this scheme action and cognition always go hand in hand, and are closely interrelated.[20]

(2) The Freudian way is one way in which the prevailing view that the Vedic pantheon represents the personification of the forces of nature could be interpreted. Oddly enough, the Buddhists criticize God for his ignorance of the forces, or rather elements, of nature, rather than man for deifying these forces or elements.[21]

(3) The Buddhist texts refer to the Mighty God as Father,[22] but they do not deny his existence, only his ultimacy.

(4) The Buddhist critique of *sīlavata-parāmāsa*[23] or attachment to ritual is strongly suggestive of the Freudian critique of religion.

(5) The Buddhist anticipation of the Oedipal complex even at the stage of conception is uncanny. The following account, which may be compared with the account at the end of the *Tibetan Book of the Dead*,[24] is based on Vasubandhu's account in the *Abhidharma-kośa*:

The Oedipal character of his analysis would do justice to Freud: driven by *karma*, the intermediate-state being goes to the location where rebirth is to take place. Possessing the divine eye by virtue of its *karma*, it is able to see the place of its birth, no matter how distant. There it sees its father and its mother to be, united in intercourse. Finding the scene hospitable, its passions are stirred. If male, it is smitten with desire for its mother. If female, it is seized with desire for its father. And inversely, it hates either mother or father, which it comes to regard as a rival. Concupiscence and hatred thus arise in the *gandharva* as its driving passions. Stirred by these wrong thoughts, it attaches itself to the place where the sexual organs of the parents are united, imagining that it is there joined with the object of its passion.[25]

However, the Buddhists do not use the idea to account for the origin of religion.

(6) The Buddhists, far from regarding incest as a tabu, establish the purity of Buddha's line through its practice. The context is provided by a Brahmin reviling the low origin of the Śākya tribe to which the Buddha belonged:

Then the Blessed One thought thus: "This Ambaṭṭha is very set on humbling the Śākya with his charge of servile origin. What if I were to ask him as to his own lineage."

And he said to him:

"And what family do you then, Ambaṭṭha, belong to?"

"I am a Kaṇhāyana."

"Yes, but if one were to follow up your ancient name and lineage, Ambaṭṭha, on the father's and the mother's side, it would appear that the Śākyas were once your masters, and that you are the offspring of one of their slave girls. But the Śākyas trace their line back to Okkāka the king.

"Long ago, Ambaṭṭha King Okkāka, wanting to divert the succession in favour of the son of his favourite queen, banished his elder children — Okkāmokha, Karaṇḍa, Hatthinika, and Sinipura — from the land. And being thus banished they took up their dwelling on the

slopes of the Himālaya, on the borders of a lake where a mighty oak
tree grew. And through fear of injuring the purity of their line they
intermarried with their sisters. Now Okkāka the king asked the
ministers at his court: 'Where, Sirs, are the children now?' 'There is a
spot, Sire, on the slopes of the Himālaya, on the borders of a lake,
where there grows a mighty oak (sako). There do they dwell. And lest
they should injure the purity of their line they have married their own
(sakāhi) sisters.'

"Then did Okkāka the king burst forth in admiration: 'Hearts of oak
(śakyā) are those young fellows! Right well they hold their own
(paramasakyā)!'

"That is the true reason, Ambaṭṭha, why they are known as Śākyas.
Now Okkāka had a slave girl called Disā. She gave birth to a black baby.
And no sooner was it born than the little black thing said, 'Wash me,
mother. Bathe me, mother. Set me free, mother, of this dirt. So shall I
be of use to you.'

"Now, just as now, Ambaṭṭha, people call 'devils', so then they called
devils 'black fellows' (kaṇhe). And they said: 'This fellow spoke as soon
as he was born. 'Tis a black thing (kaṇha) that is born, a devil has been
born!' And that is the origin, Ambaṭṭha, of the Kaṇhāyanas. He was the
ancestor of the Kaṇhāyanas. And thus is it, Ambaṭṭha, that if one were
to follow up your ancient name and lineage, on the father's and on the
mother's side it would appear that the Śākyas were once your masters,
and that you are the offspring of one of their slave girls."[26]

(7) The Buddhists do not associate theism with childhood but
they do quite clearly associate it with wish-fulfilment. Thus
Buddha asks his Brahmin disputants if any of them have met
Brahmā face to face and when they are compelled to say no he
implies that Brahmā is just a piece of wishful thinking, as the
following example suggests:

"Just, Vāseṭṭha, as if a man should say, 'How I long for, how I love the
most beautiful woman in this land!' And people should ask him, 'Well!
good friend! this most beautiful woman in the land, whom you thus
love and long for, do you know whether that beautiful woman is a
noble lady or a Brahman woman, or of the trader class, or a Śūdra?'

"But when so asked, he should answer: 'No.' And when people
should ask him, 'Well! good friend! this most beautiful woman in all the
land, whom you so love and long for, do you know what the name of
that most beautiful woman is, or what is her family name, whether she
be tall or short or of medium height, dark or brunette or golden in
colour, or in what village or town or city she dwells?'

"But when so asked, he should answer: 'No.'

"And then people should say to him, 'So then, good friend, whom you know not, neither have seen, her do you love and long for?'

"And then when so asked, he should answer, 'Yes.' Now what think you, Vaseṭṭha? Would it not turn out, that being so, that the talk of that man was foolish talk?"

"In sooth, Gotama, it would turn out, that being so, that the talk of that man was foolish talk!".

"And just even so, Vaseṭṭha, though you say that the Brahmans are not able to point out the way to union with that which they have seen, and you further say that neither any one of them, nor of their pupils, nor of their predecessors even to the seventh generation has ever seen Brahmā. And you further say that even the *Rishis* of old, whose words they hold in such deep respect, did not pretend to know, or to have seen where, or whence, or whither Brahmā is. Yet these Brahmans versed in the Three Vedas say, forsooth, that they can point out the way to union with that which they know not, neither have seen! Now what think you, Vaseṭṭha? Does it not follow that, this being so, the talk of the Brahmans, versed though they be in the Three Vedas is foolish talk?"

"In sooth, Gotama, that being so, it follows that the talk of the Brahmans versed in the Three Vedas is foolish talk!"

"Very good, Vaseṭṭha. Verily then, Vaseṭṭha, that Brahmans versed in the Three Vedas should be able to show the way to a state of union with that which they do not know, neither have seen — such a condition of things can in no wise be".[27]

Not only does the Freudian theory of religion contain elements which have been anticipated in Buddhism as such, modern Buddhists find it relatively easy to formulate some aspects of Buddhism in Freudian terms. Both of these points can be illustrated through the writings of K.N. Jayatilleke. In the following remarks he endorses the Freudian view that certain religious ideas may contain elements of wish-fulfilment. In relation to the desire for belief in survival or rebirth he remarks:

Freud in his work called *The Future of an Illusion* tries to show that people entertain certain religious beliefs, like the belief in the existence of God, for instance, because there is a deep-seated craving in us for security amidst the insecurity of life and the uncertainty of the beyond. According to him people believe in God dogmatically because of such a deep-seated craving. It is an object of wish-fulfilment and, in this specialised sense, an 'illusion'.[28]

His next remark is cautionary and that caution is Freudian as well:

This does not, however, necessarily mean that the belief is false. As Freud himself pointed out, a girl may believe in the existence of a Prince Charming who may one day come and propose to her because she likes to believe this, but this does not necessarily mean that such a person does not exist. So the desire to believe in rebirth or survival does not necessarily show that the belief is false just as much as the desire to disbelieve in rebirth does not imply that the contrary belief is false.[29]

The other point, that Buddhism itself can be readily formulated in Freudian terms may now be illustrated. The following passage in K.N. Jayatilleke is as good an example as any. Although he prefaces the passage by commenting that the "Buddhist theory of motivation may be compared with that of Freud although it is more adequate than the latter"[30] and he uses the language of comparison throughout the passage, it is easy to see how by a mere parenthetical reversal it would be easy to clothe Buddhism in a Freudian garb. K.N. Jayatilleke writes:

Man is motivated to act out of greed, which consists of the desire to gratify our senses and sex (*kāma-taṇhā*, comparable with the libido of Freud) as well as the desire to gratify our egoistic impulses (*bhava-taṇhā*, comparable with the ego-instincts and super-ego of Freud). He is also motivated to act out of hatred, which consists of the desire to destroy or eliminate what we dislike (*vibhava-taṇhā*, comparable with the thanatos or death-instinct of Freud) and also out of erroneous beliefs.[31]

Such convergences notwithstanding, however, Buddhism would stop short of explaining religion away in Freudian terms. For Freud God was the ultimate reality and could be thus explained away, and as the religion of Freud's culture was theistic, religion or the reality it represented could also be explained away. But in Buddhism, not only is God in the Buddhist sense not denied as unreal though "theistic hopes" pinned on him may be, the reality of an ultimate realization in Buddhism is not denied. On the contrary, this truth of *Nirvāṇa* it is asserted as in Buddha's famous declaration in *Udāna* 80, which is often cited:

There exists, monks, that sphere (*āyatana*) where there is neither solidity, nor cohesion, nor heat, nor motion, nor the sphere of infinite space, nor the sphere of infinite consciousness, nor the sphere of nothingness, nor the sphere of neither-perception-nor-non-perception; neither this world, nor a world beyond, nor both, nor sun and moon; there, monks, I say, there is no coming (*agati*) and going (*gati*), no maintenance (*thiti*) no decease (*cuti*) and rebirth (*upapatti*); that, surely, is without support, it has no functioning, it has no object (*appatittham appavattam anarammanam*) — this is just the end of *dukkha*.[32]

THE CHALLENGE OF MODERN SCIENCE

Some of the fundamental or at least the most persuasive grounds for disbelief in God have been provided by the rise of science. John H. Hick presents the situation succinctly:

Since the Renaissance, scientific information about the world has steadily expanded in fields such as astronomy, geology, zoology, chemistry, biology, and physics; contradicting assertions in the same fields, derived from the Bible rather than from direct observation and experiment, have increasingly been discarded. In each of the great battles between scientists and churchmen the validity of the scientific method was vindicated by its practical fruitfulness. Necessary adjustments were eventually made in the aspects of religious belief that had conflicted with the scientists' discoveries. As a result of this long debate it has become apparent that the biblical writers, recording their experience of God's activity in human history, inevitably clothed their testimony with their own contemporary prescientific understanding of the world.[33]

The issue, historically, has followed a very different course in the case of Buddhism. First of all, Buddhism was and is presented to the West as "rational" and scientific.[34] The rational West was thrilled by the discovery that a non-theistic religion could actually exist. Indeed, this may have been overdone. Even such a sympathetic student of Buddhism as Edward Conze is constrained to remark that "there are, of course, a few modern writers who make Buddhism quite rational by eliminating all metaphysics, reincarnation, all the gods and spirits, all miracles and supernatural powers. Theirs is not the Buddhism of the Buddhists."[35] When attention is drawn to them they are often dismissed as Hindu accretions! In fact, the self-perception of modern Buddhism about Buddhism being a religion in full accord with science is so strong that even if it were not a historical reality, it is now a phenomenological reality.

The basis for such a view[36] is the belief that (1) "the attitude of the Buddha, like that of a scientist, is one of open-mindedness, lack of prejudice and tolerance";[37] (2) Buddhism is naturalistic rather than supernaturalistic in its explanation of the universe;[38] (3) the Buddha arrived at his conclusions through observation, experimentation and research, like a scientist[39] and (4) that the certain Buddhist views, such as those of time and space, are corroborated by modern science.[40] Although an element of Buddhist apologetics may seem to be involved in the presentation of Buddhism as a "scientific religion" on the whole, even when it is admitted that "the scientific nature of Buddhism has been exaggerated",[41] it is at the same time conceded by critics that "it is still safe to say that Buddhism in its teachings and methods is closer to science than any of the other leading religions of the world. There is no question that the elasticity of Buddhism will enable it to accommodate itself to the findings of modern science."

In the Western philosophy of religion the contrast between the natural explanation of the world offered by science and the supernatural world of miraculous inspiration and miracles is much played out.[42] In view of this fact the Buddhist position on miracles, when treated philosophically, may not be without interest. A section of the *Milindapañha*, a Buddhist text from close to the beginning of the Christian era and better known by the English translation of the title, *The Questions of King Milinda*, provides a fitting conclusion to the chapter from this point of view. The dilemma is posed as follows: If, as early Buddhism maintains, nothing can be predicated of the Buddha after his death then no honours should be paid to him. In any case they should be ineffective as the recipient is no longer there. On the other hand, not only is a Buddhist encouraged to honour the Buddha, even favourable outcomes have been obtained. This dilemma, put to the Buddhist monk Nāgasena by the Greek King Menander (whose name is Indianized as Milinda), is resolved by the Buddhist savant as follows:

The Elder replied: "The Blessed One, O king, is entirely set free (from life). And the Blessed One accepts no gift. If gods or men put up a building to contain the jewel treasure of the relics of a Tathāgata who does not accept their gift, still by that homage paid to the attainment of the supreme good under the form of the jewel treasure of his wisdom do they themselves attain to one or other of the three glorious states. Suppose, O king, that though a great and glorious fire had been kindled, it should die out, would it then again accept any supply of dried grass or sticks?"

"Even as it burned, Sir, it could not be said to accept fuel, how much less when it had died away, and ceased to burn, could it, an unconscious thing, accept it?"

"And when that one mighty fire had ceased, and gone out, would the world be bereft of fire?"

"Certainly not. Dry wood is the seat, the basis of fire, and any men who want fire can, by the exertion of their own strength and power, such as resides in individual men, once more, by twirling the fire-stick, produce fire, and with that fire do any work for which fire is required."

"Then that saying of the sectarians that 'an act done to him who accepts it not is empty and vain' turns out to be false. As that great and glorious fire was set alight, even so, great king, was the Blessed One set alight in the glory of his Buddhahood over the ten thousand world systems. As it went out, so has he passed away into that kind of passing away in which no root remains. As the fire, when gone out, accepted no supply of fuel, just so, and for the good of the world, has his accepting of gifts ceased and determined. As men, when the fire is out, and has no further means of burning, then by their own strength and effort, such as resides in individual men, twirl the fire-stick and produce fire, and do any work for which fire is required — so do gods and men, though a Tathāgata has passed away and no longer accepts their gifts, yet put up a house for the jewel treasure of his relics, and doing homage to the attainment of supreme good under the form of the jewel treasure of his wisdom, they attain to one or other of the three glorious states. Therefore is it, great king, that acts done to the Tathāgata, notwithstanding his having passed away and not accepting them, are nevertheless of value and bear fruit."[43]

The savant then proceeds to provide other examples as well.[44]

CHAPTER 4

The Problem of Evil

THE PROBLEM

John H. Hick begins the chapter on The Problem of Evil in his widely-read book, *Philosophy of Religion* with the remark: "For many people it is, more than anything else, the appalling depth and extent of human suffering, together with the selfishness and greed which produce so much of this, that makes the idea of a loving Creator seem implausible and disposes them toward one of the various naturalistic theories of religion".[1]

The Buddhists may be counted among the many people for whom the existence of suffering has rendered the idea of God implausible. However, one must hasten to add, it has not led them into subscribing to various naturalistic theories of religion, for while the Buddhists reject the idea of a God, they at the same time, accept (1) freedom of will, (2) human survival, (3) need for cultivating virtue and abstaining from vice and (4) "a state when the mind is pure and cleansed of all defilements — a state of bliss, perfection, realization and ultimate freedom".[2] This should serve to make their position on the problem of evil specially interesting to philosophers of religion.

Why do the Buddhists find it difficult to reconcile the existence of evil with the existence of God? In this respect they mount a familiar challenge. "As a challenge to theism, the problem of evil has traditionally been posed in the form of a dilemma: if God is perfectly loving, God must wish to abolish all evil; and if God is all-powerful, God must be able to abolish all evil. But evil exists; therefore God cannot be both omnipotent and perfectly loving".[3] The Buddhist statement on this reads like a paraphrase of the above statement of John H. Hick or vice versa.

If God (Brahmā) is lord of the whole world and creator of the multitude of beings, then why (1) has he ordained misfortune in the world without making the whole world happy, or (2) for what purpose has he made a world with injustice, deceit, falsehood and conceit, or (3) the lord of beings is evil in that he has ordained injustice where there could have been justice (*Jātaka. VI. 208*).

Before turning to the attempted solutions of this dilemma in theistic philosophy, let us pause to examine the concept of evil itself from a Buddhist standpoint.

EVIL AND DUKKHA

While Christianity chooses to emphasize evil, Buddhism prefers to speak of suffering. The difference in emphasis is significant, though two factors tend to attenuate the difference. The first is the fact that both Christianity and Buddhism accept the existence of not just evil but of an 'evil one'. One is referring here, of course, to the devil in Christianity and Māra in Buddhism. The parallel, however, may be misleading for in the philosophy of religion the existence of evil is not discussed in relation to the devil but God, while in Buddhism Māra and the forces of Māra could be said to "constitute merely the symbolic representation of evil in various forms".[4] The second is the fact that although the issue is traditionally referred to as the problem of evil, what it actually amounts to is a discussion of suffering.[5] Nevertheless, the distinction between evil and suffering thereby does not lose its relevance, because in Buddhism suffering need not always involve evil. Evil in Buddhism by itself usually stands for evil karmic deeds and it is entirely possible for a person to suffer on account of "natural causes". The prime example here is the Buddha himself who is considered immaculate in Buddhology and yet underwent physical suffering.[6] In a Buddhist context, therefore, natural causes do not pose the same problem in Buddhism in relation to evil as they might in theism.

A difference in orientation between the conceptualization of suffering in theism and Buddhism must also be recognized. A theistic world-view recognizes the *existence of suffering* but Buddhism also proceeds to examine the *suffering of existence*.[7] The latter is a specifically Buddhist formulation which the reader may wish to pursue on one's own, bearing in mind the fact that the belief: existence is suffering, need not carry the further implication that all existence is evil.[8]

THE REALITY OF EVIL

Notwithstanding the fact that a wide gulf exists between Christianity and Buddhism on the question of belief in the existence of God, both the traditions fully acknowledge the reality of suffering. John H. Hick observes in relation to the problem of evil as formulated in Christianity:

One possible solution (offered, for example by contemporary Christian Science) can be ruled out immediately so far as the traditional Judaic-Christian faith is concerned. To say that evil is an illusion of the human mind is impossible within a religion based upon the stark realism of the Bible. Its pages faithfully reflect the characteristic mixture of good and evil in human experience. They record every kind of sorrow and suffering, every mode of 'man's inhumanity to man' and of our painfully insecure existence in the world. There is no attempt to regard evil as anything but dark, menacingly ugly, heartrending, and crushing. There can be no doubt, then, that for biblical faith evil is entirely real and in no sense an illusion.[9]

Buddha's experience of suffering, though at a more personal level, was equally graphic, when driving round the city on a chariot[10] he encountered the 'morbidity of decrepitude', the 'pathology of sickness' and the 'phobia of death'[11] in coming face to face with a sick person, an old person, and a dead person.[12]

EVIL AND FREE WILL

Before advancing to a discussion of the three major explanations of the problem of evil offered in the philosophy of religion, it might be worthwhile to investigate an assumption shared by all of them. This

Common ground is some form of what has come to be called the free-will defense, at least so far as the moral evil of human wickedness is concerned; for Christian thought has always seen moral evil as related to human freedom and responsibility. To be a person is to be a finite center of freedom, a (relatively) self-directing agent responsible for one's own decisions. This involves being free to act wrongly as well as rightly. There can therefore be no certainty in advance that a genuinely free moral agent will never choose amiss. Consequently, according to the strong form of free-will defense, the possibility of wrongdoing is logically inseparable from the creation of finite persons, and to say that God should not have created beings who might sin amounts to saying that God should not have created people.[13]

This serves to answer to some extent the Buddhist critique of theism, also voiced in the Jātakas as follows: "If God designs the life of the entire world — the glory and misery, the good and the evil acts — man is but an instrument of his will and God (alone) is responsible".[14] However, the free-will argument has come under attack in Christianity itself as follows:

If there is no logical impossibility in a man's freely choosing the good on one, or on several occasions, there cannot be a logical impossibility in his freely choosing the good on every occasion. God was not, then, faced with a choice between making innocent automata and making beings who, in acting freely, would sometimes go wrong: there was open to him the obviously better possibility of making beings who would act freely but always go right. Clearly, his failure to avail himself of this possibility is inconsistent with his being both omnipotent and wholly good.[15]

This argument has elicited the following response:

This argument has considerable power. A modified form of free-will defense has, however, been suggested in response to it. If by free actions we mean actions that are not externally compelled but flow from the nature of agents as they react to the circumstances in which they find themselves, then there is indeed no contradiction between our being free and our actions being 'caused' (by our own God-given nature) and thus being in principle predictable. However, it is suggested, there is a contradiction in saying that God is the cause of our acting as we do and that we are free beings specifically in relation to God. The contradiction is between holding that God has so made us that we shall of necessity act in a certain way, and that we are genuinely independent persons in relation to God. If all our thoughts and actions are divinely predestined, then however free and responsible we may seem to ourselves to be, we are not free and responsible in the sight of God but must instead be God's puppets. Such 'freedom' would be comparable to that of patients acting out a series of post hypnotic suggestions: they appear to themselves to be free, but their volitions have actually been predetermined by the will of the hypnotist, in relation to whom the patients are therefore not genuinely free agents. Thus, it is suggested, while God could have created such beings, there would have been no point in doing so — at least not if God is seeking to create sons and daughters rather than human puppets.[16]

Buddhist thought is sympathetic to such an argument. The reason for this is historical. A contemporary of the Buddha, Makkhali Gosāla believed in predetermination. He is credited with developing the following simile: "Just as a ball of thread, when flung on the ground unravels itself until it comes to an end, so the wise and the fools alike fare on in *saṁsāra* and eventually attain salvation".[17] His doctrines are known as *niyati-vāda* and *saṁsāraśuddhi* and he explained them as follows:

There is no deed performed either by oneself or by others [which can affect one's future births], no human action, no strength, no courage, no human endurance or human prowess [which can affect one's destiny in this life]. All beings, all that have breath, all that are born, all that have life, are without power, strength, or virtue, but are developed by destiny, chance, and nature.... There is no question of bringing unripe *karma* to fruition, nor of exhausting *karma* already ripened, by virtuous conduct, by vows, by penance, or by chastity. That cannot be done. *Saṁsāra* is measured as with a bushel, with its joy and sorrow and its appointed end. It can neither be lessened nor increased, nor is there any excess or deficiency of it. Just as a ball of thread will, when thrown, unwind to its full length, so fool and wise alike will take their course, and make an end of sorrow.[18]

K.N. Jayatilleke refers to Makkhali Gosāla's view as the "puppet argument" and this enables us to set up a comparison with the modified free-will defense. The Buddha was extremely critical of Makkhali Gosāla's position. He said that he knew of "no other person than Makkhali born for the detriment and disadvantage of so many people" and compared him "to a fisherman casting his net at the mouth of a river for the destruction of many fish".[19] In fact, the Buddha himself subscribed to a modified free-will theory[20] in a nontheistic context in the sense that past acts influence present acts without conditioning them, and

Buddhism states that man is conditioned by his heredity (*bīja-niyāma*), by his physical, social and ideological (*salāyatana paccayā phasso*, etc.), environment, by his psychological past (*citta-niyāma*) including his karmic heritage (*karma-niyāma*), but he is not determined by any or all of them. He has an element of free-will (*attakāra*), or personal endeavour (*purisa-kāra*) by exercising which he can change his own nature as well as his environment (by understanding it) for the good of himself as well as others. In this sense man is master of his fate (*atta hi attano natho*).[21]

One may now turn to a discussion of the

Three main Christian responses to the problem of evil: the Augustinian response, hinging upon the concept of the fall of man from an original state of righteousness; the Irenaean response, hinging upon the idea of the gradual creation of a perfected humanity through life in a highly imperfect world; and the response of modern process theology, hinging upon the idea of a God who is not all-powerful and not in fact able to prevent the evils arising either in human beings or in the processes of nature.[22]

Interestingly, each of these can be brought in relation to the three major ways of solving the problem identified by Gunapala Dharmasiri,[23] namely, (1) by redefining the nature of God;[24] (2) by redefining the concept of evil[25] and (3) by not tackling "the problem of evil directly as it exists"[26] but to see "design and purpose"[27] in it. The Augustinian response redefines evil; the Irenaean response faces up to the fact of evil but sees purpose in it, and the response from modern process theology redefines God.

THE AUGUSTINIAN THEODICY

Augustine (354–430) had to reconcile the biblical idea that creation was good with the fact that evil existed. To achieve this reconciliation Augustine looked upon evil as something which had not been set there by God but represented the going wrong of something which was inherently good. The example of blindness is usually invoked as a useful illustration of the point. "Blindness is not a 'thing'. The only thing involved is the eye, which is in itself good; the evil of blindness consists in the lack of a proper functioning of the eye. Generalizing the principle, Augustine holds that evil always consists of the malfunctioning of something which is in itself good".[28]

This is what evil is but how does it come to be? Augustine links it to the exercise of free-will by angels and human beings in undesirable ways so that "all evil is either sin or punishment of sin".[29]

This theodicy has been subjected to three basic criticisms:[30] (1) if the creation was "good", that is, flawless, how could it go wrong; (2) the human species cannot be pronounced as "good" in evolutionary terms and (3) Augustine's system includes eternal damnation and this renders "impossible any solution to the problem of evil, for it would build both the sinfulness of the damned and the non-moral evil of their pains and sufferings into the permanent structure of the universe".[31]

The Buddhist point of view, however, calls the basic premise of Augustine into question. According to Buddhism, the universe is not inherently good; rather, suffering is inherent in it. The first two noble truths of Buddhism pertain to the existence of suffering. And they are found as such in what is traditionally considered the very first sermon preached by the Buddha.

"The Noble Truth of suffering (*Dukkha*) is this: Birth is suffering; aging is suffering; sickness is suffering; death is suffering; sorrow and lamentation, pain, grief and despair are suffering; association with the unpleasant is suffering; dissociation from the pleasant is suffering; not to get what one wants is suffering — in brief, the five aggregates of attachment are suffering.

"The Noble Truth of the origin of suffering is this: It is this thirst (craving) which produces re-existence and re-becoming, bound up with passionate greed. It finds fresh delight now here and now there, namely, thirst for sense-pleasures; thirst for existence and becoming; and thirst for non-existence (self-annihilation)".[32]

The aphoristic style, to a certain extent, conceals the full thrust of the passage. This is particularly true of the statement: "the five aggregates of attachment are suffering". Buddhism resolves the entire psycho-physical organism of what we call a living human being into these five aggregates such as body, sensations, perceptions, etc. The fivefold enumeration is not illustrative but exhaustive of the human personality. In brief then, according to Buddhism, suffering is quite pervasive.

It has even been said of the Buddha that,

As a real thinker he tried to find an axiom, a self-evident formulation of truth, which could be universally accepted. Descartes, the famous French philosopher, started his philosophy with the formula: *'Cogito ergo sum'*, 'I think, therefore I am'. The Buddha went one step further in starting with an even more universally established principle, based on an experience that is common to all sentient beings: the fact of suffering (*'sabbe saṅkhārā dukkhā'*).[33]

Thus, given the Buddhist doctrine of *Dukkha*, Augustine's argument becomes very interesting from a Buddhist point of view because for the Buddha the fundamental truth of the world was the truth of suffering. His main thesis was that "birth is a suffering, decay is a suffering, disease is a suffering, death also is a suffering and, in short, all the five forms of grasping lead to suffering (or non-satisfaction)". *For the Buddha, the worldly forms of happiness were essentially temporary and leading to various forms of suffering or non-satisfaction. Happiness or good is always a 'privation' of evil or suffering!*[34]

The Augustinian position becomes open to another criticism if certain Buddhist categories are applied to it. Buddhist thought distinguishes, for instance, between pleasurable feelings, painful feelings *and* neutral feelings.[35] It is possible, on this pattern, to posit a neutral condition between good and evil. In that case the privation of good need not necessarily produce an evil condition, it could as well only produce a neutral condition. In other words, the Augustinian model operates only in a strictly dualistic mode of thought. It is interesting to speculate if he intellectually inherited this dualistic mode from his Manichean background. Be that as it may, it is quite clear that the privation of good need not necessarily produce evil. For instance, the privation, that is, the deprivation of love, may produce indifference, for it to produce hatred may require an extra movement.

THE IRENAEAN THEODICY

Irenaeus (*c*. 130–*c*. 202) represents another approach to the problem of evil. He was a predecessor of Augustine and his theodicy is particularly interesting, if not intriguing, in that it takes into account both the past and future of humanity and also tries to account for the fact of natural evil.

Like Augustine, Irenaeus starts with Genesis, but his key

passage is I.26. In the reference to the two terms by which human resemblance to God is described — "image" and "likeness", Irenaeus distinguished two stages in the creation of the human race, one in which they were more like 'intelligent animals' (rather than perfect beings as supposed by Augustine) and a second in which they were "gradually being transformed through their own free responses from human animals into 'children of God'."[36] John H. Hick offers two logical reasons for why human beings should strive towards perfection rather than have it conferred on them: (1) perfection achieved is superior to perfection conferred and (2) proximity obtained is superior to proximity offered — this last point relating to the 'epistemic distance' God might place between himself and human beings.

Such a theodicy is also a prophecy of post-mortem existence for three reasons: (1) if there is no afterlife, failure would be final and therefore pointless; (2) the joys of afterlife would render any suffering undergone *en route* justifiable and (3) an afterlife would provide for universal salvation in principle.

The discussion of natural evil we shall postpone to a later section. We may note here that this doctrine has been criticized because it runs counter to the traditional doctrines of the Fall. Others claim, however, "that this theodicy does succeed in showing why God's world, as a sphere involving contingency and freedom, is such that even these things can, alas, happen — even though human history would have been much better without such conspicuous crimes and horrors".[37]

The Buddhist response to these views may be considered under two headings: mythological and doctrinal.

Although in general the Buddha discouraged speculation on the origin of the universe there is at least one context in which etiological views have been expressed.[38] These views reflect a cosmogonal decline as when "the good *karma* of beings in the highest heaven begins to fail, and the 'world of form', a lower heaven evolves".[39] Subsequently, too, as part of the same process the "first men are fairy-like beings, but they gradually degenerate and become earthbound".[40] While it is true that cosmological details involved vary considerably, the cosmic trend in Buddhism is downwards and more in keeping with the Augustinian view.

The doctrinal difficulty from the point of view of Buddhism

must naturally be accorded more importance. Just as the Augustinian theodicy clashed headlong with the first noble truth, the Irenaean theodicy clashes with the third noble truth, the truth of the *extinction* of suffering. The "Christian cannot make the idea of the extinction of suffering very meaningful if he accepts the utility theory of suffering because the existence of evil has its own justification".[41] Two more points may be noted. The idea of trial seems central to the Irenaean theodicy but "the idea that suffering is a trial is foreign to Buddhism".[42] Similarly, Irenaean theodicy in relation to post-mortem existence assumes a single afterlife. Such views were held in Buddha's time,[43] but in Buddhism post-mortem existence is not confined to a single afterlife.

PROCESS THEODICY

The kind of theology associated with A.N. Whitehead (1861–1947) has developed its own theodicy. The following points may be identified as constituting its key elements. (1) Traditional theology avers that the universe was created *ex nihilo* by God. According to process theology, God has not created the universe but interacts with it. (2) This interaction of God with the universe is persuasive rather than coercive. (3) The universe represents "an uncreated process which includes the deity".[44] (4) Traditional theology implants a 'Godward bias' in the creatures by virtue of God, being the creator, but in process thought "their very creation came about in struggle with primordial chaos, so that the divine purpose is only imperfectly written into their nature". (5) The process of the universe as pictured in this theology is presented in the following passage in some detail for reasons which will become obvious later:

The ultimate reality, according to process theology, is creativity continually producing new unities of experience out of the manifold of the previous moment. Creativity is not, however, something additional to actuality — that is, to what actually exists at a given instant — but is the creative power within all actuality. Every actuality, or 'actual entity', or 'actual occasion', is a momentary event, charged with creativity. As such it exerts some degree of power. It exerts power first in the way in which it receives and organizes the data of the preceding moment. This is a power of selection, exercised in positive and negative 'prehensions' of the data of which it thus becomes the unique 'concrescence'. Thus each wave of actual occasions, constituting a new moment of the universe's life, involves an element of creativity of self-causation. An actual occasion is never completely determined by the past. It is partly so determined and partly a determiner of the future, as the present occasion is itself prehended by succeeding occasions. As part determiner of the future it is again exercising power. This dual efficacy is inseparable from being actual, and so every actual occasion, as a moment of creativity, necessarily exerts some degree of power.[45]

The Buddhist response to the first point will be positive. Buddhist texts accept Brahmā as part of the cosmos. "Although Brahmā is believed to be creator of the cosmos, he is no other than a temporary regent of the cosmos, an office to which any being in the cosmos can aspire".[46] In the Buddhist version too God seems to possess power[47] and is part of the cosmos. His interaction is not coercive but exemplary — he serves as an example of moral perfection.[48] The universe includes the deity but there is this wrinkle in the Buddhist version that, "As Brahmā was first to be born in the World of Form, and ... [as the birth of other beings] agrees with his wishes, he imagines that he is the creator of the other Gods, and of all the world, which actually comes into existence through cosmic law".[49]

On points (4) and (6) the divergence is even greater, in the sense that the human being possesses far greater autonomy in Buddhism. In relation to (6) one should note that in Buddhism "the germ, the arising of *Dukkha* is within *Dukkha* itself, and not outside"[50] and this has a direct bearing on point (4) as follows:

Thus, the germ of their arising as well as that of their cessation are both within the Five Aggregates. This is the real meaning of the Buddha's well-known statement: "Within this fathom-long sentient body itself, I postulate the world, the arising of the world, the cessation of the world, and the path leading to the cessation of the world." This means that all the Four Noble Truths are found within the Five Aggregates, i.e., within ourselves. (Here the word 'world' (*loka*) is used in place of *dukkha*.) This also means that there is no external power that produces the arising and the cessation of *dukkha*.[51]

The fifth point, however, represents a philosophical convergence with Buddhism which is nothing short of startling, a convergence which has not escaped the notice of both Buddhist scholars[52] and scholars of process philosophy.[53] The formulation of creativity in process theology bears a close family resemblance to the Buddhist doctrine of momentariness, a theory which, "means not only that *everything* has conditional and therefore non-permanent existence, but that things last not even for short periods of time but exist for one *partless moment only*, for to exist means to produce an effect and as nothing stays unchanged during any two moments because it does not produce an identical effect during those two moments". Hence, every moment is creative according to the doctrine of momentariness and there is a succession of such moments according to the doctrine of conditioned co-ordination. The difference between Buddhist and process thought, though both are equally dynamic, lies in the anthropocentric nature of the former and the theocentric nature of the latter.[54] The similarities, nevertheless, are suggestive, and extend further.

As in the theodicy of process theology, there are also trends in Buddhism involving the notions of harmony/discord and intensity/triviality. On the one hand the universe consists of flashes of reality moving in quick succession. "The series of indivisible point-instants ... is the only thing in the universe which is not a fictitious construction, but the real basis on which our whole erroneous view of the universe ultimately rests." How successfully, then, we conceptualize around this series represents harmony or discord. Moreover, living in a universe consisting of such horizontal series, we also aspire vertically for the attainment of *Nirvāṇa*, moving to ontological intensity from mundane triviality. However, harmony and intensity do not come in conflict in Buddhism because here the higher level of intensity is made possible not by increased conceptual complexity but its reduction to experiential simplicity.

Process theodicy has been criticized on several grounds. (1) Its implied elitism has been criticized along the following lines:

The process theodicy does not suggest that it is their own individual fault that hundreds of millions of human beings have been born into and have had to endure this situation. The high intensity of physical and mental suffering that is possible at the human level of experience is just part of the actual process of the universe. What makes it acceptable to God, according to the process theodicy, is the fact that the same complex process that has produced all this suffering has also produced the cream of the human species.[55]

It is not suggested that the "unfortunate have suffered deprivation *in order that* the fortunate may enjoy their blessings"[56] but
rather that according to it "the universe may be good as a whole
even though it contains considerable evil in its details".[57] The
Buddhist criticism of this is interesting. First, the Buddhist
doctrine of *karma* would make it hard to accept that individuals
are not responsible, at least in good measure, for their condition. And secondly, as Buddhists are dubious of elevating the
whole over and above the sum of the parts, and even regard this
as a dangerous deification, the idea that something is evil in
details but is good as a whole would be considered suspect.

(2) The God of process theology has also been criticized. On
the positive side, it renders the problem of a theistic theodicy
less acute by shedding transcendental omnipotence in favour of
an immanentist involvement and by enthusing human beings to
fight on behalf of "a finite God who claims our support in the
ongoing battle of light against darkness".[58] From the traditional
point of view, however, such a God cannot be equated with
"the God of the New Testament ... who values all human
creatures with a universal and impartial love".[59] The Buddhist
difficulties with the traditional concept have been mentioned
earlier, while the modifications suggested in the attributes of
God now only confirm the worst fears of the Buddhist, that the
concept of God is "full of theoretical problems".[60]

Buddhist scholars also criticize process theology on its own
ground by pointing out that while it is an attempt to integrate
modern science, especially the concepts of cosmos and the
doctrine of evolution with theistic theology ontologically, it is
unable to produce an adequate soteriology to go with it, leaving
its theodicy as a half-way house from where the other house
cannot even be seen, since it equivocates on the issue of post-
mortem survival. Buddhists might even consider it a house
divided.

WHY NATURAL EVIL?

In our discussion of the problem of evil we have so far skirted
this issue. As John H. Hick points out:

Even though the bulk of actual human pain is traceable, as a sole or part cause, to misused human freedom, there remain other sources of pain that are entirely independent of the human will — for example, bacteria, earthquake, hurricane, storm, flood, drought, and blight. In practice it is often impossible to trace a boundary between the suffering that results from human wickedness and folly and that which befalls humanity from without; both are inextricably mingled in human experience. For our present purpose, however, it is important to note that the latter category does exist and that it seems to be built into the very structure of our world.[61]

Modern theology seems to adopt what Hick calls "a negative path" in facing this issue. We saw how process theodicy argued that this kind of evil more or less went with the territory. This is in line with Irenaean theodicy as well, for the

Irenaean answer to the question, why natural evil? is that only a world which has this general character could constitute an effective environment for the second stage (or the beginning of the second stage) of God's creative work whereby human animals are being gradually transformed, through their own free responses into 'children of God'.[62]

The case for a theodicy for natural evil has been strengthened by the following "counter-factual hypothesis":

Suppose that contrary to fact, this world were a paradise from which all possibility of pain and suffering were excluded. The consequences would be very far-reaching. For example, no one could ever injure anyone else: the murderer's knife would turn to paper or the bullets to thin air; the bank safe, robbed of a million dollars, would miraculously become filled with another million dollars; fraud, deceit, conspiracy, and treason would somehow leave the fabric of society undamaged. No one would ever be injured by accident: the mountain climber, steeple-jack, or playing child falling from a height would float unharmed to the ground; the reckless driver would never meet with disaster. There would be no need to work, since no harm could result from avoiding work; there would be no call to be concerned for others in time of need or danger, for in such a world there could be no real needs or dangers.

This would have startling consequences for the structure of the world as we know it.

To make possible this continual series of individual adjustments, nature would have to work by "special providences" instead of running according to general laws that we must learn to respect on penalty of pain or death. The laws of nature would have to be extremely flexible: sometimes gravity would operate, sometimes not; sometimes an object would be hard and solid, sometimes soft. There could be no sciences, for there would be no enduring world structure to investigate. In eliminating the problems and hardships of an objective environment with its own laws, life would become like a dream in which, delightfully but aimlessly, we would float and drift at ease.[63]

As the hypothesis is developed it seems to gain in imaginative cogency:

One can at least begin to imagine such a world — and it is evident that in it our present ethical concepts would have no meaning. If, for example, the notion of harming someone is an essential element in the concept of a wrong action, in a hedonistic paradise there could be no wrong actions — nor therefore any right actions in distinction from wrong. Courage and fortitude would have no point in an environment in which there is, by definition, no danger or difficulty. Generosity, kindness, the *agape* aspect of love, prudence, unselfishness, and other ethical notions that presuppose life in an objective environment could not even be formed. Consequently, such a world, however well it might promote pleasure, would be very ill adapted for the development of the moral qualities of human personality. In relation to this purpose it might well be the worst of all possible worlds!

Through this exercise in counterfactuality one is led to a very different assessment of actuality.

It would seem, then, that an environment intended to make possible the growth in free beings of the finest characteristics of personal life must have a good deal in common with our present world. It must operate according to general and dependable laws, and it must present real dangers, difficulties, problems, obstacles, and possibilities of pain, failure, sorrow, frustration, and defeat. If it did not contain the particular trials and perils that — subtracting the considerable human contribution — our world contains, it would have to contain others instead.[64]

The Buddhist response to this may be identified at three levels. One of them may be identified in the following comment by K.N. Jayatilleke:

The Buddhist is under no compunction to deny or explain away the fact of evil. If we deny the existence of evil, there would be no reason nor even the possibility of getting rid of it. If we justify it, it would still be unnecessary to try and eliminate it. *But evil is real for the Buddhist and must be removed* as far as possible at all its levels of existence for the good and happiness of mankind, by examining its causal origins.[65]

The theodicy proposed earlier seems to represent, from a Buddhist point of view, a *compromise* with evil — a theological and philosophical compromise with evil — while Buddhism is intent on *overcoming* it. For according to Buddhism it must be removed because it can be removed *entirely* at the level of the individual. The Arhat, while alive, may not be free from pain but the Arhat is free of suffering.[66]

At another level, the Buddhist position approximates the Irenaean position but at a specific and not cosmic level. This becomes clear from the following account:

The presence of some forms of evil, such as suffering has, it is said, a tendency to awaken us from our lethargic state of existence and induce belief in moral and spiritual values (*dukkhūpanisāsaddhā*) (S.II.1).

We are attached to the world because of the joys and satisfactions it affords us by way of the gratification of our desires. But because of the disappointments, frustrations, anguish and suffering that we also experience in the process, we seek to understand and transcend our finite conditioned existence.

So some forms of evil, such as suffering have a tendency to make us seek the good. But, in general, the problem of evil for the Buddhist is to recognise evil as such, to look for its verifiable causes and, by removing the cause, eliminate evil as far as possible at all its levels of existence.[67]

At a third level the Buddhist would be inclined to question the Irenaean assessment of human nature, of which in general it takes a more positive view than the Christian. There are two points at issue here: (1) which of the two, good and evil, predominates in general and (2) which of the two predominates in the human constitution. As to the first the following possibilities exist:

We can say that (1) good predominates over evil although both exist, or that (2) good alone exists but not evil, or that (3) evil predominates over good although both exist, or that (4) evil alone exists but not good or that (5) both good and evil exist with equal strength and vigour (dualism) and there is a perpetual battle in the universe between them, or that (6) neither good nor evil exist in any strict sense e.g. relativism, amoralism, illusionism (*māyāvāda*).[68]

On this point, according to K.N. Jayatilleke, "Buddhism seems to favour the first point of view. It accepts the reality of both good and evil and seems to uphold the view that good predominates over evil".[69]

It is also claimed by modern exponents of Buddhism that according to Buddhism:

Man is fundamentally good by nature, and the evil in him is an extraneous outcome of his *saṃsāric* conditioning. The mind of man is compared in the Buddhist texts to gold ore, which is said to have the defilements of iron, copper, tin, lead and silver, but when these impurities are removed, then the gold shines with its natural lustre. So does the mind when the evil is got rid of.[70]

It is further pointed out that according to the Buddha,

The mind is naturally resplendent, though it is corrupted by adventitious defilements (*pabhasaraṃ idaṃ cittaṃ taṃ ca kho āgantukehi upakkilesehi upakkiliṭṭhaṃ*). Man, therefore, despite the fact that he has committed sin (*pāpa*) and is capable of sinning is not addressed as a 'sinner' but as a 'meritorious being' (e.g. *Siṇhala, piṇvatnī*) because of his potentiality for good.[71]

This last statement invites comparison with some unflattering assumptions about human nature in some forms of Christian theism.

Even the evil that he commits is not due to his basic depravity or wickedness but to his ignorance. This ignorance can be got rid of and man himself is capable of doing so. Buddhism does not agree with the theist who holds that man in his present condition is so degenerate by nature that he is incapable of saving himself without the grace of an external power. The future of man is in his own hands; he is master of his fate. In denying an eternal hell, in not regarding man as a sinner who is incapable of attaining salvation by his own efforts, Buddhism gives a less pessimistic account of man and nature than is to be found in some forms of theism.[72]

THE QUESTION OF ANIMAL SUFFERING

Most discussions of the problem of evil are confined to the problem of human suffering. The large and intractable problem of animal pain is not taken up in these discussions. This may be a consequence of the distinction drawn between animals and human beings in traditional Christian theology on the basis of only the latter possessing a soul and on the assumption that the latter have dominion over the former. Process theology helps overcome this divide to some extent, for as John B. Cobb, Jr. has pointed out: "In contrast to some Christian views of the soul, it should also be noted at the outset that Whitehead's understanding of the soul applies to higher animals as well as man".[73] The religions of India, including Hinduism and Jainism, do not draw as sharp a distinction between animal and human forms of life[74] as traditional Christianity and in the Jātaka stories the Buddha is often depicted as an animal in a previous existence.[75]

Animal existence is one of the *five* (sometimes six)[76] modes of existence accepted in Buddhism, sometimes classified as 'beasts'. Two key points emerge from a survey of the Buddhist material in this regard: (1) that although animal existence represents a form of existence in which suffering far outweighs happiness, such suffering seems to be essentially karmic in nature and (2) whether animals can attain Buddhahood has been a matter of much debate. While the above-mentioned classification militates against this view, it was its *six*fold version which was used "almost without exception in China and Japan" (where the Mahāyāna claim that "all sentient beings without exception have Buddha nature") that represents the other side of the picture. A famous Zen koan turns on the question whether a dog possesses Buddha-nature or not. The response it offers to the question — namely, *mu*, remains mysterious,[77] and may indicate "that the problem denies the possibility of an answer in the affirmative or the negative".[78]

It is interesting, however, that as human beings can be reborn as animals, animal suffering *can* be connected with freedom of will in Buddhism. It is however not possible in Christianity to regard it as due to the grant of free-will to human beings, "especially that occurring before — or after — the human period".[79]

FREEDOM OF WILL AND THE PROBLEM OF EVIL

John H. Hick links the problem of evil to the question of free will early in his discussion of the issue[80] and the point has been identified for comment by modern Buddhist scholars. He is often quoted as stating that "the origin of moral evil lies forever concealed within the mystery of human freedom".[81]

Buddhist scholars have been critical of the theistic matrix in which this statement is made, which by itself, independent of such a context, would probably not cause much stir, as even in a Buddhist context the statement is not entirely meaningless. The theistic context is essential to assessing the significance of it. K.N. Jayatilleke, after citing the Buddhist position that if theism is assumed "then certain evils are inexplicable" goes on to say:

Here again, leading modern philosophers endorse the argument after showing that all the attempts to explain away evil are unsatisfactory. It will not do to say that evil is negative or unreal, for suffering, ignorance, poverty and ugliness are as real as their opposites. It will not do to say that evils (like wilful injury) are necessary for the existence of higher-order goods (like forgiveness), for there are still many evils unaccounted for in this fashion. Nor will it do to say that the evils in the world are due to the grant of free-will to human beings (quite apart from the difficulty of reconciling this with divine providence, as indicated above). For as Professor Flew has shown, "There are many evils which it scarcely seems either are or could be redeemed in this way: animal suffering, for instance, especially that occurring before — or after — the human period".

In the face of such criticism John H. Hick has argued that "The origin of moral evil lies forever concealed within the mystery of human freedom" but this line of argument leaves Buddhist scholars unmoved: "Here again the inability to give a rational explanation leads the theist to a confession that it is a mystery.... So there is the mystery or the incompatiblity between divine providence and human freedom as well as the mystery or the contradiction between belief in divine goodness and the existence of certain evils".[82]

Gunapala Dharmasiri voices his criticism even more strongly. It has been, he remarks,

... argued that without freedom to do moral evil, the idea of free will does not make any sense. But the problem takes a different turn when one looks at certain aspects of moral evil. Hitler's killing of six million Jews can ultimately be traced to the free will of Hitler. Is that a justification? Hick tries to give a mysterious justification of moral evil in terms of free will: "The origin of moral evil lies forever concealed within the mystery of human freedom". But does that furnish a justification for the suffering and death of six million Jews? Here the more important problem is the problem of suffering and death of six million rather than the free will of one man. Morally speaking, it is a very dubious explanation or justification to say that the safeguarding of one man's free will involves the suffering and death of six million people. One can say that man himself is responsible for it, but as a justification it would be saying too much. From the point of view of those who suffered and died, what form of justification can they find for their destiny? It is here that moral evil starts to assume a great similarity to physical evil. From the standpoint of those who suffered and the dead, both an earthquake and Hitler's extermination campaign would look very much the same. If the earthquake follows from physical regularity and moral evil from mental regularity, both become only factual justifications. One cannot say that moral evil, here, admits of a moral justification, because the one who has suffered does not, and cannot, share the justification. The problem becomes important when God is regarded as all-loving and omnipotent. If God is such why does he allow the innocent to suffer at the hand of a mass-murderer like Hitler? Therefore, it is sensible to maintain, as the Buddha did, that moral and physical evils stand on a par in many respects and hence one can sensibly ask, why God did not, if he were good, create the world otherwise than as he has created it.[83]

This last point is significant because it suggests that, from a Buddhist point of view, a "counterfactual hypothesis" *against* Irenaean theodicy is as much of a possibility as one in support *of* it.

The modified "free will defense" also, according to modern scholars, requires further modification, for here again, one could argue "giving due allowance to the utility of moral evil" that

God could have created a will less free, i.e. limited in several respects, that is, so that it would limit a man from perpetrating Hitlerian types of crime. Even now, though man is theoretically free, there are many things that he cannot actually do. Some things can be done only by a very few men, like knowing other peoples' minds. Having telepathic powers can increase man's degree of free will in the sense that the degree of one's free will increases when a man knows more, because one is less free when one knows less. This is only an example to illustrate how it would be possible for man's free will to be limited by God to avert 'unnecessary moral evil' without making man completely devoid of free will. It would be, of course, a limited form of free will. To speak of practically realizable unlimited free will would be to talk of an unrealizable ideal. If the Christians think, to argue from within the tradition, that they can reconcile predestination and free will, there is every reason why God should intervene in man's free will to avoid morally unjustifiable evils that happen due to the existence of free will.[84]

The Buddhists also like to raise the question: how free is free will? This is not meant to deny its existence but to recognize its conditional character often overlooked in the West. As Walpola Sri Rahula points out:

The question of Free Will has occupied an important place in Western thought and philosophy. But according to Conditioned Genesis, this question does not and cannot arise in Buddhist philosophy. If the whole of existence is relative, conditioned and interdependent, how can will alone be free? Will, like any other thought, is conditioned. So-called 'freedom' itself is conditioned and relative. Such a conditioned and relative 'Free Will' is not denied. There can be nothing absolutely free, physical or mental, as everything is interdependent and relative. If Free Will implies a will independent of conditions, independent of cause and effect, such a thing does not exist. How can a will, or anything for that matter, arise without conditions, away from cause and effect, when the whole of existence is conditioned and relative, and is within the law of cause and effect? Here again, the idea of Free Will is basically connected with the ideas of God, Soul, justice, reward and punishment. Not only is so-called free will not free, but even the very idea of Free Will is not free from conditions.[85]

CONCLUSION

John H. Hick begins his chapter, as we noted earlier, by saying that "For many people it is, more than anything else, the appalling depth and extent of human suffering, together with the selfishness and greed which produce so much of this, that makes the idea of a loving Creator seem implausible".[86]

One will have to count the Buddhists among such people.

CHAPTER 5

Revelation and Faith

INTRODUCTION

After examining the grounds for belief and disbelief in God as well as the problem of evil, John H. Hick offers two conclusions: (1) that it is "not possible to establish either the existence or the non-existence of God by rational arguments proceeding from universally accepted premises"[1] and (2) that "arguments to the effect that theism is more probable than naturalism, or naturalism than theism, are basically defective, since the term 'probable' lacks a precise meaning in the context".[2]

The first conclusion will be acceptable within Buddhism. In Buddhism 'perverted views' are "fourfold when we consider the features of the objective world which they distort. They are threefold when we consider their location in our minds — for they may concern perception, or thought, or theoretical opinion".[3] Theories about God would fall in the last category of perverted views and Buddhist logicians have taken pains to refute belief in God by resorting to reasoning.[4]

However, although the first conclusion will be thus acceptable within Buddhism, perhaps a Buddhist philosopher of religion would like to offer some remarks before passing on to a consideration of the second.

(1) Inasmuch as the word God implies the separation of the sacred from the profane, and to the extent that one is functioning within such a universe of discourse, the use of the word God may be an acceptable locution:

Some words ... [are] 'numinous', others rational or ordinary. If treated as though purely rational, numinous terms suffer a great deal of distortion. An easy example is the word 'God'. 'Natural theology', or the Deists, used it as a 'rational' term. But, as Pascal put it, this 'god of the philosophers' is something quite different from 'the god of Abraham and Isaac'. An Oxford don showed his blindness for this distinction when he criticized Jehovah for describing himself by the tautological phrase 'I am that I am', when in fact he ought to have told us exactly what he was. M. Eckhart's beautiful meditation on this phrase from the 'Book of Exodus' shows that *Ho Ōn* is clearly a numinous term of great profundity. No student of the Buddhist scriptures in the original can fail to notice that they abound in numinous words, such as *Dharma, Buddha, Bhagavat, Arhat, Nirvana* and *Tathagata*. Their prominence has many important consequences.[5]

(2) If a distinction is drawn between God and Godhead, then the Buddhist may re-evaluate his position in relation to God-head but not God.[6]

(3) It must not be overlooked that

Buddhism does not reject theism outright. While the Buddha was critical of theistic religions, he accepted that they had a limited value: he referred to them as 'unsatisfactory religions' (*anassāsika*) rather than as 'unreligious religions' (*abrahmacariyavāsa*) such as Materialism. The Buddha, very often, showed great respect to leaders and followers of other religions and strongly recommended his followers to show respect to other faiths.[7]

(4) "Buddhism is atheistic, but we need to remember, as already noted that Buddhist atheism has to be distinguished from materialistic atheism".[8]

As regards the second conclusion pertaining to probability, the Buddhists may be inclined to accept it as according to Buddhism "what is 'in the nature of things' (*Dhammatā*) is only a probability and not a necessity, *when psychological factors are involved*".[9] At least in early Buddhism, causation is "not subjective and is not a category imposed by the mind on phenomena",[10] so that the introduction of psychological factors would tend to vitiate any conclusion based on probability.[11]

John H. Hick then proceeds to offer a conclusion specific to Christian theism when he writes:

In spite of the immense intellectual investment that has been going into the various attempts to demonstrate the existence of God, the conclusion which many have reached that this is indemonstrable agrees both with the contemporary philosophical understanding of the nature and limits of logical proof and with the biblical understanding of our knowledge of God.[12]

Buddhist thought, like modern philosophical thought, recognizes the limits of logic, especially in relation to its central experience of *Nirvāṇa*. These limits are explained both literally and figuratively. Thus K.N. Jayatilleke remarks:

However, all these phrases, 'exists', 'ceases to exist', etc. are misleading since they have a spatio-temporal connotation. *Nirvāṇa* is not spatially located (*na katthaci, na kuhiñci*), nor located in time so that 'one cannot say of *Nirvāṇa* that it is past, present or future'. It is also not causally conditioned (*na paṭiccasamuppannaṃ*). It is therefore not capable of conceptual formulation (*asaṅkhiyo*) or literal description.[13]

He also goes on to say:

So the explanations given to us who have not attained it are compared to the attempt to explain the nature of light or colour to a man born blind. To tell him that light or colour is not a sound, nor a taste, nor smell, nor touch, is literally true, but since he is only acquainted with sounds, tastes, smells and touches he may think that colours are nothing or cannot exist. The problem with *Nirvāṇa* is analogous. What we have to do with the blind man is to evolve a method of restoring his sight. When this is done, no explanation is necessary, but before that strictly no explanation was possible. So to explain *Nirvāṇa* by some form of rational demonstration is impossible — it falls beyond the pale of logic (*atakkāvacara*).[14]

However, a nuance may be identified in relation to the limit of logic. While Christian theism uses the limits of logic to indicate the mystery of God[15] and to demonstrate how God may not be exhaustively known through logic, the Buddhist position with respect to the limit of logic would be that *Nirvāṇa* transcends logic (*attakāvacāra*)[16] and cannot at all be conventionally known.

Similarly, the question of the knowledge of God is also significant. There are, for instance, passages in the Hindu texts[17] which are reminiscent of passages in Buddhist texts.[18] K.N. Jayatilleke maintains that "it would be quite misleading to identify the two".[19] The similarity, nevertheless, is so striking that perhaps it would be wiser to keep an open mind regarding the possibility of the same experience being expressed in two modes — theistic[20] and non-theistic. The main point here, however, pertains to the fact of our *knowledge* — whether biblical or otherwise and of God or *Nirvāṇa*. This leads to the question: How do we know what we know?

RATIONALISM AND EMPIRICISM

Modern philosophical thought has basically recognized two ways of knowing and has debated their respective merits.

Philosophy recognizes two ways in which human beings may come to know whatever there is to be known. One way (stressed by empiricism) is through experience, and the other (stressed by rationalism) is through reasoning. The limitation of the rationalist way is that the only truths capable of being strictly proved are analytic and ultimately tautological. We cannot by logic alone demonstrate any matters of fact and existence; these must be known through experience. That two and two equal four can be certified by strict proof; but that we live in a world of objects in space, and that there is this card table and that oak tree and those people, are facts that could never be known independently of sense perception. If nothing were given through experience in its various modes, we should never have anything to reason about. This is as true in religion as in other fields. If God exists, God is not an idea but a reality outside us; in order to be known to men and women, God must become manifest in some way within their experience.[21]

In this debate John H. Hick seems to come out on the side of empiricism. In this respect his stand is very similar to that of the Buddha. It is important to distinguish here between 'recommending doctrines on rational grounds' and doctrines 'derived by reason'.[22] The term rationalism is used here in the latter sense. "Rationalism is used in philosophical language in opposition to empiricism and it is defined as 'a theory of philosophy in which the criterion of truth is not sensory but intellectual and deductive — usually associated with an attempt to introduce mathematical methods into philosophy as in Descartes, Leibnitz and Spinoza'."[23] K.N. Jayatilleke demonstrates conclusively that Buddha was not a rationalist in this sense.

When we thus examine whether the Buddha was a rationalist in this sense, we find that he rejected such claims. It is stated that according to a contemporary of his, Buddha's doctrines were a product of pure reasoning and were not based on any extrasensory perception or extraordinary insight. Sunakkhatta, who left the order dissatisfied, observes that 'the recluse Gotama does not have a distinctive knowledge and vision more than that of (other) men; he preaches a doctrine, which is a product of reasoning and speculation and is self-evident'.... The Buddha denies that it is so and it is a veritable denial that he was a rationalist in the above sense of the term. We have no reason to doubt this claim, since nothing in the Nikāyas suggests that any doctrines were taught or were considered to follow from premises which were held to be true in an *a priori* sense. On the contrary, we always find the Buddha recommending doctrines which are claimed to be true in an empirically or experientially verifiable sense. We have already seen that the reason for the rejection of theories based on *takka* was that the reasoning may be valid or invalid and even if the reasoning was valid and consistent, the theories may be true or false in the light of facts. Pure reason was therefore no safe guide for the discovery of truth.[24]

In view of the contemporary dissatisfaction with being trapped in "a self-imposed state of Cartesian doubt" it may be worth pointing out that, if anything, even at a purely philosophical level, Buddhist thought represents a very different tendency. It maintains that

there is no unmoving mover behind the movement. It is only movement. It is not correct to say that life is moving, but life is movement itself. Life and movement are not two different things. In other words, there is no thinker behind the thought. Thought itself is the thinker. If you remove the thought, there is no thinker to be found. *Here we cannot fail to notice how this Buddhist view is diametrically opposed to the Cartesian cogito ergo sum: "I think, therefore I am".*[25]

If Buddha was not a rationalist, then can Buddha be described as an empiricist? K.N. Jayatilleke considers this to be a far more accurate characterization of Buddha's position. "The emphasis that 'knowing' (*jānam*) must be based on 'seeing' (*passam*) or direct perceptive experience, makes Buddhism a form of Empiricism. We have, however, to modify the use of the term somewhat to mean not only that all our knowledge is derived from sense-experience but from extrasensory experience as well".[26]

The inclusion of extrasensory perception within empiricism seems to represent no greater an accommodation to Buddhism than the acceptance of the conscious theistic experience within its range in the context of Christianity,[27] especially if one uses the term empiricism "to include the entire conscious content of the mind and not merely the data of the senses: 'the sole source of knowledge is experience ... experience may be understood as either all conscious content data of the senses only or *other designated content'*."[28]

When Buddhist logic emerged as a developed school from around fifth century onwards, it admitted only two means of knowledge namely, perception and inference.[29] These seem to correspond to empiricism and rationalism in a general way. However, prior to these developments, it underwent a period reminiscent of the remarks made by John H. Hick that "really radical and thorough doubt can never be reasoned away, since it includes even our reasoning powers within its scope".[30] The Mādhyamika School of Buddhism came close to adopting this position, especially by claiming that everything is empty or void (*śūnya*), and who, when challenged "that the argument that proves the voidness of *all* things is itself void", replied that, "this only serves to bring out the universal applicability of the law; the proof that all things are *śūnya* is itself *śūnya*, within appearance".[31] The extent to which doubting may be carried varies in different strands of the school, but the rival school of Yogācāra did argue that at least the reality of consciousness must be conceded to justify the validity of logical and soterio-logical operations.[32] In other words, the "only way of escaping such doubt is to avoid falling into it in the first place".[33] "The Buddhist refers in this connection to a maxim — *vyāghātāvadhirā-śaṅkā* — which means that we cannot go on doubting for ever, but must desist from doing so when it results in a self-contra-diction in thought or leads to a practical absurdity".[34]

John H. Hick questions the use of pushing free inquiry to the very limits of scepticism when he writes:

It has also been argued that when doubt becomes universal in its scope, it becomes meaningless. To doubt whether some particular perceived object is real is to doubt whether it is *as real as* the other sensible objects that we experience. "Is that chair really there?" means "Is it there in the way in which the table and the other chairs are there?" But what does it mean to doubt whether there is really anything whatever there? Such 'doubt' is meaningless. For if nothing is real, there is no longer any sense in which anything can be said to be unreal.[35]

Although the reaction to such developments in India did not lead to a revival of realism *vis-à-vis* scepticism, it did open up the discussion for similar questions to be raised, namely, that nothing can be said to be false unless something is admitted to be as true.

REVELATION AND FAITH

John H. Hick has observed that "empiricist reasoning is in agreement with the unformulated epistemological assumptions of the Bible".[36] Our brief excursion into the realm of Buddhist epistemology showed that the same could be said of early Buddhism. In later Buddhism, the dimension of experience is more explicitly employed and is identified as a means of direct knowledge. Several modes of direct knowledge are acknowledged but the one most relevant here is the intuition of a Yogin (*yogipratyakṣa*) and the Buddha is acknowledged as the supreme exemplar of such direct intuition.[37] Whether statements based on such intuition can be accorded the status of revelation as commonly understood is a moot point in Buddhism and most Buddhist scholars would prefer to distinguish their position from the Christian example. The Christian concept, of course, represents the paradigmatic example in Western thought and it is to its consideration that we must now turn, with the realization that Christian thought contains "two very different understandings" of the nature of revelation and faith: a propositional one and a non-propositional one.

THE PROPOSITIONAL VIEW OF REVELATION AND FAITH

The propositional view of revelation and faith characterizes (1) medieval Christianity; (2) traditional Roman Catholicism and (3) conservative Protestantism. At its core lies the idea that the "content of revelation is a body of truths expressed in statements or propositions".[38] These are contained in the Bible and faith is the proper response to these statements communicated by God. "To a Catholic, the word 'faith' conveys the notion of an intellectual assent to the content of revelation as true because of the witnessing authority of God the Revealer."[39] Some important aspects of the propositional view of revelation and faith may now be identified: (1) Catholicism accepts the authority of both the text of the Bible as well as "traditions concerned with faith and morals as having been received orally from Christ or inspired by the Holy Spirit and continuously preserved in the Catholic Church".[40] Protestantism stands by the text as such (*sola scriptura*). (2) The propositional view of revelation and faith involves a distinction between natural and revealed theology, the former consisting of those insights which could be arrived at by the human intellect by itself (that 'God exists') and the latter consisting of those truths not so accessible (e.g. the doctrine of the Trinity). (3) Most modern critics of religion assume a propositional view of revelation and faith. (4) Faith itself is considered a product of God's grace, like revelation, so that a "tightly circular system of theology"[41] is involved which is apparent in the following pronouncement of the Vatican Council of 1870, when it defined faith as "a supernatural virtue whereby, inspired and assisted by the grace of God, we believe that the things He has revealed are true".[42] Finally, (5) faith involves "believing of propositions upon insufficient evidence" and the "most popular way of bridging the evidential gap is by an effort of will". This final point naturally paves the way for the discussion of various theories of faith.

Before embarking on that discussion it might be worthwhile to offer a Buddhist assessment of revelation. In relation to the first point it is worth observing that Theravāda and Mahāyāna Buddhism have a parallel difference of opinion in the matter of Buddhist texts. Theravāda Buddhism takes its stand on the text of the Pali canon just as conservative Protestantism does on the biblical, but Mahāyāna Buddhism believes in an extra esoteric transmission.[43] (2) The distinction of natural and revealed theology can be applied, *mutatis mutandis*, to Buddhist doctrines. For instance, Buddhists distinguish among three kinds of *Dukkha*: "(1) *Dukkha* as ordinary suffering (*dukkha-dukkha*); (2) *Dukkha* as produced by change (*viparināma-dukkha*) and (3) *dukkha* as conditioned states (*saṃkhāra-dukkha*)".[44] Walpola Sri Rahula explains:

All kinds of suffering in life like birth, old age, sickness, death, association with unpleasant persons and conditions, separation from beloved ones and pleasant conditions, not getting what one desires, grief, lamentation, distress — all such forms of physical and mental suffering, which are universally accepted as suffering or pain, are included in *dukkha* as ordinary suffering (*dukkha-dukkha*).

A happy feeling, a happy condition in life, is not permanent, not everlasting. It changes sooner or later. When it changes, it produces pain, suffering, unhappiness. This vicissitude is included in *dukkha* as suffering produced by change (*vipariṇāma-dukkha*).

It is easy to understand the two forms of suffering (*dukkha*) mentioned above. No one will dispute them. This aspect of the First Noble Truth is more popularly known because it is easy to understand. It is common experience in our daily life.

But the third form of *dukkha* as conditioned states (*saṃkhāra-dukkha*) is the most important philosophical aspect of the First Noble Truth, and it requires some analytical explanation of what we consider as a 'being', as an 'individual', or as 'I'.[45]

It will be clear from this passage that while the first two understandings of *dukkha* can be encompassed within our normal understanding of *dukkha*, the third, the further insight, is a peculiarly Buddhist one[46] and a particularly recondite one[47] with which the Buddhists themselves have had trouble. This third type of *dukkha* would be analogous to 'revealed theology' and the first two to 'natural theology'.

As to the third point, the Buddhist understanding of revelation is propositional and its criticism of the position has a modern ring to it. In this respect the most trenchant Buddhist critique takes the form that if "nobody has seen god face to face ... it is difficult to talk of a revelation given by god".[48] Although this criticism is developed originally in a Hindu context,[49] it can easily be extended to Christianity. And it becomes particularly forceful in a Christian context because "... any type of seeing god is, by definition, ruled out in the teaching of Christianity",[50] according to which no human being could survive such an encounter.[51]

As for the fourth point, faith in Buddhism has a very different connotation, which will be specified soon. However, to the extent that its more usual sense is recognized in Buddhism in the category of the *saddhānusārī*[52] (follower in faith) and the analysis of the term *saddhā*[53] (faith) itself, there are two crucial differences from the Christian position here: (1) faith is but *one* element in *one* particular formulation of the celebrated Buddhist tripod of *śīla, samādhi* and *prajñā* and (2) faith-response is a distinguishing characteristic of *some* followers of the Buddha; it is not intended as a universal response of all believers the way it is in Christianity.

On the fifth point, Buddhism is quite explicit in *not* encouraging belief based on insufficient evidence and in preferring knowledge to faith. In the face of insufficient evidence Buddha would seem to recommend abandoning the revelation if the following discourse is taken into account:

Herein a certain religious teacher is a revelationist, who holds to the truth of revelation and preaches a doctrine according to revelation, according to what is traditionally handed down, according to the authority of scripture. Now a teacher who is a revelationist and holds to the truth of revelation may have well-heard it or ill-heard it and it may be true or false. At this, an intelligent person reflects thus — this venerable teacher is a revelationist, etc. ... so seeing that his religion is unsatisfactory he loses interest and leaves it.[54]

As Buddhism allows for pre-mortem attainment of its religious goals and accepts extrasensory phenomena it is able to accord primacy to knowledge over belief or faith. Two dialogues from the Buddhist texts are relevant here. One is between the leader of the Jainas, Nigaṇṭha Nātaputta and a follower of the Buddha, Citta by name. The other is between the Buddha and Ānanda on the eve of Buddha's death. The first one runs as follows:

NIGANTHA NATHAPUTTA: Do you *believe* in (*saddahasi*) the statement of the recluse Gotama that there is a *jhanic* state (trance) in which there is no discursive or reflective thought there and is a cessation of discursive thought and reflection?

CITTA: I do not accept this as a *belief.*

NIGANTHA NATHAPUTTA: See what an honest, straightforward and upright person the householder Citta is...

CITTA: What do you think? Which is better, *knowledge or belief?*

NIGANTHA NATHAPUTTA: Surely, knowledge is better than belief.

CITTA: (I can attain up to the fourth *jhana*) ...*Knowing and seeing thus,* why should I accept this on the grounds of faith in any recluse or brahmin, that there is a trance in which there is no discursive or reflective thought....[55]

The background of the second dialogue is provided by the Buddha who asked all assembled, as he lay close to death, whether they had any vestigial doubts about his teachings, for now was the time to remove them. When no one raised a doubt his cousin and loyal attendant Ānanda exclaimed: "I have this faith, Sir, in the community of Bhikkus here, that not even one of them has any doubt of perplexity...."[56] Buddha responded: "You speak of faith, Ānanda. But in this matter Ānanda the [Buddha] knows and knows for certain".[57]

It will be clear from the above discussion that faith in its Christian sense does not have a direct role to play in Buddhism for, "faith in Buddhism resembles very much the faith a scientist reposes in a particular hypothesis. He has faith that the latter might work because of the credibility and reliability that is suggested by the preliminary observations. Faith in Buddhism works only as a starting point in the scientist's sense and therefore it has necessarily to be replaced later by direct personal knowledge. Consequently, an Arahant is described as 'one devoid of faith' and it is often pointed out that the Arahant must be in a position to claim the highest knowledge without having to rely on faith."[58]

There are, however, situations, when even in Buddhism one has to function on the basis of "insufficient evidence", and these would perhaps provide interesting parallels to Christian theories of faith, some of which may now be identified. These are known as voluntarist theories of faith as they involve the "acceptance of certain beliefs by a definite act of will".[59]

BLAISE PASCAL'S VIEW

This view is popularly known as Pascal's wager. Blaise Pascal (1628-62) perhaps himself did not need it after his experience of mystical certitude on 23 November, 1654 but it will be of interest to those less convinced. Pascal's position can be stated in the form of two statements (1) that given the enigmatic nature of the existence of god, it is still a better bet to assume that he does exist rather than not and (2) if one is thus rationally convinced, the rational conclusion can be converted into a fideist position for oneself by an act of will.

We start with the initial position that we do not know whether

God exists or not. Now if we assume that God exists and act accordingly, we have a lot to gain and nothing to lose if God does in fact exist. But if we assumed God did not exist, and God did, we have a lot to lose. "Let us weigh the gain and the loss in wagering that God is. Let us estimate these two chances. If you gain, you gain all; if you lose, you lose everything. Wager, then, without hesitation that He is."[60]

However, if one wagers thus, can one coax oneself into believing in God? Pascal thinks it is possible to do so:

You would like to attain faith, and do not know the way; you would like to cure yourself of unbelief, and ask the remedy for it. Learn of those who have been bound like you.... Follow the way by which they began; by acting as if they believed, taking the holy water, having masses said, etc. Even this will naturally make you believe, and deaden your acuteness.[61]

This approach to faith has been advocated by some as probabilistically rational and criticized by others as mercenary. Be that as it may, it finds an interesting parallel in the idea of post-mortem survival in Buddhism, which again, to the unconvinced, presents a case of insufficient evidence, as demonstrated by Pāyāsi's inconclusive experiments at the time in this regard.[62] When faced with two doctrines, one asserting and the other denying survival and moral responsibility, the Buddha recommended the acceptance of the former as a rational choice. K.N. Jayatilleke writes that one may

... represent this "wager argument", which reminds us of a similar argument of Pascal, as follows:

	If p is true	If not-p is true
We wager p	We are happy in the next life	We are praised by the wise in this life
We wager not-p	We are unhappy in the next life	We are condemned by the wise in this life.

The conclusion (logical) is that it would be better to wager p than not-p because in this alternative we win whatever happens, while in choosing not-p we lose whatever happens. The two theories that are contrasted above are the theories of *atthikavāda* and *natthikavāda*, between which it was urged on rational grounds that it would be better to choose the former, irrespective of their truth-value.[63]

Similar arguments are used in early Buddhism to demonstrate the rationality not only of accepting belief in life after death (*attikavāda*) over the opposite (*natthikavāda*) but also of belief in efficacy of action (*kiriyavāda*) over lack of it (*akiriyavāda*) and belief in causality (*hetuvāda*) over the opposite (*ahetuvāda*).[64]

WILLIAM JAMES'S VIEW

William James (1842–1910) recommends faith on the ground that the enormity of what is at stake calls for a commitment. The following extracts from his writings indicate his position:

We cannot escape the issue by remaining skeptical and waiting for more light, because, although we do avoid error in that way if religion be untrue, we lose the good, if it be true, just as certainly as if we positively chose to disbelieve.[65]

William James then argues that the matter is too grave for not going ahead rather than waiting for proof as a scientist does. He says:

Better risk loss of truth than chance of error — that is your faith-vetoer's exact position. He is actively playing his stake as much as the believer is; he is backing the field against the religious hypothesis, just as the believer is backing the religious hypothesis against the field. To preach scepticism to us as a duty until 'sufficient evidence' for religion be found, is tantamount therefore to telling us, when in presence of the religious hypothesis, that to yield to our fear of its being error is wiser and better than to yield to our hope that it may be true.... Dupery for dupery, what proof is there that dupery through hope is so much worse than dupery through fear? I, for one, can see no proof; and I simply refuse obedience to the scientist's command to imitate his kind of option, in a case where my own stake is important enough to give me the right to choose my own form of risk.[66]

He also suggests that some overture on our part (rather than on God's) may be necessary to set the process in motion. Why, if one never asked someone for a date, what could then possibly ensue? His example is less romantic but contains the same message:

Just as a man who in a company of gentlemen made no advances, asked a warrant for every concession, and believed no one's word without proof, would cut himself off by such churlishness from all the social rewards that a more trustworthy spirit would earn — so here, one who would shut himself up in snarling logicality and try to make the gods extort his recognition willy-nilly, or not get it at all, might cut himself off forever from his only opportunity of making the gods' acquaintance.[67]

James's position has been criticized as constituting "an unrestricted license for wishful thinking" and as amounting "to an encouragement to us all to believe at our own risk, whatever we like. However, if our aim is to believe what is *true*, and not necessarily what we *like*, James's universal permissiveness will not help us".[68]

The material from Buddhism in this respect is relevant and helpful. It seems to suggest an angle which might help soften our criticism of James's position by suggesting that sometimes, in order to know what is true, we may have no choice but to believe, on good grounds no doubt, but at our own risk. The Pali canon contains the account of one Pukkusāti, who, unbeknown to him, encountered the Buddha in a potter's shed. He had already decided to join the Buddha's Order without having met the Buddha and at the end of the conversation he realized that he had been conversing with the Buddha himself! However, as he went out to obtain the robes and alms-bowl required for initiation he was savaged by a cow and died.[69]

It seems to me that Pukkusāti had acted on the Jamesian intuition. In the Pali canon itself Buddha points out the need of testing a master before accepting one,[70] but Pukkusāti had dispensed with those requirements. The Buddha declared that Pukkusāti "was a wise man, who had already seen the truth, and attained the penultimate stage in the realization of *Nirvāṇa*".[71]

F.R. TENNANT'S VIEW

F.R. Tennant's doctrine of voluntaristic faith is best developed in the context of the position developed by William James. In one respect it diverges from James's position on faith, but in another it converges with James's position on saintliness. It diverges from James's position on faith by being more rigorous in its approach. First of all, Tennant distinguishes between faith and belief as follows:

Belief is more or less constrained by fact or Actuality that already is or will be, independently of any striving of ours, and which convinces us. Faith, on the other hand, reaches beyond the Actual or the given to the ideally possible, which in the first instance it creates, as the mathematician posits his entities, and then by practical activity may realize or bring into Actuality. Every machine of human invention has thus come to be. Again, faith may similarly lead to knowledge of Actuality which it in no sense creates, but which would have continued, in absence of the faith-venture, to be unknown: as in the discovery of America by Columbus.[72]

Then he proceeds to show how science involves elements analogous to faith:

Science postulates what is requisite to make the world amenable to the kind of thought that conceives of the structure of the universe, and its orderedness according to quantitative law; theology, and sciences of valuation, postulate what is requisite to make the world amenable to the kind of thought that conceives of the why and wherefore, the meaning or purpose of the universe, and its orderedness according to teleological principles.[73]

The "scientific" proof of faith he offers, however, is saintliness.

Successful faith ... is illustrated by numerous examples of the gaining of material and moral advantages, the surmounting of trials and afflictions, and the attainment of heroic life, by men of old who were inspired by faith. It is thus that faith is pragmatically 'verified' and that certitude as to the unseen is established.[74]

In the end, Tennant has used James's criterion: 'not by the roots but by the fruits ye shall know them', although in the beginning his position is far less open-ended than that of James.

From the perspective of Buddhism the points on which Tennant has been criticized are potentially of even greater interest than Tennant's own position. John H. Hick remarks that

Tennant's bracketing together of religious faith and scientific 'faith' is highly questionable. A scientist's 'faith' is significant only as a preliminary to experimental verification. It is often a necessary stage on the way to tested knowledge, and it has value only in relation to subsequent verification. In science, verification '... consists in finding that the postulate or theory is borne out by appeal to external facts and tallies with them'.[75]

He goes on to note that such verification is not possible in the case of faith according to Tennant and therefore subjective sanctification must take the place of objective verification. The Buddhist position is one of great sympathy with that of Tennant. We saw earlier how the Buddhist concept of faith tends to assimilate the scientific and how, as the results of Buddhist practices can be experienced in this life, "objective" verification may not be out of the question. A second criticism of Tennant by John H. Hick is based on Tennant's claim that

The fruitfulness of a belief or of faith for the moral and religious life is one thing, and the reality or existence of what is ideated and assumed is another. There are instances in which a belief that is not true, in the sense of corresponding with fact, may inspire one with lofty ideals and stimulate one to strive to be a more worthy person.[76]

John H. Hick remarks that "This admission reduces religious faith, as Tennant conceives it, to an unverifiable hope, and thereby undermines his attempt to assimilate religious to scientific cognition".[77] From the Buddhist point of view, however, "assimilation of religious to scientific cognition" does not pose any special problem and may even be welcomed; and because Buddhism accepts the position that a belief may not be true and yet be morally uplifting, the Buddhist position is also close to that of Tennant in this regard.

PAUL TILLICH'S VIEW

Paul Tillich (1886-1965) is an extremely influential figure in modern thinking about faith. As a preliminary to the presentation of his views we may cite his definition of faith as "the state of being ultimately concerned".[78] The expression "ultimate concern" has gained wide currency as a definition of faith and even of religion and its flavour can perhaps be conveyed to a Buddhist if one chose to describe *Nirvāṇa* as *parama dharma*. The following comments could be understood in the same light: "People are in fact, ultimately concerned about many different things — for example, their nation, or their personal success and status; but these are properly only preliminary concerns, and the elevation of a preliminary concern to ultimacy is idolatry." Tillich describes ultimate concern in an often-quoted passage:

Ultimate concern is the abstract translation of the great commandment: "The Lord, our God, the Lord is one; and you shall love the Lord your God with all your heart, and with all your soul, and with all your mind, and with all your strength." The religious concern is ultimate; it excludes all other concerns from ultimate significance; it makes them preliminary. The ultimate concern is unconditional, independent of any conditions of character, desire, or circumstance. The unconditional concern is total; no part of ourselves or of our world is excluded from it; there is no 'place' to flee from it. The total concern is infinite: no moment of relaxation and rest is possible in the face of a religious concern which is ultimate, unconditional, total, and infinite.[79]

The recognition of the ultimacy of *Nirvāṇa* in Buddhism provides the cue here, for it represents "the culmination of that freedom of mind and freedom through extrasensory wisdom which, as the crown of renunciation and the casting aside of all unskills, dominates the Teaching: 'Even as the great ocean has but one flavour, that of salt, so has this *Dharma* and Discipline but one flavour, that of freedom' (*Vinaya-Piṭaka* ii. 239; *Anguttara-Nikāya* iv. 206; *Udāna* 54), 'that freedom which is analogous to knowledge on the one hand and *Nirvāṇa* on the other' (*Majjhima-Nikāya* i. 304; *Samyutta-Nikāya* iii. 189; v. 218)..."[80]

To revert now to a further consideration of Tillich's ideas prior to comparing them with the Buddhist, it has been pointed out that the phrase "ultimate concern" is ambiguous as it "may refer either to an *attitude* of concern or to the (real or imagined) *object* of that attitude. Does 'ultimate concern' refer to a concerned state of mind or to a supposed object of this state of mind?"[81]

The Buddhist response to this dilemma can take two forms. If the question is transposed in terms of *Nirvāṇa* and the question is asked whether it refers to a subjective attitude or an object, the Buddhist response is likely to be that it represents an experience which is "free from any partiality or dualism", an experience which has overcome "the extremes of emphasizing subject or object", that it is an experience in which "the Infinite is not only conceptualized but realized".[82] The famous passage from the Pali text (*Udāna* 80) deserves to be cited here.

O bhikkhus, there is the unborn, ungrown, and unconditioned. Were there not the unborn, ungrown, and unconditioned, there would be no escape for the born, grown, and conditioned. Since there is the unborn, ungrown, and unconditioned, so there is escape for the born, grown, and conditioned.

Here the four elements of solidity, fluidity, heat and motion have no place; the notions of length and breadth, the subtle and the gross, good and evil, name and form are altogether destroyed; neither this world nor the other, nor coming, going or standing, neither death nor birth, nor sense-objects are to be found.[83]

It is interesting that in his own efforts to solve the dilemma posed earlier, Tillich seems to espouse an isomorphic solution.

In his later book, *Dynamics of Faith,* this ambiguity is resolved. Tillich explicitly adopts both of these two possible meanings by identifying the attitude of ultimate concern with the object of ultimate concern. "The ultimate of the act of faith and the ultimate that is meant in the act of faith are one and the same." This means the "... disappearance of the ordinary subject-object scheme in the experience of the ultimate, the unconditional."[84]

If, however, the question is not transposed in terms of *Nirvāṇa* but is restricted to faith as understood in its accepted connotation, then the Buddhist answer will assume a very different form. For if it is faith one is dealing with through the intermediary expression of "ultimate concern" then for the Buddhist faith is clearly a matter of *attitude and not object* in both Theravāda and Mahāyāna Buddhism. The question is raised in Theravāda Buddhism that if the Buddha and the Buddhist saints have, after their death, passed into a state about which nothing empirically valid can be predicated then how can offerings made to them earn merit? The answer of the elder Nāgasena to the Indo-Greek king Menander (or Milinda), who asked the question, is worth citing:

'Does the broad earth acquiesce, O king, in all kinds of seeds being planted all over it?'
'Certainly not, Sir.'
'Then how is it those seeds, planted without the earth's consent, do yet stand fast and firmly rooted, and expand into trees with great trunks and sap and branches, and bearing fruits and flowers?'

'Though the earth, Sir, gives no consent, yet it acts as a site for those seeds, as a means of their development. Planted on that site they grow, by its means, into such great trees with branches, flowers, and fruit.'

'... As the broad earth, O king, is the Tathāgata, the Arahat, the Buddha supreme. Like it he accepts nothing. Like the seeds which through it attain to such developments are the gods and men who, through the jewel treasures of the relics and the wisdom of the [Buddha] — though he have passed away and consent not to it — being firmly rooted by the roots of merit, become like unto trees casting a goodly shade by means of the trunk of contemplation, the sap of true doctrine, and the branches of righteousness, and bearing the flowers of emancipation.... Therefore is it, great king, that acts done to the [Buddha], notwithstanding his having passed away and not accepting them, are still of value and bear fruit.'[85]

The evidence from Mahāyāna Buddhism on this point is more risible but no less pertinent. Both Theravāda and Mahāyāna believe that the sanctity of any object was to a great extent generated by the faith and worship bestowed upon it.

A well-known story may illustrate this. An old woman in China heard that a friend of hers was going on a trade journey to India, and she asked him to bring her back one of the Buddha's teeth. The trader went to India, but forgot all about the old woman's request, which he remembered only when he was nearly back home again. He saw a dead dog lying by the wayside, took one of the teeth and gave it to the old woman as his present from India. The old woman was overjoyed, built a shrine for the tooth, and she and her friends worshipped it daily. After a time the tooth became radiant, and emitted a strange light. Even after the merchant had explained that it was only a dog's tooth, the halo round the tooth persisted, so strong was the faith and devotion of this old woman.[86]

We must now consider faith as ultimate concern not as it is ordinarily accepted but as it is understood by Tillich in terms of his own profound theology. According to such a view,

ultimate concern is not a matter of the human subject adopting a certain attitude to a divine Object but is, in Tillichian language, a form of the human mind's participation in the Ground of its own being. This notion of participation is fundamental to Tillich's thought. He contrasts two types of philosophy of religion, which he describes as ontological and cosmological. The latter (which he associates with Aquinas) thinks of God as being 'out there', to be reached only at the end of a long and hazardous process of inference; to find him is to meet a Stranger. For the ontological approach, which Tillich espouses and which he associates with Augustine, God is already present to us as the Ground of our own being, yet at the same time God infinitely transcends us. Our finite being is continuous with the infinity of Being; consequently, to know God means to overcome our estrangement from the Ground of our being. God is not Another, an Object which we may know or fail to know, but Being-itself, in which we participate by the very fact of existing. To be ultimately concerned about God is to express our true relationship to Being.[87]

From a Buddhist point of view, two elements in such a worldview and godview are of special interest: (1) the distinction between the ontological and the cosmological and (2) the concept of participation which goes with the ontological type of philosophy of religion. The general trend of Buddhist thought is ontological rather than cosmological, that is why, as indicated in an earlier chapter, "monotheism has never appealed to the Buddhist mind. There has never been any interest in the origin of the Universe — with only one exception",[88] when allegedly under Islamic influence it came up with the idea of a primeval Buddha (*Ādibuddha*),[89] and in doing this it may have even prepared "the way for its own extinction".[90]

The development of the idea of participation in Tillich naturally assumes a theistic background. However, similar thought-patterns can be identified within Buddhism if the theistic discontinuity between creature and god is temporarily suspended. This is, for instance, the clear thrust of the following comment, *although from an opposite angle*:

the emphasis on the identity of the Buddha with this world had accustomed the Mahayanists to the idea that the Buddha nature dwells in every part of the universe, and therefore in the heart of each one of us.

> *"The Lord Buddha on his lion-throne*
> *Dwells in each particle of sand and stone."*

If one assumes that by our own efforts we ourselves strive for salvation, which part of ourselves is it then that seeks Nirvana? Is it our individual self, or perhaps our 'higher self', our 'Buddha-self', which does the seeking? The Mahayana came to the conclusion that it is really the Buddha in us who does the seeking and that it is the Buddha nature in us which seeks Buddha-hood.[91]

Here then lies the great difference in how ultimate concern may be interpreted in the Christian and Mahāyāna Buddhist contexts: their different conceptions of the *ultimate* have a profound implication for the nature of the *concern*. In Mahāyāna Buddhism the final development of this concern leads to a complete identificatin with the absolute, while in Christianity it can lead to a complete distancing from it.[92] The point calls for elaboration which may also result in its clarification. In Mahāyāna,

Nirvana is that mental state in which one realizes that all things are really non-existent and they are ultimately all the same. The moment an individual realizes this state of mind he is enlightened and realizes the Buddha-nature within himself. He eradicates from his own mind not only the concept of his own individuality but also the concept of the substantiality of everything. He cannot distinguish himself from any other thing or even from the absolute, for he has merged into the absolute. Since the absolute or the Buddha-nature is eternal, he also becomes eternal.[93]

We have here, in Tillich's words, the "disappearance of the ordinary subject–object scheme", a point also made earlier in the case of *Nirvāṇa* in the context of Theravāda Buddhism. However, in a Christian context, this disappearance sends the needle plunging to the opposite end of the compass. As John H. Hick explains:

Stressing the removal of the subject–object dichotomy, his [Tillich's] definition of faith can be seen as pointing to humanity's continuity or even identity with God as the Ground of one's being. But it can also be seen as pointing in the opposite direction, toward so extreme a sundering of God and man that faith can operate as an autonomous function of the mind whether God be a reality or not. Tillich presents this view in the following passage:

" 'God' ... is the name for that which concerns man ultimately. This does not mean that first there is a being called God and then the demand that man should be ultimately concerned about him. It means that whatever concerns a man ultimately becomes god for him, and conversely, it means that a man can be concerned ultimately only about that which is god for him."[94]

Paul Tillich's discussion of faith can also be aligned with the equation of *saṁsāra* with *Nirvāṇa* in Buddhism. In the following passage Tillich's claim of developing a standpoint 'beyond naturalism and supernaturalism' is reminiscent of Nāgārjuna's claim of Emptiness representing a superior standpoint beyond *samsāra* and *Nirvāṇa*.

Thus, with Tillich's formula, one can either define faith in terms of God, as one's concern about the Ultimate, or define God in terms of faith, as that — whatever it may be — about which one is ultimately concerned. This permissiveness between supranaturalism and naturalism is regarded by Tillich as constituting a third and superior standpoint "beyond naturalism and supranaturalism". Whether Tillich is justified in regarding it in this way is a question for the readers to consider for themselves.[95]

The same may be said of Nāgārjuna's claim.

A NON-PROPOSITIONAL VIEW OF REVELATION AND FAITH

The thought of Paul Tillich provides a convenient bridge over which one may pass from a consideration of a propositional view of revelation and faith to a non-propositional one.

The documentary character of the Bible is identical with the fact that it contains the original witness of those who participated in the revealing events. Their participation was their response to the happenings which became revealing events through their response. The inspiration of the biblical writers is their receptive and creative response to potentially revelatory facts. The inspiration of the writers of the New Testament is their acceptance of Jesus as the Christ, and with him, of the New Being, of which they became witnesses. Since there is no revelation unless there is someone who receives it as revelation, the act of reception is a part of the event itself. The Bible is both original event and original document; it witnesses to that of which it is a part.[96]

This

different view of revelation, which can be called in contrast the 'non-propositional' view (or, if a technical term is desired, the *heilsgeschichtliche* view), has become widespread within Protestant Christianity during the present century. This view claims to have its roots in the thought of the Reformers of the sixteenth century (Luther and Calvin and their associates) and still further back in the New Testament and the early Church.[97]

The chief feature of this non-propositional view as distinguished from the propositional view is that

According to this non-propositional view, the content of revelation is not a body of truths about God, but God coming within the orbit of human experience by acting in history. From this point of view, theological propositions, as such, are not revealed but represent human attempts to understand the significance of revelatory events. This non-propositional conception of revelation is connected with the modern renewed emphasis upon the personal character of God and the thought that the divine–human personal relationship consists of something more than the promulgation and reception of theological truths.[98]

As in the case of the propositional view of revelation and faith, the non–propositional view has its own implications for the Bible and for theological thinking:

The conception of revelation as occurring in the events of history — both world history and individual history — and the conception of faith as the experiencing of these events as God's dealings with human creatures, also suggest a different conception of the Bible from that which accompanies the propositional theory. Within the propositional circle of ideas, the Bible is customarily referred to as 'the Word of God'. This phrase is understood in practice as meaning 'the words of God'. However, within the contrasting set of ideas associated with the non-propositional view of revelation there is a tendency to return to the New Testament usage in which Christ, and only Christ, is called the divine Word (*Logos*). According to this view the Bible is not itself the Word of God but is rather the primary and indispensable witness to the Word. The New Testament is seen as the human record of the Incarnation, that is, of the 'fact of faith' which is expressed in such statements as "the Word became flesh and dwelt among us, full of grace and truth; we have beheld his glory, glory as of the only Son from the Father".[99]

The Buddhist response to the non-propositional view of revelation and faith may be presented in two parts. In the first part the Buddhist response in general to such a view may be identified. Subsequently, in the second part, the Buddhist responses to the specific issues raised by the non-propositional view may be discussed.

The Buddhist attitude, in general, towards the non-propositional view of revelation and faith will be more critical than towards the propositional, on account of the non-historical nature of the Buddhist assessment of the human condition. It is not being suggested here that the Buddha was not a historical person; the implication is that the insights, though arrived at by the Buddha, are independent of the person of the Buddha. This accounts for the anecdotal irreverence of the Buddha encountered in Zen in such statements which purportedly answer the question: Who is Buddha?

"One made of clay and decorated with gold."
"Even the finest artist cannot paint him."
"The one enshrined in the Buddha Hall."
"He is no Buddha."
"Your name is Yecho."
"The dirt-scraper all dried up."
"See the eastern mountains moving over the waves."
"No nonsense here."
"Surrounded by the mountains are we here."
"The bamboo grove at the foot of Change-lin hill."
"Three pounds of flax."
"The mouth is the gate of woe."
"Lo, the waves are rolling over the plateau."
"See the three-legged donkey go trotting along."
"A reed has grown piercing through the leg."
"Here goes a man with the chest exposed and the legs all naked."

After providing this list D.T. Suzuki remarks:

How difficult and how misleading it would be to try and understand Zen literally and logically, depending on those statements which have been given above as answers to the question "What is the Buddha?" Of course, so far as they are given as answers they are pointers by which we may know where to look for the presence of the Buddha; but we must remember that the finger pointing at the moon remains a finger and under no circumstances can it be changed into the moon itself. Danger always lurks where the intellect slyly creeps in and takes the index for the moon itself.[100]

Even early Buddhism shares this attitude to Buddha's personal existence.[101] The following statement in the Pali canon serves to illustrate the point:

Whether Buddhas arise, O priests, or whether Buddhas do not arise, it remains a fact and the fixed and necessary constitution of being, that all its constituents are transitory. This fact a Buddha discovers and masters, and when he has discovered and mastered it, he announces, teaches, publishes, proclaims, discloses, minutely explains, and makes it clear, that all the constituents of being are transitory.[102]

This is then repeated verbatim with respect to the other two marks or characteristics of existence as well.

Similarly, although the Buddhists generated, elaborated and transmitted an enormous mass of sacred literature, the words of the Buddha possessed a soteriological rather than historical significance. It is true that this is also true of the Bible; the crucial difference, however, lies in the fact that neither the Buddha nor his teachings as such possessed that power: the same insights received from anyone else and couched in a different pedagogy would be as effective, for it is the insight which saves, neither the person who communicates it nor the words through which it is communicated. Moreover, the insights may need to be communicated to different audiences or at different times in a different manner.

On more specific points, however, the parallels from Buddhism are closer.

(1) The point is raised in relation to the non-propositional view of revelation and truth that "if it is God's intention to confront men with God's presence, as personal will and purpose, why has this not been done in an unambiguous manner, by some overwhelming manifestation of divine glory and power?"[103]

The answer to the question in Christianity is given in terms of freedom of will and the exercise of choice related to it in responding to God's message. Thus,

the process of becoming aware of God, if it is not to destroy the frail autonomy of the human personality, must involve the individual's own freely responding insight and assent. Therefore, it is said, God does not become known to us as a reality of the same order as ourselves. If God were to do that the finite being would be swallowed by the infinite Being. Instead, God has created space-time as a sphere in which we may exist in relative independence, as spatiotemporal creatures. Within this sphere God is self-discovered in ways that allow us the fateful freedom to recognize or fail to recognize God's presence. The divine actions always leave room for that uncompelled response that theology calls faith. It is this element in the awareness of God that reserves man's cognitive freedom in relation to an infinitely greater and superior reality. Faith is thus the correlate of freedom: faith is related to cognition as free will to conation. As one of the early Church Fathers wrote, 'And not merely in works, but also in faith, has God preserved the will of man free and under his own control'.[104]

The Buddhist position is in some ways similar. Buddhism is against predeterminism and emphasizes freedom of will[105] and the Buddha, though not above displaying miracles on occasion,[106] was in general opposed to their performance even by his gifted monks.[107] The adoption of Buddhism had to be voluntary. The Buddha did not demand the abandonment of previous adherence from those who became his followers.[108] In fact, the experience of the person who met Buddha on the road to Benaras hardly compares with the experience of Paul on the road to Damascus.

On the road, Gautama met an ascetic who remarked on his clear eyes and radiant complexion and asked about his religion. The Buddha declared that he was a Victor, that he had no equal in the world of gods and men, that he had become omniscient and had reached *nirvāṇa*. The ascetic answered in one word which means either 'it may be so' or 'let it be so', shook his head, and walked away on another road. This curious encounter seems like historical fact rather than pious invention. Gautama's first proclamation of his Buddhahood was not heeded.[109]

Moreover, in Buddhism not only is it the individual's decision to follow its teachings; it is the individual's effort, as opposed to God's grace, which determines the outcome of the decision.

(2) In Christianity,

the non-propositional view of revelation also tends to be accompanied by a different conception of the function of theology from that operating in the propositional system of ideas. The strong emphasis upon God's self-revelation in and through the stream of saving history (*Heilsgeschichte*) recorded in member of this distinction. The notion of revealed theology is rejected on the ground that revelation means God's self-disclosure in history (rather than the disclosure of a set of theological propositions) to mankind; natural theology is rejected as a series of attempts to establish without faith what can only be given to faith.[110]

Buddhist thought also would be inclined to reject both revealed and natural theology, but on different grounds. The grounds on which it would reject revealed theology have already been discussed. As for natural theology, it has provoked two responses. The first response rejects natural theology without rejecting theism. The second response shows how the non-propositional view may not be able to do without natural theology!

The first response takes the position that, "The Western God was a conceptual phenomenon, while the Eastern God was an intuitive experience. That is why the question about the proofs of God's existence never arises in Eastern philosophy. There is no natural theology in the East. For them, the god-concept carries only a phenomenological significance."[111]

The second response is specific to Christianity and takes the altered conception of revelation in the non-propositional view into account. The criticism then runs as follows:

The theist can argue that the special revelation of Christ is particularly within revealed theology and has nothing to do with natural theology. This may be true to a certain extent because there is hardly any empirical fact to make the idea of the savior Christ meaningful, and therefore positively, its meaning owes much to revealed theology. But on the other hand, it gets very closely related to factual statements. The revealed figure of Christ depends on many objectively factual premises like 'God created man and the world and Christ is his incarnation; Man has sinned; This sin is transmitted on a social scale; Christ did attain resurrection', etc., etc. And these statements are meaningful only in terms of natural theology and factual statements.[112]

REVELATION AND REASON IN THE NON-PROPOSITIONAL VIEW OF REVELATION AND FAITH

The role of reason in the non-propositional view of revelation and faith has been succinctly outlined by John H. Hick as follows:

This modern theological rejection of natural theology is not necessarily motivated by an irrationalist distrust of reason. It may represent an empiricism which recognizes that human thought can deal only with material that has been given in experience. Just as our knowledge of the physical world is ultimately based upon sense perception, so any religious knowledge must ultimately be based upon aspects of human experience that are received as revelatory. Thus, reason can never

replace experience as the source of the basic religious data. Nevertheless, in its proper place and when allowed to fulfil its proper role,
reason plays an important part in the religious life. Negatively, it can
criticize naturalistic theories that are proposed as ruling out a rational
belief in the reality of God; and in this way it may have the effect of
removing blocks in the way of belief. Positively, it must seek to
understand the implications of what is known by faith: in a famous
phrase of Anselm's, this is 'faith seeking understanding.' Of course,
reason is at work also in the systematic formulation of what is believed
on the basis of faith.

This statement can be reduced to five main propositions: (1)
"reason can never replace experience as the source of basic
religious data"; (2) it can, however, serve both a negative and
positive function in this context; (3) it can render naturalistic
theories improbable; (4) it can render faith plausible; and (5)
reason can elucidate faith.

Buddhism is in complete agreement on the first point. The
basic component of Buddhism is *Nirvāṇa* and it is consistently
described in terms of experience in the Buddhist texts. Two
examples should suffice, (1) one in which the Buddha describes
Nirvāṇa as experienced by him and (2) another in which he
speaks of it as experienced by his followers.

(1) In seeking for 'salvation' I reached in experience the *nibbāna* which is
unborn, unrivalled, secure from attachment, undecaying, unailing,
undying, unlamenting and unstained.... This condition is indeed
reached by me which is deep, difficult to see, difficult to understand,
tranquil, excellent, beyond the reach of mere logic, subtle and to be
realized only by the wise (each individually for himself).[114]
(2) Well expounded by the master is the doctrine which bears the
desired fruit here and now, which has 'Come and See' for its motto,
which assuredly leads to the goal, the truth whereof is to be experienced by the wise, each individually for himself, namely, the one
which consists essentially in subduing the haughty spirit, the perfect
control of thirst, the upsetting of the very storage of creative energy,
the arrest of the course of *saṁsāra* as regards the fate of an individual,
the rare attainment of the state of the void, the waning out of desire,
the dispassionate state, the cessation of all sense of discordance, the
nibbāna.[115]

Not only is experience emphasized, the limits of reason in
arriving at religious truth are clearly recognized. In his last

section on the Buddhist attitude to reason, K.N. Jayatilleke offers the conclusion that,

one cannot hope to have perfect knowledge (*ñāṇa*) of a proposition or theory by the consideration of some reasons for it (*ākāra-parivitakka-*) or by the conviction that dawns by merely reflecting on it (*diṭṭhi-nijjkāna-kkhanti*). Belief on the basis of these two kinds of rational reflection, is placed on the same footing on epistemological grounds as faith (*saddhā*), authority (*anussava-*) or purely subjective considerations like likes or dislikes (*ruci*).[116]

The *nature* of the experience differs in the two traditions but if the non-propositional view of revelation and reason is taken into account then both Christianity and Buddhism accord a common epistemological primacy to experience. Again, Buddhism would probably have little difficulty in accepting the dual role played by reason. Buddha clearly reasons *against*[117] the opposing views and reasons *for*[118] his own position. Interestingly, the Buddha also criticises naturalistic beliefs which question not the reality of God but the reality of post-mortem survival.[119] One also encounters a version of 'faith seeking understanding' in the context of Buddhism:

Saddhā (faith, belief) being used for different stages and types of acceptance of a proposition or doctrine. The first was that of accepting for the purpose of testing, the stage in which one 'safeguards the truth'. The stage in which one reposes faith in a person after realizing that he was honest, unbiased and intelligent is perhaps the second. The next stage is the one in which there was a partial and personal verification of the doctrine and it is at this stage that one is said to have a 'rational faith'. The word 'faith' here may seem less preferable than belief though we have used it to translate the word *saddhā*.[120]

K.N. Jayatilleke remarks that it "is this last stage that is greatly valued in Buddhism. The person who has developed this "rational faith" seems to be identical with the person who is described as being "emancipated by faith" (*saddhāvimutto*).[121]

The use of reason to elucidate matters of faith and doctrine is as much attested to in Buddhism as in Christianity. The entire text of *The Questions of King Milinda* illustrates the point, as also the numerous commentaries and independent works.

There is, however, the danger of overestimating these parallels if one focuses only on structure and overlooks the content.

One must not overlook the "contrasting situations of Christianity and Buddhism with regard to their respective means of knowledge. For Christianity the basic and fundamental, and sometimes the only, means of knowledge are grace, revelation and authority".[122] On the other hand, "Buddhism emphasizes the necessity of rational understanding, experience and verification in the field of religion".[123]

SOME GENERAL BUDDHIST CRITICISMS OF REVELATION AND FAITH IN CHRISTIANITY

Some modern Buddhist scholars who are familiar with Christian theology have offered some fresh criticisms of the Christian concepts of revelation and faith by applying the traditional Buddhist critique in a modern context. Three such criticisms may be of particular interest.

(1) Gunapala Dharmasiri is familiar with the propositional and non-propositional views of revelation and faith in Christianity. He even offers the opinion that

the traditional view about revelation is a much more coherent attempt to answer the problems of revelation. The traditional way was to take the scriptures as the basis of revelation. But some contemporary theologians try to relegate scripture to the background and emphasize the special revelation of Christ, taking scripture only as a commentary on the special revelation.

Herein Dharmasiri is expressing an opinion, an interesting one, but still an opinion. Subsequently, however, he cites James J. Packer as follows:

So the revealing facts of history are only accessible to those who are already sure that Christianity is true. And how do we become sure of this?... Before I can find revelation in history, I must first receive a private communication from God: and by what objective standard can anyone check this? There is no norm for testing private revelations. We are back in subjectivism with a vengeance.... Only when we abandon the liberal view that Scripture is no more than fallible human witness, needing correction by us, and put in its place the Biblical conviction that Scripture is in its nature revealed truth in writing, an authoritative norm for human thought about God, can we, in principle, vindicate the

Christian knowledge of God from the charge of being the incorrigibly arbitrary product of our own subjective fancy. Reconstructed liberalism, by calling attention to the reality of sin, has shown very clearly our need of an objective guarantee of the possibility of right and true thinking about God; but its conception of revelation through historical events and personal encounter with the speaking God ends, as we saw, in illuminism or mysticism, and is quite unable to provide us with such a guarantee. No guarantee can, in fact, be provided except by a return to the old paths — that is, by a renewed acknowledgement of, and submission to, the Bible as an infallible written revelation from God.[124]

Gunapala Dharmasiri bases his criticism on the above assessment and comments:

Packer is here pointing to an unavoidable problem in Christian theology. Every theologian who has tried to overemphasize the special revelation of Christ has got repeatedly entangled in this problem. Therefore what really happens with these theologians is that they usually confuse the general and special revelations together and do not, in practice, stand up to their theoretical dogma of the exclusive predominance of the special revelation. Barth also exemplifies this dilemma when he says that the hearing of the Word of God 'can only be attested in the realm of humanity by an appeal to proclamation through the Church, to Holy Scripture, to revelation....'[125]

A parallel problem in Buddhism would arise if one rejected authority as a general source of knowledge and then proceeded to assert that the Buddha's words were especially authoritative. This epistemological sleight of hand, as it were, is actually attempted by Dharmakīrti![126]

(2) Buddhist scholars reject the distinction between revealed and natural theology, as well as both as sources of knowledge, in keeping with the non-propositional view of revelation and faith, but for different reasons. Their rejection is based on the rejection of authority and tradition itself as constituting a valid epistemology. Thus it is argued that

revealed theology can hardly keep to itself as an independent branch of knowledge. Here, one can always say that revealed theology can be an independent branch of knowledge on a completely different epistemological basis. This is what Barth tries to do; God being completely transcendent and 'wholly other' he can be known only through his own revelations to us. This makes tradition and authority its own epistemological basis. Revealed theology has also been treated as supplementing natural knowledge or as supplying the basis for natural theology in the sense that natural theology is said to be trying to prove and clarify what revealed theology has already stated. Thus, revealed theology can assume a great significance, not only in its Barthian form, but also in its many other variations. Whatever the form it takes, it always bases itself on authority and tradition as its only epistemological basis.[127]

(3) When Christian scholars offer rational grounds for theistic beliefs, modern Buddhist scholars, not sharing such belief, accuse them of confusing coherence and rationality.

Any two related fictional concepts are always coherent as [a] system, but it does not say anything at all about their rationality. Coherence may be a form of rationality, and what is actually meant by rationality here is clarity or coherence: it is always advisable to distinguish between rationality and coherence in such instances. Novels and fictional stories though coherent are hardly spoken of as being rational. This distinction is an important one and should always be made.[128]

CHAPTER 6

Problems of Religious Language

THE PECULIARITY OF RELIGIOUS LANGUAGE

In the philosophy of religion as it has developed in the West, two main questions may be identified as representing problems associated with the religious use of language: (1) what "special sense" do "descriptive terms bear when they are applied to God"?[1] and (2) what is "the basic function of religious language"?[2] In relation to this last question one would want to ask, "In particular, do those religious statements that have the form of factual assertions (for example, "God loves mankind") refer to a special kind of fact — religious as distinguished from scientific fact or do they fulfil a different function altogether?"[3]

When one examines the descriptive terms that are applied to God in Christianity, two points at once become quite clear: (1) that although words from everyday life are used to make theological statements such as "God said", clearly a "long shift of meaning between the familiar secular use of these words and their theological employment",[4] is involved. When it is stated that "God said", it is hardly implied that "God has a physical body with speech organs which set in motion sound waves" which impinge on somebody's ears. (2) It is equally clear, however, "that in all cases in which a word occurs both in secular and in theological contexts, its secular meaning is primary in the sense that it developed first and has accordingly determined the definition of the word".[5] Thus if it is said that "God loves mankind" then the meaning of the statment is derived from our experience of love as human beings, yet "God is said to be 'without body, parts, or passions'. God has then, it would seem, no local existence or bodily presence through which to express love. But what is disembodied love, and how can we ever know that it exists?"[6]

The Buddhist response to these issues can take several forms. As Buddhism does not acknowledge a God and maintains that the concept of God has not been "meaningfully established", "it becomes pointless to build a religion or a religious language based on the concept of God".[7] Another less extreme[8] but more general criticism could flow from the fact that the meaning of the words used in everyday life is so nebulous that even if the existence of God was conceded hypothetically, the discourse about God would still be seriously compromised by this nebulousness. Edward Conze suggests that if the Buddhists have "never stated that God is *love* ... that may be due to their preoccupation with intellectual precision, which must have perceived that the word 'love' is one of the most unsatisfactory and ambiguous terms one could possibly use".[9]

The one point on which the Buddhist position would seem closest to that in the Western philosophy of religion would relate to the primacy of the secular meaning. Indeed, Buddha is sometimes quoted as stating that "one should not overstep the limits of conventional usage".[10] The point, however, must be elaborated to avoid any misunderstanding, for the Buddha also declares that there were "expressions, turns of speech, designations in common use in the world which the [Buddha] uses without being led astray by them"[11] — an aspiration which Christian theology could well share with him. In fact, if we recognize that the kind of role God plays in theism seems to be played by a Bodhisattva in Buddhism,[12] then we find that Buddhist discourse is also compelled to contend with the peculiarities of religious language as identified in a Christian context. Edward Conze writes that in Mahāyāna Buddhism:

The Buddhas and Bodhisattvas become an object of the desire to *love* Now the word *love* is extremely ambiguous, and harbours a great multiplicity of meanings. In this context, *love* in the sense of *Bhakti* means a personal relationship with a person whom one not only cherishes and adores, but whom one wishes to see, wishes to be with, whom one does not want to let go, whom one wants to persist. The orthodox view which the *"Wise"* had formed of the Buddha had made him quite unsuitable as an object of such love. He was said to be *extinct*, and, after his *Nirvana*, to have gone to nowhere at all. He was really lost to the world, quite isolated from it. Only his *Dharma*, an impersonal entity, remained. This theory had, from the very start, proved emotionally quite unsatisfactory to those whose religion meant *love*. Ananda, among the immediate disciples of the Buddha the chief representative of bhaktic mentality, a man who *loved* the Lord as a person, could not resign himself to his loss. He formed the quite heretical opinion that, when he entered *Nirvana*, the Buddha had gone up to the Heavens of Brahma, just as at birth he had come down from the Tushita Heavens....

As time went on, the bhaktic trend grew in India. Buddhism was not exempt from it. Increasingly the faithful wished to *"dwell in the sight of the Buddha,"* or to *"see the Tathagatas"*. In spite of official discouragement, they wished to believe that the Lord Buddha was not really extinct, but that somewhere he was present and in existence. Wisdom and devotion were in open conflict. Wisdom consisted in giving up all supports whatsoever. Devotion was unhappy without some persisting person as its support. The Mahasanghikas came to the rescue of the devotional needs of the laity by fostering the belief that the Buddha, as a supramundane being had not quite passed away, but persisted after his *Nirvana* in some form or other. The Mahayana greatly developed this idea, and filled the entire universe to the utmost limits of space with Buddhas and Bodhisattvas who were alive and thus could be loved and treasured.[13]

This citation extends the discussion of the issue on hand to a form of Buddhism which is as popular as the Theravāda but whose philosophy has often not been taken as much into account in intellectual comparisons of Christianity and Buddhism as Theravāda Buddhism. The relevance of such an extension becomes apparent the moment one focuses on a term which plays as key a role in Buddhism, and especially in Mahāyāna Buddhism, as 'love' does in Christianity; namely, compassion (*karuṇā*). In Mahāyāna Buddhism, in the context of the Bodhisattva, its complexity begins to parallel Christian discussions of *agape, eros*, etc. For,

Compassion itself is capable of three degrees of perfection: at first the Bodhisattva is compassionate to living beings; then he realizes that these do not exist, and directs his compassion on the impersonal events which fill the world; finally, the compassion operates within one vast field of Emptiness. The last two stages are unattested by our everyday experience. Nevertheless, it is not necessarily absurd to speak of a compassion which "has no object at all", for we know of other emotions which arise inwardly, without the stimulus of outside objects. Under the influence of excessive adrenalin a person may feel very angry, and will then look round for an object to vent his wrath on. An elderly spinster is full of more love and tenderness than she knows what to do with, and accordingly she will not rest until she has found someone to bestow it upon, even if only a cat or a parrot. Similarly a Bodhisattva's compassion springs from the depths of his heart, and from there it spreads over to that which he knows to be illusory.[14]

This discussion was set in motion by a consideration of the "special sense" that "descriptive terms bear when they are applied to God". In Buddhism a similar issue arises in the context of descriptive terms when they are applied to *Nirvāṇa*. Much has been written on this point[15] but the following passage serves to illustrate the issue:

Nirvāṇa is beyond all terms of duality and relativity. It is therefore beyond our conceptions of good and evil, right and wrong, existence and non-existence. Even the word 'happiness' (*sukha*) which is used to describe *Nirvāṇa* has an entirely different sense here. Sāriputta once said: 'O friend, *Nirvāṇa* is happiness! *Nirvāṇa* is happiness!' Then Udāyi asked: 'But, friend Sāriputta, what happiness can it be if there is no sensation?' Sāriputta's reply was highly philosophical and beyond ordinary comprehension: 'That there is no sensation itself is happiness'.[16]

This makes us revert to a point common to the philosophy of religion and to Buddhism — that even though the teaching may not be conventional it has necessarily to be conveyed by resorting to conventional language. How might this be possible?

THE DOCTRINE OF ANALOGY OF THOMAS AQUINAS
(1224/5 – 74)

In discussing the doctrine of analogy in preparation for instituting a comparison with Buddhist thought one needs to be clear about what the doctrine is, what it does *not* accomplish and what it *does* accomplish. The doctrine may be briefly recapitulated as follows:

Aquinas's basic and central idea is not difficult to grasp. He teaches that when a word such as 'good' is applied both to a created being and to God, it is not being used univocally (that is, with exactly the same meaning) in the two cases. God is not good in identically the sense in which human beings may be good. Nor, on the other hand, do we apply the epithet 'good' to God and man equivocally (that is, with completely different and unrelated meanings), as when the word 'bat' is used to refer both to the flying animal and to the instrument used in baseball. There is a definite connection between divine and human goodness, reflecting the fact that God has created mankind. According to Aquinas, then, 'good' is applied to creator and creature neither univocally nor equivocally but analogically.[17]

What the doctrine does *not* accomplish may now be recognized as follows:

Since the deity is hidden from us, the question arises of how we can know what goodness and the other divine attributes are in God. How do we know what perfect goodness and wisdom are like? Aquinas's answer is that we do not know. As used by him, the doctrine of analogy does not profess to spell out the concrete character of God's perfections, but only to indicate the relation between the different meanings of a word when it is applied both to humanity and (on the basis of revelation) to God. Analogy is not an instrument for exploring and mapping the infinite divine nature; it is an account of the way in which terms are used of the Deity whose existence is, at this point, being presupposed. The doctrine of analogy provides a framework for certain limited statements about God without infringing upon the agnosticism, and the sense of the mystery of the divine being which have always characterized Christian and Jewish thought at their best.[18]

However, while the doctrine does not tell us what divine attributes such as goodness are, and offer proof that they are attributes of God, it does tell us how we might begin to grasp what they are like. A canine analogy has often been used quite helpfully in this connection.

We sometimes say of a pet dog that it is faithful, and we may also describe a man as faithful. We use the same word in each case because of a similarity between a certain quality exhibited in the behavior of the dog and the steadfast voluntary adherence to a person or a cause that we call faithfulness in a human being. Because of this similarity, we are not using the word 'faithful' equivocally (with totally different senses). On the other hand, there is an immense difference in quality between a dog's attitudes and a person's. The one is indefinitely superior to the other in respect of responsible, self-conscious deliberation and the relating of attitudes to moral purposes and ends. Because of this difference, we are not using 'faithful' univocally (in exactly the same sense). We are using it analogically, to indicate that at the level of the dog's consciousness there is a quality that corresponds to what at the human level we call faithfulness. There is a recognizable likeness in structure of attitudes or patterns of behavior that causes us to use the same word for both animals and people. Nevertheless, human faithfulness differs from canine faithfulness to all the wide extent that a person differs from a dog. There is thus both similarity within difference and difference within similarity of the kind that led Aquinas to speak of the analogical use of the same term in two very different contexts.[19]

The analogy is pressed further by Baron von Hügel (1852 – 1925) as follows:

The source and object of religion, if religion be true and its object be real, cannot indeed, by any possibility, be as clear to me even as I am to my dog. For the cases we have considered deal with realities inferior to our own reality (material objects, or animals), or with realities level to our own reality (fellow human beings), or with realities no higher above ourselves than are we, finite human beings, to our very finite dogs. Whereas, in the case of religion — if religion be right — we apprehend and affirm realities indefinitely superior in quality and amount of reality to ourselves, and which, nevertheless (or rather, just because of this), anticipate, penetrate, and sustain us with a quite unpicturable intimacy. The obscurity of my life to my dog must thus be greatly exceeded by the obscurity of the life of God to me. Indeed the obscurity of plant life — so obscure for my mind, because so indefinitely inferior and poorer than is my human life — must be greatly exceeded by the dimness, for my human life, of God — of His reality and life, so different and superior, so unspeakably more rich and alive, than is, or ever can be, my own life and reality.[20]

One may now turn to an examination of the Buddhist critique of this doctrine. Often when the Buddhists criticize God they are told that they are taking the attributes ascribed to God "too literally when they are meant to be taken only analogically. To answer this we shall look at the problem of analogy."[21] Gunapala Dharmasiri points out that

The theists have always believed that the doctrine of analogy could answer some of the problems raised by non-believers. But actually the doctrine of analogy raises and emphasizes the real problems in the doctrine of God rather than solves any. Wittgenstein points out the central problem involved here. "... in the ethical and religious language we seem constantly to be using similes. But a simile must be the simile for something. And if I can describe a fact by means of a simile I must also be able to drop the simile and describe the facts without it." Nielsen comments, "If ... we can *only* talk about God in images, then we cannot intelligibly speak of faithful or unfaithful images any more than we can speak of married or widowed stones". Therefore the doctrine of analogy does not improve the situation. The theist has to explain how the doctrine of analogy started and how it works. To do this he has to go behind the analogies, which he confesses to be unable to do even in principle. What this amounts to is that the doctrine of analogy, as used by the theist, is meaningless because he only knows and uses the analogies which do not serve any useful purpose without a knowledge of the original data.[22]

In a sense it could be argued that the Buddhists are asking the doctrine of analogy to do something which at the outset it was pointed out it does not set out to. But the scepticism cuts deeper. The doctrine of analogy assumes that there is something to be analogically described but the Buddhists are not certain that such is the case.

The ontologies of Christianity and Buddhism have clear implications for epistemology and for the use of analogy. As the ultimate in Christianity is God whose conception is personal and we are persons, analogy can bridge this gap as some sort of continuity may be discerned or posited. The ultimate in Buddhism, however, is impersonal, so that the gulf fixed between it and us may be conventionally unbridgeable. This seems to be the reason why the analogue to the doctrine of analogy in Christianity is, (1) the two types of discourses in Theravāda Buddhism and (2) the two types of truth in Mahāyāna Buddhism.

The *Aṅguttara-Nikāya*, for instance, states that there are two kinds of persons who misrepresent the Buddha: "which two? He who represents a *Sutta* of indirect meaning as a *Sutta* of direct meaning and he who represents a *Sutta* of direct meaning as a *Sutta* of indirect meaning",[23] the word *nītattha* being used for one with the direct meaning and *neyyāttha* for one with indirect meaning. However, although "no examples are given in the Canon of the two kinds of Suttas",[24] it is clear from the clues provided by the commentaries that when the Buddha

... is speaking about things or persons we should not presume that he is speaking about entities or substances; to this extent his meaning is to be inferred (*neyāttha*). But when he is pointing out the misleading impli- cations of speech or using language without these implications, his meaning is plain and direct and nothing is to be inferred (*nīttatha-*).[25]

The commentaries, however, go further and "characterize these two kinds of discourse ... as two kinds of *truth*".[26] They also use the words *sammuti* and *paramattha* for "commonly accepted beliefs" and "in the absolute sense" respectively,[27] though they "are nowhere contrasted in the Canon"[28] of Theravāda Buddhism.

It is clear, however, that the distinction of two types of discourse in apposition to two types of truth paved the way for the distinction in Mahāyāna Buddhism between conventional (*samvṛtti*) and absolute (*paramārtha*) truth, a distinction which Nāgārjuna, (second century) the famous Buddhist philosopher, made the cornerstone of his doctrine by declaring: "Those who are unaware of the distinction between these two truths are incapable of grasping the deep significance of the teaching of Buddha."[29] The significance of this distinction from the point of view of linguistic discourse is that while conventional (*samvṛtti*) truth is "the truth that does not do any violence to what obtains in our everyday word, being in close conformity with linguistic conventions and ideas", the absolute (*paramārtha*) truth "is unsignified by language and belongs to the realm of the unutterable, and is experienced by the wise in a very intimate way".[30]

Thus while Aquinas could find a middle way between the univocal and the equivocal through the analogical, Buddhism could only find the middle way between affirmation and negation in Buddha's "roaring silence". Buddhism may choose to be silent on some points, but it is not mute. A contemporary illustration might be of help.

Modern science finds it necessary to distinguish between the conven- tional conception of stones and tables as hard, inert objects, which undergo no change, with the scientific conception of them as composed of atoms and molecules, whose inner content consists largely of empty space and whose fundamental elements have such a tenuous existence that they may be regarded as particles in some respects and waves in other respects, if at all it is possible to conceptualise their existence. Still, from a conventional standpoint we need to talk of stones and tables and there is no harm in doing so, provided we are aware of the false assumptions and misleading implications. As the Buddha would say, "They are expressions, turns of speech, designations in common use in the world which the Tathāgata (the Transcendent One) makes use of without being led astray by them".[31]

THE SYMBOLIC NATURE OF RELIGIOUS STATEMENTS
ACCORDING TO PAUL TILLICH (1886 – 1965)

Paul Tillich emphasized the symbolic nature of the language of religious discourse. He distinguished between a sign and a symbol. A sign is the product of arbitrary convention — like halting at a red light — but a symbol participates in what it represents. Tillich's famous example here is the flag which "participates in the power and dignity of the nation it represents". It does so because symbols are not the result of mere convention but "grow out of the individual or collective unconscious".[32]

A symbol performs a twofold function: it "opens up levels of reality that were otherwise closed to us" and also "unlocks dimensions and elements of our soul". The arts provide an example of this *par excellence*.

On the specific point of religion, or as Tillich would prefer to call it, religious faith, Tillich offered the following conclusions: (1) That religious faith could only be expressed in symbolic language: "Whatever we say about that which concerns us ultimately, whether or not we call it God, has a symbolic meaning. It points beyond itself while participating in that to which it points. In no other way can faith express itself adequately. The language of faith is the language of symbols."[33] (2) That "one and only one literal nonsymbolic statement could be made about the religious reality which religion calls God — that God is being-itself".[34] (3) That the symbol had a dual relationship with what it symbolized which he elaborated as follows:

There can be no doubt that any concrete assertion about God must be symbolic, for a concrete assertion is one which uses a segment of finite experience in order to say something about him. It transcends the content of this segment, although it also includes it. The segment of finite reality which becomes the vehicle of a concrete assertion about God is affirmed and negated at the same time. It becomes a symbol, for a symbolic expression is one whose proper meaning is negated by that to which it points. And yet it also is affirmed by it, and this affirmation gives the symbolic expression an adequate basis for pointing beyond itself.[35]

Buddhism would seem to agree on the role of symbolic language in religious discourse, but its reason for doing so would appear to differ from that of Tillich. That which concerns Buddhists ultimately is an *experience*, not a person or principle. It needs to be expressed in symbolic language because language is only capable of conveying meaning based on shared experience. If I have never experienced a toothache myself I will have difficulty in understanding what is meant by it; a difficulty which is multiplied manifold if I have not experienced pain of any kind. Symbolism is an effort to indicate the unknown in terms of the known. It was mentioned earlier that the *summum bonum* of Buddhism is represented by *Nirvāṇa*.

Now you will ask: But what is *Nirvāṇa*. Volumes have been written in reply to this quite natural and simple question; they have, more and more, only confused the issue rather than clarified it. The only reasonable reply to give to the question is that it can never be answered completely and satisfactorily in words, because human language is too poor to express the real nature of the Absolute Truth or Ultimate Reality which is *Nirvāṇa*. Language is created and used by masses of human beings to express things and ideas experienced by their sense organs and their mind. A supramundane experience like that of the Absolute Truth is not of such a category. Therefore there cannot be words to express that experience, just as the fish had no words in his vocabulary to express the nature of the solid land. The tortoise told his friend the fish that he (the tortoise) just returned to the lake after a walk on the land. "Of course" the fish said, "You mean swimming." The tortoise tried to explain that one couldn't swim on the land, that it was solid, and that one walked on it. But the fish insisted that there could be nothing like it, that it must be liquid like his lake, with waves, and that one must be able to dive and swim there.[36]

Let us carry this illustration a little further and the role of symbolism will become apparent. If the tortoise were to dive to the bottom of the lake and to say to the fish: 'You see this solid surface, this bottom of the lake. Now imagine it without this whole body of water and you and me. That is what land is like!' In other words, for the fish the bottom of the lake could symbolize dry land. In that sense, to apply Tillich further, the symbol does participate in what it symbolizes, in being land; but it also negates what it symbolizes in that it is wet but is made to represent dry land.

The Buddhist will have a real problem with the second point, however. For the word *being* carries with it connotations rather alien to Buddhist thought. Being-itself would appear to denote absolute truth. "Now, what is Absolute Truth? According to Buddhism, the Absolute Truth is that there is nothing absolute in the world, that everything is relative, conditioned and impermanent, and that there is no unchanging, everlasting, absolute substance like Self, Soul or *Ātman* within or without. This is the Absolute Truth."[37]

Even here though there is some scope to presenting the situation in a Tillichian light. Whatever the Buddhists and others might say about *Nirvāṇa*, they will all doubtless agree that according to Buddhism "*Nirvāṇa is*",[38] or as the Buddhist thinker Asaṅga says: "There *is* the fact of no-selfness (*nairātmyā-stitā*)"[39] which may be translated as 'there is the being of the non-being of the soul'. Thus *is-ness* might, as a literal statement of the ultimate in Buddhism, compare favourably with Tillich's Christian "Being-itself". However, if one presses for a symbol which might represent *Nirvāṇa* symbolically in *saṁsāra* (although space may be a good choice in this regard), the general thrust of Tillich's discussion, especially the idea of participation, becomes enormously intriguing when we realize that in Mahāyāna Buddhism rather than anything in the world of *saṁsāra* symbolizing *Nirvāṇa*, *Nirvāṇa* was identified with *saṁsāra* in the following manner. In early Buddhism "every being is a conglomeration of elements, just as a chariot is a combination of axle, wheel, rim, yoke, spokes, and so forth. The axle, wheel, rim, and spokes are the elements that compose the chariot and are considered as real and existing, but the chariot as the sum total of the parts is not considered as real",[40] because the chariot could not exist without the parts but the parts could exist independently of the chariot.

Likewise, the human individual is considered as the combination of the five aggregates, material body, perception, sensation, predispositions, and consciousness. These five aggregates are considered as real whereas the living being is not. Now the Mahayana comes forward with a very bold idea. Since these elements come into existence as a result of causes and conditions, they do not have an independent existence of their own, hence they are said to be void or empty. Take away the causes and conditions and the elements no longer exist. This is one of the daring and far-reaching doctrines taught by the Mahayana, that all the elements of existence are empty, void, and unreal. The Mahayana now goes one step further and teaches that not only all phenomenal elements but also *nirvana* is also void or empty, since *nirvana* is devoid of all discriminations, particularities, and definitions. One cannot predicate anything of this *nirvana*. Now if the phenomenal elements of existence and *nirvana* are both empty, then the phenomenal world and *nirvana* may be equated with one another. The Mahayana thus arrived at their second great thesis, the phenomenal world is *nirvana*, *nirvana* is the phenomenal world.[41]

This creates a situation tantamount to John Hick's query that if "according to Tillich, everything that exists participates in Being-itself, what then is the difference between the way in which symbols participate in Being-itself and the way in which everything else participates in it?"[42]

Moreover, "Tillich's tendency to assimilate religious in aesthetic awareness"[43] is also significant from the point of view of Buddhism when one takes the close association of Zen Buddhism with the aesthetic dimension of life in China[44] and Japan. D.T. Suzuki has remarked:

The doctrine of ascetic aestheticism is not so fundamental as that of Zen aestheticism. Art impulses are more primitive or more innate than those of morality. The appeal of art goes more directly into human nature. Morality is regulative, art is creative. One is an imposition from without, the other is an irrepressible expression from within. Zen finds its inevitable association with art but not with morality. Zen may remain unmoral but not without art.[45]

INCARNATION AND THE PROBLEM OF MEANING

It has been suggested that the Christian doctrine of the Incarnation "offers the possibility of a partial solution to the problem of theological meaning" in two ways: a long-standing one and a relatively new one. As John H. Hick points out:

There is a long-standing distinction between the metaphysical attributes of God (aseity, eternity, infinity, etc.) and God's moral attributes (goodness, love, wisdom, etc.). The doctrine of the Incarnation involves the claim that the moral (but not the metaphysical) attributes of God have been embodied, so far as this is possible, in a finite human life, namely that of the Christ. This claim makes it possible to point to the person of Christ as showing what is meant by assertions such as 'God is good' and 'God loves his human creatures'. The moral attitudes of God toward mankind are held to have been incarnated in Jesus and expressed concretely in his dealings with men and women. The Incarnation doctrine involves the claim that, for example, Jesus' compassion for the sick and the spiritually blind was God's compassion for them; his forgiving of sins, God's forgiveness; and his condemnation of the self-righteously religious, God's condemnation of them. On the basis of this belief, the life of Christ as depicted in the New Testament provides a foundation for statements about God.[46]

A relatively new approach is suggested by Ian Crombie when he writes:

The things we say about God are said on the authority of the words and acts of Christ, who spoke in human language, using parable; and so we too speak of God in parable — authoritative parable, authorized parable; knowing that the truth is not literally that which our parables represent, knowing therefore that now we see in a glass darkly, but trusting, because we trust the source of the parables, that in believing them and interpreting them in the light of each other we shall not be misled, that we shall have such knowledge as we need to possess for the foundation of the religious life.[47]

The solution offered by the doctrine of incarnation is not available to Buddhism (should it need it) the way it is in Christianity because Theravāda Buddhism insists on the humanity as opposed to the divinity of the Buddha[48] and Mahāyāna Buddhism, which did develop the belief that the Buddha was a special type of being, concedes him only *fictive* humanity.[49] These differences are deeply rooted in the original matrix of the two traditions — Jesus Christ underwent resurrection after his death, while nothing can be predicated of the Buddha after his death except that he is then "immeasurable, unfathomable" like the ocean.[50] However, the Buddha identified himself with his doctrine (wherein lay the salvific potency, rather than in him) during his lifetime[51] and after his death he was identified with the surviving "body of his teachings"

The epithet of *dhamma-kāya* (*Dīgha-Nikāya* iii. 84), the body of *Dharma*, applicable only to the Lord and not even to Arhants, points in this same direction. So the *Milindapañha*, a later and post-canonical work, can say: 'The Lord can be designated by means of the *Dharma*-body' (*Milinda-pañha* 75), even though he himself has entered on *parinirvāṇa*, has 'gone home' or 'set' like the sun whose kinsman he was, and cannot be pointed to any longer as being either here or there. Thus while the unending *Dharma* exists the Lord exists and cannot be called extinct. And though we are here touching on a tenet that was to be developed and made much of in some of the Mahāyāna Buddhist Sūtras its core is already apparent in the Pali writings.[52]

Thus in Buddhism Buddha may exemplify his teachings, but *these teachings were ultimately considered as dispensable as the Buddha himself, even if one may be said to incarnate the other.* In Mahāyāna Buddhism the concept of *dharmakāya* underwent a change[53] and the Buddha became identical with everything,[54] whereas earlier he could be identified with nothing.[55] Hence, the traditional concept of incarnation in either case could not offer a solution to the problem of religious language in the context of Buddhism.

In another sense, however, Christ in Christianity and Buddha in Buddhism speak in "human language, using parables" as a way of indicating ultimate verities. And attempts to decipher them certainly represent a parallel approach. It may not be an accident that Harvey Cox has compared some of the parables to Zen Koans "that leave the listener shocked and perplexed, the taken-for-granted world turned upside-down". The difference is that "while Koans subvert reality as such, Jesus' parables overturn social and religious conventions".[56]

RELIGIOUS LANGUAGE AS NON-COGNITIVE

The development of the non-cognitive approach to religious language is a relatively new development within Christianity. As John Hick remarks:

> There is no doubt that as a matter of historical fact religious people have normally believed such statements as 'God loves mankind' to be not only cognitive but also true. Without necessarily pausing to consider the difference between religious facts and the facts disclosed through sense perception and the sciences, ordinary believers within the Judaic-Christian tradition have assumed that there are religious realities and facts and that their own religious convictions are concerned with such.[57]

But then he goes on to add that "today, however, a growing number of theories treat religious language as non-cognitive".[58]

No such clear-cut division in its approach to religious language is discernible in Buddhism, which has always tended to feel that verbal language has no direct relation to what really exists, and is essentially misleading not merely in relation to the absolute but even in empirical matters. It bears little resemblance to reality though it may serve a useful purpose just as our phone number bears little resemblance to us but is useful in contacting us, or our address, written out on a slip of paper, bears no resemblance to the apartment we live in but helps people to reach it. In this very fundamental sense, therefore, Buddhism has always tended to consider language non-cognitive.

The sense, however, in which in modern times religious language has come to be considered non-cognitive in the West is quite different. It is to a consideration of these developments that we now turn.

RANDALL'S NON-COGNITIVE THEORY

According to J.H. Randall, Jr. the role of religious language is symbolic not in the sense that it is symbolic in relation to some transcendental reality but in the following sense:

> What [it] is important to recognize is that religious symbols belong with social and artistic symbols, in the group of symbols that are both

nonrepresentative and *noncognitive*. Such noncognitive symbols can be said to symbolize not some external thing that can be indicated apart from their operation, but rather what they themselves *do*, their peculiar functions.[59]

Thus understood, Randall assigns four functions to religious language as engaging an individual's affective dimension of being; as binding a community; as expressing that which cannot be expressed literally and, finally, to "both evoke and foster and clarify the human experience of an aspect of the world that can be called the 'order of splendour' or the divine".[60] It is of key importance that "Randall does not mean to imply that God or the divine exists as a reality independently of the human mind",[61] for the religious dimension involved here is "a quality to be discriminated in human experience of the world, the splendour of the vision that sees beyond the actual into the perfected and eternal realm of the imagination".[62]

The Buddhist response to this position would probably be brief. It would accept the statement that God is a product of our imagination but would hesitate to celebrate it in the manner suggested by Randall. However, the growth of the cult of Buddhas and Bodhisattvas in Mahāyāna Buddhism suggests that Mahāyāna Buddhism allows for some reinterpretation of Buddhism along Randall's lines. If the Mādhyamika form of Buddhism came to view empirical reality as an illusion, the Yogācāra school came to regard it as a projection. This meant that

the world which besets man so mercilessly is as much his mental creation as the fellow-beings whom he believes that he 'perceives'. It was but a small step for the Vajrayāna ... to regard the Transcendent Buddhas and Bodhisattvas as well as ideations. There is only one difference between the ideation of a world from the ideation of Transcendent beings. The latter are not readily visible, because the ability to see them has to be acquired through spiritual practices. The world-ideation, on the other hand, is an effect of old Karman and automatically forces itself on to everybody.[63]

Although this is clearly not what Randall had in mind, it does suggest a novel interpretation of his views in a Buddhist context with reference to Tantra.

BRAITHWAITE'S NON-COGNITIVE THEORY

Another theory which asserts the non-cognitive nature of religious language is associated with the name of R.B. Braithwaite. According to him "religious assertions serve primarily an ethical function".[64] It is interesting that for Braithwaite religions are in a sense really stories with a moral or perhaps many morals. Thus for

> Braithwaite, Christianity is a matter of a big story. In that sense, all religions are, according to Braithwaite, sets of stories. Even a fiction can be a religion according to him, because sometimes fictions can advocate moral standards rather effectively. He says, "Next to the Bible and the Prayer Book the most influential work in Christian religious life has been a book whose stories are frankly recognized as fictitious — Bunyan's *Pilgrim's Progress*; and some of the most influential works in setting the moral tone of my generation were the novels of Dostoevsky." The logical priority of morality is clearly accepted by Braithwaite when he agrees with Matthew Arnold in saying "wisdom and goodness, they are God". Therefore, the Christian stories become meaningful and important only in so far as they reinforce the accepted moral values.[65]

Braithwaite, fortunately for us, offers a comparison between Christianity and Buddhism. It is worth remembering that at the heart of Buddhism, according to some scholars, is also a great story.[66]

> On the assumption that the ways of life advocated by Christianity and Buddhism are essentially the same, it will be the fact that the intention to follow this way of life is associated in the mind of a Christian with thinking of one set of stories (the Christian stories) while it is associated in the mind of a Buddhist with thinking of another set of stories (the Buddhist stories) which enables a Christian assertion to be distinguished from a Buddhist one.[67]

The Buddhist response to this view has been formulated by a Buddhist in two parts. Gunapala Dharmasiri has demonstrated both the extent to which the Buddhist position diverges with that of Braithwaite on this point as well as the extent to which it is convergent with it. Dharmasiri identifies the divergence as follows:

> Braithwaite's remarks about Buddhism can be true only if Buddhism shares the problems of Christian theology, which, in fact, it does not.

For Buddhism, moral perfection is the ideal in the sense that it leads to spiritual perfection. Morality, as we shall see later on, is generically related to the spiritual ideal. In Buddhism, morality is based on two fundamental facts. One is that humanity has a set of basic needs and the other is that moral values generically effect a spiritual perfection. The validity of Buddhist morals depends on these two facts and therefore if these two facts are false, then the morality becomes necessarily invalid. But stories of fictions can never be falsified. Therefore it would be a grave misinterpretation to say that in Buddhism to follow a religious morality is to act in conformity to a collection of stories.[68]

However, Dharmasiri also hastens to add that

there is an important place for fictions in Buddhist morality. The Buddha had preached stories of his past lives for the moral edification of his followers. He had in mind the psychological impact those stories could make on his followers and therefore utilized them to reinforce and support the moral system he was preaching. These stories have always belonged more to the popular stratum of Buddhism than to the intellectual. They have no credal significance in Buddhism.[69]

It is perhaps important to realize in this context that both Buddhism and Braithwaite are willing to concede moral value to what may otherwise be metaphysically questionable. As K.N. Jayatilleke explains:

Another test that Buddhism applies in gauging the validity of a belief is the 'fruit test', or the attempt to see what consequences a belief or set of beliefs, when acted upon, has led to. With regard to theism it may be held that it has given people a sense of security and inspired them to various kinds of activity. This does not prove that the belief is true but suggests that it may be useful. A realistic survey would show that while beliefs in theism have done some good, they have brought much evil in their train as well.[70]

In these terms Braithwaite may be seen as suggesting a moral fruit test.

THE LANGUAGE GAME THEORY

This theory was developed by Ludwig Wittgenstein (1889 – 1951) and then applied to Christian themes by D.Z. Phillips. The Buddhist response to the original theory will be considered in this section and to its development by D.Z. Phillips in the next.

It may be hypothesized that a Christian or a theist, or a Christian theist, who subscribes to the standpoint that the function of religious language is non-cognitive might claim that "just as 'an electron exists' is meaningful only within the language game of physics so 'God exists' is meaningful only within the language game of religion".[71]

The Buddhist critique of this suggestion would point out that (1) "while the electron's indeterminability in nature and location is experimentally demonstrable; in the case of God, to say that the nature of his existence is different, is only to advance an hypothesis about the possibility of the existence of God".[72] (2) That this is so "because the concept of electron is meaningful prior to the question of the nature of its existence, while the concept of God is not meaningful prior to the question of the nature of his existence".[73] Moreover, (3)

we posit the 'existence' of [the] electron because certain very unambiguous, clear consequences follow from this position. We first see the consequences and then posit the 'existence' of the electron. Now, we can accept that 'God exists' but we cannot see any consequence at all which follows from that acceptance. Here we are back at the problem of the evidence of the proofs for the existence of God.[74]

Furthermore (4) in

the context of physics the concept of electron is a meaningful term, while in the context of religion God is not a meaningful term. Notwithstanding the characterizations of God as Being, Love, etc. which are too ambiguous to mean anything definite, the problems of the contradictory or the meaningless nature of the divine attributes insistently militate against the possibility of giving any meaning to the concept of God.[75]

(5) Finally,

by the fact that 'electron' is meaningful only within the context of physics, it should not be understood that 'electrons' cease to exist if the science of physics ceases to exist. It is true that the terms 'electrons' cease to exist, but the series of events denoted by the term 'electrons' do not cease to exist in any sense. On the other hand, if the theistic religious language game ceases to exist, the whole idea of God will cease to exist and no corresponding events will be left because the idea of God cannot be made meaningful in terms of any form of event. If the idea of God could be made meaningful in this way, then the theists could have easily met Flew's Challenge and shown the events that would falsify the belief in God. In fact, however, even such a possibility is precluded by the prior meaninglessness of the concept of God.[76]

D.Z. PHILLIPS'S NON-COGNITIVE THEORY

The language-game theory may now be applied to Christianity as well as to theism. In that case the argument would run that:

> To participate wholeheartedly in, say, the Christian 'form of life' is, among other things, to use distinctively Christian language, which has its own internal criteria determining what is true and false within this universe of discourse. The internal transactions constituting a given language-game are thus invulnerable to criticism from outside that particular complex of life and language — from which it follows that religious utterances are immune to scientific and other nonreligious comment.[77]

If this is granted then,

> It would, for example, be an authentic piece of traditional Christian discourse to refer to the first man and woman, Adam and Eve, and to their fall from grace in the Garden of Eden, a fall that has made us, along with all their other descendants, guilty before God. According to this Neo-Wittgensteinian theory of religious language, such a way of talking does not clash with the scientific theory that the human race is not descended from a single primal pair, or that the earliest humans did not live in a paradisal state, for science is a different language-game, with its own quite different criteria.[78]

D.Z. Phillips has applied this view to "two themes in particular: prayer and immortality".[79] The theme of immortality may be explored further as an illustration of his approach. The traditional cognitive understanding of the Christian concept of "the life everlasting" is a view about continued existence subsequent to death. For Phillips, however, a non-cognitive understanding yields a very different meaning:

> Eternal life is the reality of goodness, that in terms of which human life is to be assessed.... Eternity is not an extension of this present life, but a mode of judging it. Eternity is not more life, but this life seen under certain moral and religious modes of thought.... Questions about the

immortality of the soul are seen not to be questions concerning the extent of a man's life, and in particular concerning whether that life can extend beyond the grave, but questions concerning the kind of life a man is living.[80]

The moral quality of this interpretation lies in the freedom it affords from egocentricity. As he explains:

This renunciation [of the idea of a life to come] is what the believer means by dying to the self. He ceases to see himself as the centre of his world. Death's lesson for the believer is to force him to recognise what all his natural instincts want to resist, namely, that he has no claims on the way things go. Most of all, he is forced to realise that his own life is not a necessity.[81]

The Buddhist will be quick to criticise this view because according to Buddhism it is the craving of the ego for permanence which generates a belief in everlasting life[82] and thus, from the Buddhist point of view, the argument has not merely been reversed, the proverbial cart has been put before the horse.

As a Christian thinker, Phillips has also used his non-cognitive approach to religious language to strengthen the moral justification of God's existence by suggesting that such a belief is conducive to moral progress, a point touched upon earlier. The following extracts from his works represent his argument:

In order to renounce one's power one must not fix one's attention on *how* people are: useful or useless for one, desirable or undesirable, morally deserving or undeserving, but on the fact *that* they are. This is a prerequisite of compassion. When it is achieved in the presence of suffering, the giver is able to give without feeling that he has done anything deserving of praise, and the sufferer is able to receive without feeling bought or degraded. It might be said that in this attitude, people are seen, not as the world sees them, but as God sees them.... The believer, if his faith is at all deep, is not concerned with his rights. He is not concerned with receiving thanks for the good he does, or recompense for the harm he suffers. What he considers to be advantage, disadvantage, happiness or misery is determined by his relationship to the love of God.... Without his belief he could not be said to have the same relationship or experience the same events.... The reason why [the] love of God is said to be *other than* the world, is, as I have tried to illustrate, because it entails dying to the world's way of regarding things.... The love of God is manifested in the believer's relationship to people and things.... To see the world as God's world, would primari-

ly be to possess this love. To say that God created a world would not
be to put forward a theory, hypothesis, or explanation of the world.[83]

Phillips himself recognizes that his mode of discussion seems
to "deny the objective reality of God". He goes on to observe:

The term 'objective reality' is a hazy one. The objector may be
suggesting that the believer creates his belief, or decides that it should
be the kind of thing it is. This obviously is not the case. The believer is
taught religious beliefs. He does not create a tradition, but is born into
one. He cannot say whatever he likes about God, since there are criteria
which determine what it makes sense to say. These criteria may
develop or change partly as the result of personal decisions. But not
anything can count as a religious decision or a religious development.[84]

Gunapala Dharmasiri has pointed out that to do justice to
Phillips's position one must distinguish between "existential"
and "objective" reality. God may be rendered an "existential"
reality for a Christian but if it is his claim that even the "objective
reality of God is to be established on grounds of tradition" then
the objective reality of unicorns in certain societies may also
have to be accepted "because they have behind them a strong
tradition which gives criteria for talking about them".[85] This
would then represent a special case of Gunapala Dharmasiri's
general argument that there is a close relationship "between
superstitious types of thinking and theological thinking".[86]

John Hick offers the following general criticism of this line of
approach:

Indeed, the basic criticism that has been made of the Neo-Wittgen-
steinian theory of religious language is that it is not (as it professes to
be) an account of normal or ordinary religious language use but rather
is a proposal for a radical new interpretation of religious utterances. In
this new interpretation, religious expressions are systematically de-
prived of the cosmic implications that they have always been assumed
to have. Not only is human immortality reinterpreted as a quality of
this present mortal life but, more fundamentally, God is no longer
thought of as a reality existing independently of human belief and
disbelief. Rather, as Phillips says, "What [the believer] learns is religious language; a language which he participates in along with other
believers. What I am suggesting is that to know how to use this
language is to know God." Again, "To have the idea of God is to know
God". The skeptical possibility for which such a position does not allow

is that people have the idea of God, and participate in theistic language, and yet there is no God.[87]

Buddhism advances precisely this sceptical possibility when it suggests that certain beliefs may be useful without being true,[88] and true without being useful or no longer useful.[89]

CHAPTER 7

The Problem of Verification

THE QUESTION OF VERIFIABILITY

In the previous chapter several non-cognitive theories of religious language were examined. It nevertheless remains true that the way in which religious language "operates within historic Judaism and Christianity is much closer to ordinary factual asserting than to either the expressing of aesthetic intuitions or the declaring of ethical policies".[1] In other words, religious language makes factual assertions. Modern Western philosophy, especially the form of it known as logical positivism, has devoted considerable attention to the issue of how the truth or falsity of factual statements is to be established. Originally it was thought that 'a direct examination' as to the truth or falsity of a proposition would suffice but subsequently another condition was attached, namely, that the proposition be 'meaningful' when the word is understood in a logical rather than a psychological sense, namely, that "its truth or falsity must make some possible experienceable difference".[2]

The application of the idea of verifiability in this sense led to two interesting developments in the context of religious language. It soon became apparent that (1) an event may make an experienceable difference even when its status as a fact is not in doubt; and (2) an event may make an experienceable difference irrespective of its truth or falsity.

The first approach is represented by a parable made famous by John Wisdom. It runs as follows:

Two people return to their long-neglected garden and find among the weeds a few of the old plants surprisingly vigorous. One says to the other, "It must be that a gardener has been coming and doing something about these plants." Upon inquiry they find that no neighbor has ever seen anyone at work in their garden. The first man says to the other "He must have worked while people slept." The other says, "No, someone would have heard him and besides, anybody who cared about the plants would have kept down these weeds." The first man says, "Look at the way these are arranged. There is purpose and a feeling for beauty here. I believe that someone comes, someone invisible to mortal eyes. I believe that the more carefully we look the more we shall find confirmation of this." They examine the garden ever so carefully and sometimes they come on new things suggesting the contrary and even that a malicious person has been at work. Besides examining the garden carefully they also study what happens to gardens left without attention. Each learns all the other learns about this and about the garden. Consequently, when after all this, one says "I still believe a gardener comes" while the other says "I don't" their different words now reflect no difference as to what they have found in the garden, no difference as to what they would find in the garden if they looked further and no difference about how fast untended gardens fall into disorder. At this stage, in this context, the gardener hypothesis has ceased to be experimental, the difference between one who accepts and one who rejects it is not now a matter of the one expecting something the other does not expect. What is the difference between them? The one says, "A gardener comes unseen and unheard. He is manifested only in his works with which we are all familiar," the other says, "There is no gardener" and with this difference in what they say about the gardener goes a difference in how they feel towards the garden, in spite of the fact that neither expects anything of it which the other does not expect.[3]

Two aspects of the situation are worth noting here: (1) that the two parties do not differ as to the set of facts; (2) the two parties do differ in their reaction to the same set of facts. The thrust of John Wisdom's position is that "there is no disagreement about the experienceable facts, the settlement of which would determine whether the theist or the atheist is right. In other words, neither of the rival positions is, even in principle, verifiable".[4]

One can, however, go a step further. One of the points raised by Wisdom's parable is that both the parties in the parable really felt "about the world in the way their words indicate. Nevertheless, expressions of feeling do not constitute assertions about the world".[5] However, although there may be no 'disagreement about experienceable facts', yet the situation may involve an 'experienceable difference'. As Norman Malcolm points out:

> One may have the feeling that unless religious belief somewhere involved empirical consequences which can provide verification or falsification of the belief, then it does not 'get a grip' on the world; it does not really deserve the name of 'belief'. But a belief can get a grip on the world in another way. The man who believes that his sins will be forgiven if he is truly repentant, might thereby be saved from despair. What he believes has, for him, no verification or falsification; yet the belief makes a great difference to this action and feeling.[6]

Buddhism subscribes to a correspondence theory of truth rather than to a pragmatic theory of truth.[7] It is nevertheless "pragmatic although it does not subscribe to a pragmatic theory of truth".[8] K.N. Jayatilleke even states that the "pragmatic theory of truth was put forward to accommodate theistic beliefs".[9] From this it is clear that as the 'meaningfulness' of theism is psychological while meaningfulness in the present context is "a logical term; it is not a psychological term, as when we speak of 'a very meaningful experience' or say of something 'it means a lot to me',"[10] theism is not verifiable.

The position of the Buddha, both on the meaning of "meaningful" and on the verifiability of theism seems to be logical positivist in nature. Gunapala Dharmasiri writes on the question of the nature and existence of God:

> Some of the Buddha's comments on the meaningfulness of questions become very relevant in this context. He said that there were two types of questions: meaningful (*sappāṭihīrakatam*), and meaningless (*appāṭihīrakatam*). If one asks a question that is meaningless then, he said, there is no way to answer because one does not understand the question. The Buddha refers to a person who says: 'Whoever is the beauty queen of this countryside, I want her, I desire her'. Another man might say to him, 'My good man, do you know whether this beauty queen of the countryside whom you want and desire is a noble maiden or a brahmin or a merchant or a worker?' Asked this, he would say: 'No'. The other might say to him: 'My good man, do you know the name or the clan of this beauty queen of the countryside whom you want and desire ... whether she is tall or short or of medium height, or dark or brown or sallow; or what village or market town or what town she belongs to?' Asked this, he might say: 'No'. The other might speak

to him thus: 'My good man, do you want and desire her whom you know not, see not?' Asked this he might say: 'Yes'. What do you think about this ...? this being so, surely that man's meaningless talk does not prosper him?[11]

What he goes on to say further illustrates how the Buddha at least considered theism unverified and in the state of affairs he encountered also unverifiable:

The Buddha says that the people who talk about God (Brahma) and talk about ways of attaining union with God are making meaningless statements because nobody can make the concept of God meaningful in any way, nobody can give any criteria for discriminating God from other entities. To understand a concept one must have delineating criteria for making that concept meaningful. These criteria can be derived either from knowledge by acquaintance or from knowledge by description. The Buddha says that the theistic believers can furnish none of these criteria: "Then you say, Vasettha, that none of the brahmins, or of their teachers, or of their pupils, even up to the seventh generation, has ever seen God face to face. And that even the sages of the old, the authors and utterers of the verses, of the ancient form of words which the brahmins of today so carefully intone and recite precisely as they have been handed down — even they did not pretend to know or to have seen where or whence or whither God is. So that the brahmins versed in the three Vedas have forsooth said thus: 'What we know not, what we have not seen, to a state of union with that we can show the way, and can say: "This is the straight path, this is the direct way which makes for salvation, and leads him, who acts according to it, into a state of union with God." ' Now what think you, Vasettha? Does it not follow, this being so, that the talk of the brahmins, versed though they be in the three Vedas, turns out to be foolish talk? ... In sooth, Gotama, that being so, it follows that the talk of the brahmins versed in the three Vedas is foolish talk.... verily, Vasettha, that brahmins versed in the three Vedas should be able to show the way to a state of union with that which they do not know, neither have seen — such a condition of things can in no wise be! Just, Vasettha, as when a string of blind men are clinging one to the other, neither can the foremost see, nor can the middle one see, nor can the hindmost see — just even so, methinks, Vasettha, is the talk of the brahmins versed in the three Vedas but blind talk: the first sees not, the middle one sees not, nor can the latest see. The talk then of these brahmins versed in the three Vedas turns out to be ridiculous, mere words, a vain and empty thing!"[12]

THE QUESTION OF FALSIFIABILITY

The weight may now be shifted on to the other leg: perhaps theism cannot be verified but is there "any conceivable event, if it were to occur, [which] would decisively refute theism?"[13] In other words, theism may not be verifiable but is theism falsifiable! Antony Flew has stated this point of view eloquently:

Now it often seems to people who are not religious as if there was no conceivable event or series of events the occurrence of which would be admitted by sophisticated religious people to be a sufficient reason for conceding "There wasn't a God after all" or "God does not really love us then". Someone tells us that God loves us as a father loves his children. We are reassured. But then we see a child dying of inoperable cancer of the throat. His earthly father is driven frantic in his efforts to help, but his Heavenly Father reveals no obvious sign of concern. Some qualification is made — God's love is "not a merely human love" or it is "an inscrutable love", perhaps — and we realize that such sufferings are quite compatible with the truth of the assertion that "God loves us as a father (but, of course...)". We are reassured again. But then perhaps we ask: what is this assurance of God's (appropriately qualified) love worth, what is this apparent guarantee really a guarantee against? Just what would have to happen not merely (morally and wrongly) to tempt but also (logically and rightly) to entitle us to say "God does not love us" or even "God does not exist"? I therefore put ... the simple central questions, "What would have to occur or to have occurred to constitute for you a disproof of the love of, or of the existence of, God?"[14]

Buddhist scholars are much impressed by the challenge thrown by Flew as it seems to conform to their own critique of theism.[15]

R.M. HARE'S RESPONSE

R.M. Hare is responsible for introducing the concept of a *blik* in the context of the current discussion. Very simply, a *blik* is "an unverifiable and unfalsifiable interpretation of one's experience".[16] However, it is possible to have (1) a right or wrong *blik* and (2) and a positive or negative *blik*. The first distinction is clearly made by Hare on the basis of the following example:

Suppose, for example, a lunatic is convinced that all the professors in a certain college are intent upon murdering him. It will be vain to try to allay his suspicions by introducing him to a series of kindly and inoffensive professors, for he will see only a particularly devious cunning in their apparently friendly manner. He does not hold his belief in a way that is open to confirmation or refutation by experience; he has a *blik* about them. "It is [says Hare] important to realize that we have a sane one, not no *blik* at all; for there must be two sides to any argument — if he has a wrong *blik*, then those who are right about dons must have a right one. Flew has shown that a *blik* does not consist in an assertion or system of them; but nevertheless it is very important to have the right *blik*."[17]

The second distinction is implicit in another example of a *blik* given by Hare. It runs as follows:

Suppose we believe that everything that happened, happened by pure chance. This would not of course be an assertion; for it is compatible with anything happening or not happening, and so, incidentally, is its contradictory. But if we had this belief, we should not be able to explain or predict or plan anything. Thus, although we should not be *asserting* anything different from those of a more normal belief, there would be a great difference between us; and this is the sort of difference that there is between those who really believe in God and those who really disbelieve in him.[18]

Let us suppose that whether events occur by accident or by causality cannot be conclusively established, hence both are *blik*s. It is clear, however, that Hare regards belief in causality as a positive *blik* as opposed to the belief that things happen by accident, which is a negative *blik*. It is better to believe that occurrences are causal rather than casual, even if there is no way of proving this to be the case. The essence of Hare's reply to Flew seems to consist in the suggestion that although theism is unverifiable and unfalsifiable, it does not follow that it does not involve a rational choice. If one only takes Hare's first example into account this point does not come across clearly and the following criticism of John Hick seems justified:

Hare abandons as indefensible the traditional view of religious statements as being or entailing assertions that are true or false. Probably everyone would agree that, when sincerely held, religious beliefs make an important difference *to the believer*. They affect the ways he or she feels, talks, and acts — as does the lunatic's *blik* about the professors.

But a serious and rational concern with religion will inevitably make us want to know whether the way the believer feels and acts is appropriate to the actual character of the universe, and whether the things a believer says are true. We want to distinguish, in Hare's terminology, between right and wrong *bliks*. In the previously quoted passage, Hare assumes that one can make this distinction, for he identifies one *blik* as sane and the contrary *blik* as insane. However, there seems to be an inconsistency in his position here, for a discrimination between sane (= right) and insane (= wrong) *bliks* is ruled out by his insistence that *bliks* are unverifiable and unfalsifiable. If experience can never yield either confirmation or disconfirmation of *bliks*, there is no basis for speaking of them as being right or wrong, appropriate or inappropriate, sane or insane. These distinctions make sense only if it also makes sense to refer to tests, evidence, and verification. It is precisely this confirmation that Flew has demanded in relation to religious beliefs. It seems then, that Hare has neither met Flew's challenge nor shown a way of avoiding it.[19]

It seems, however, that the second illustration given by Hare does make it possible to distinguish between *bliks* on the basis of the difference they make *to the believer*. The verification which Hare is suggesting is through the *value* or otherwise of theistic belief rather than the *fact* or otherwise of theism. This is a position with which Buddhism could resonate positively to some extent. In the *Karaṇḍa-vyūha*, for instance, a Mahāyāna text, the Bodhisattva Avalokiteśvara "even takes the form of Hindu Gods, Maheśvara, etc., and preaches according to the doctrine of each".[20] However, the Theravāda position, although allowing for value, remains more tied to fact. For instance, the Buddha concedes the role of the God Mahā Brahmā as a moral exemplar but denies the claim that God is omniscient and omnipotent.[21]

BASIL MITCHELL'S RESPONSE

R.M. Hare, in response to the Flew's challenge, conceded the non-falsifiability of theism. Basil Mitchell, however, suggests a different tack.

Mitchell recounts his own parable. A member of the resistance movement in an occupied country meets a stranger who deeply

impresses him as being truthful and trustworthy and who claims to be
the resistance leader. He urges the partisan to have faith in him
whatever may happen. Sometimes the stranger is seen apparently
aiding the resistance and sometimes apparently collaborating with the
enemy. Nevertheless the partisan continues in trust. He admits that on
the face of it some of the stranger's actions strain this trust. However,
he has faith, even though at times his faith is sorely tried, that there is a
satisfactory explanation of the stranger's ambiguous behavior. "It is
here [says Mitchell] that my parable differs from Hare's. The partisan
admits that many things may and do count against his belief: whereas
Hare's lunatic who has a *blik* about dons doesn't admit that anything
counts against his *blik*. Nothing *can* count against *blik*s. Also the
partisan has a reason for having in the first instance committed himself,
viz. the character of the Stranger; whereas the lunatic has no reason for
his *blik* about dons — because, of course, you can't have reasons for
*blik*s."[22]

It is clear then, as John Hick points out that

Mitchell's parable is concerned with a straightforward matter of fact
which can, in principle, be definitely ascertained. The stranger himself
knows on which side he is, and after the war, when all the facts are
brought to light, the ambiguity of his behavior will be resolved and his
true character made clear. Thus, Mitchell is concerned with stressing
the similarity rather than the dissimilarity between religious beliefs and
ordinary, unproblematic factual beliefs.[23]

The parable poses a slight problem in the Christian context.
Whereas the 'war' is supposed to be over in this lifetime and the
true identity of the character revealed, this does not happen in
Christianity till after death. One is, therefore, automatically led
towards the idea of eschatological verification which has been
developed by John Hick and which is discussed in the next
section. Suffice it to indicate here that from a Buddhist point of
view verifiability does not pose the same kinds of problem for
Buddhism as it does for Christianity. K.N. Jayatilleke observes:

The statements of the *Dhamma* are meaningful (*sappāṭihāriyaṃ*) and are
supported by reason and experience (*sanidāhaṃ*) and are hence verifiable (*ehipassika*). It is the duty of each Buddhist to try and verify their
truth in practice. The Buddhist starts with right beliefs in his *sammā-
diṭṭhi* endeavour gradually to eliminate greed and hatred and ends his
quest for truth with right knowledge (*sammāñāṇī*) and emancipation of
mind (*sammāvimutti*). In the process, each person has to verify the

truths of Buddhism for himself. Verifiability in the light of reason and experience is thus a characteristic of the truths of Buddhism.[24]

However, as this is apparently not the case in Christianity, a different approach is called for.

JOHN HICK'S RESPONSE

The suggestion made by Basil Mitchell is carried a step further by John Hick, who narrates his own parable.

Two people are travelling together along a road. One of them believes that it leads to the Celestial City, the other that it leads nowhere, but since this is the only road there is, both must travel it. Neither has been this way before; therefore, neither is able to say what they will find around each corner. During their journey they meet with moments of refreshment and delight, and with moments of hardship and danger. All the time one of them thinks of the journey as a pilgrimage to the Celestial City. She interprets the pleasant parts as encouragements and the obstacles as trials of her purpose and lessons in endurance, prepared by the sovereign of that city and designed to make of her a worthy citizen of the place when at last she arrives. The other, however, believes none of this, and sees their journey as an unavoidable and aimless ramble. Since he has no choice in the matter, he enjoys the good and endures the bad. For him there is no Celestial City to be reached, no all-encompassing purpose ordaining their journey; there is only the road itself and the luck of the road in good weather and in bad.[25]

The parable is then commented upon as follows:

This parable, like all parables, has narrow limitations. It is designed to make only one point: that Judaic-Christian theism postulates an ultimate unambiguous existence *in patria*, as well as our present ambiguous existence *in via*. There is a state of having arrived as well as a state of journeying, an eternal heavenly life as well as an earthly pilgrimage. The alleged future experience cannot, of course, be appealed to as evidence for theism as a present interpretation of our experience, but it does apparently suffice to render the choice between theism and atheism a real and not merely an empty or verbal choice.[26]

John Hick is suggesting that the Christian theism contains a clear concept of post-mortem verification which is not merely religious; it can be formulated philosophically as follows:

1. The verification of a factual assertion is not the same as a logical demonstration of it. The central core of the idea of verification is the removal of grounds for rational doubt. That a proposition, p, is verified means that something happens that makes it clear that p is true. A question is settled, so that there is no longer room for rational doubt concerning it. The way in which such grounds are excluded varies, of course, with the subject matter, but the common feature in all cases of verification is the ascertaining of truth by the removal of grounds for rational doubt. Whenever such grounds have been removed, we rightly speak of verification having taken place.

2. Sometimes it is necessary to put oneself in a certain position or to perform some particular operation as a prerequisite of verification. For example, one can only verify "There is a table in the next room" by going into the next room; however, it is to be noted that no one is compelled to do this.

3. Therefore, although "verifiable" normally means "publicly verifiable" (i.e. capable in principle of being verified by anyone), it does not follow that a given verifiable proposition has in fact been or will in fact ever be verified by everyone. The number of people who verify a particular true proposition depends upon all manner of contingent factors.

4. It is possible for a proposition to be in principle verifiable but not in principle falsifiable. Consider, for example, the proposition that "there are three successive sevens in the decimal determination of π." So far as the value of π has been worked out, it does not contain a series of three sevens; but since the operation can proceed *ad infinitum* it will always be true that a triple seven may occur at a point not yet reached in anyone's calculations. Accordingly, the proposition may one day be verified if it is true but can never be falsified if it is false.

5. The hypothesis of continued conscious existence after bodily death provides another instance of a proposition that is verifiable if true but not falsifiable if false. This hypothesis entails a prediction that one will, after the date of one's bodily death, have conscious experiences, including the experience of remembering that death. This is a prediction that will be verified in one's own experience if it is true but that cannot be falsified if it is false. That is to say, it can be false, but *that* it is false can never be a fact that anyone has experientially verified. This principle does not undermine the meaningfulness of the survival hypothesis, for if its prediction is true, it will be known to be true.[27]

Hick's position has drawn criticism from Buddhist scholars. Gunapala Dharmasiri writes, for instance:

In theology, sometimes the verificatory procedures are claimed in terms of other realms of reality. They usually posit two such realms. One is the mystical realm. The other is the eschatological realm. As we discussed in the previous chapter, a theist could claim that the propositions about God could be verified in a mystical realm by the mystics. In terms of visions, manifestations, illuminations, etc., they claim, the mystics can experience the truths propounded and claimed by theology. Thus the theological truths are made meaningful in terms of another reality. Some thinkers like Hick maintain that the claims of theology may be verified eschatologically. Thus, the realm of eschatological reality which is, of course, a future reality, also functions as another realm where the claims of theology are verified. It is to be noted that these realms themselves are posited by the theological claims. That is, the contents of the mystical realm are produced by the theistic beliefs and the eschatological realm itself is a theological claim. The mystical realm is more relevant to our discussion because though the contents are theologically produced, it exists in the present. Also, the theologians attach a great significance to this realm as giving meaning and verifiability to the theistic beliefs.[28]

The analysis of this criticism leads to some interesting conclusions. First, while after-life plays an important role in Christianity, Buddhism is very much here-and-now religion (*ehipassika*).[29] Hence Dharmasiri's assessment of the mystical realm as "more relevant" reflects to some extent the orientation of the Buddhist tradition itself. Second, it is claimed that the eschatological realms are posited by the theology itself; but so is the realm of *Nirvāṇa* posited by Buddhism itself. Moreover, along the same lines, one must pause to consider whether external criteria are at all feasible in some cases. Although "as a child, one does not yet know exactly what it means to be grown-up", yet "when one reaches adulthood, one is nevertheless able to know that one has reached it, for one's understanding of adult maturity grows as one matures".[30] In other words, the process which generates the experience to be judged may also provide the criteria for judging them. Third, the concept of eschatological verification is not entirely absent in Buddhism. Of the four stages of sanctification in Theravāda Buddhism, the third — that of the *anāgāmi* involves attaining *Nirvāṇa* from a celestial realm, without having to return to this world. In Mahāyāna Buddhism, the confirmation of the existence of the Pure Land could be considered a matter of eschatological verification, not to speak of attaining Buddhahood there.

CHAPTER 8

The Conflicting Truth Claims of Different Religions

INTRODUCTION

In order to grasp the full significance of what is at stake in the conflicting truth claims of different religions the

... problem can be posed very concretely in this way. If I had been born in India, I would probably be a Hindu; if in Egypt, probably a Muslim; if in Sri Lanka, probably a Buddhist; but I was born in England and am, predictably, a Christian. These different religions seem to say different and incompatible things about the nature of ultimate reality, about the modes of divine activity, and about the nature and destiny of the human race. Is the divine nature personal or nonpersonal? Does deity become incarnate in the world? Are human beings reborn again and again on earth? Is the empirical self the real self, destined for eternal life in fellowship with God, or is it only a temporary and illusory manifestation of an eternal higher self? Is the Bible, or the Qur'an, or the Bhagavad Gita the Word of God? If what Christianity says in answer to such questions is true, must not what Hinduism says be to a large extent false? If what Buddhism says is true, must not what Islam says be largely false?[1]

Presented in this way the problem of conflicting truth claims appears very modern. However, already in the time of the Buddha religious doctrines and practices had attained such bewildering variety in north India that people were beginning to feel confused. Thus when Heinrich Zimmer says that "We of the Occident are about to arrive at a crossroads that was reached by the thinkers of India some seven hundred years before Christ"[2] his statement may be stating a truth in a way he never intended!

Between the seventh and the fifth centuries B.C. the intellectual life of India was in ferment. It has been pointed out many times that this period was a turning point in the intellectual and spiritual development of the whole world, for it saw the earlier philosophers of Greece, the great Hebrew prophets, Confucius in China, and probably Zarathustra in Persia. In India this crucial period in the world's history was marked on the one hand by the teaching of the Upanishadic sages, who admitted the inspiration of the Vedas and the relative value of Vedic sacrifices, and on the other hand by the appearance of teachers who were less orthodox than they, and who rejected the Vedas entirely. It was at this time that Jainism and Buddhism arose, the most successful of a large number of heterodox systems, each based on a distinctive set of doctrines and each laying down distinctive rules of conduct for winning salvation.[3]

The situation at the time of the Buddha does seem to illustrate the point well historically. The *Brahmajāla Sutta* not only spreads its net to cover 62 views as such,[4] one source mentions 363 schools of thought among which 67 'types' of sceptics are identified.[5] Small wonder, then, that the people then as now were a bit confused, as a story about the Buddha tells us:

The Buddha once visited a small town called Kesaputta in the kingdom of Kosala. The inhabitants of this town were known by the common name Kālāma. When they heard that the Buddha was in their town, the Kālāmas paid him a visit, and told him:

"Sir, there are some recluses and *brāhmaṇas*, and they, too, in their turn, explain and illumine only their own doctrines, and despise, condemn and spurn others' doctrines. But, for us, Sir, we have always doubt and perplexity as to who among these venerable recluses and *brāmaṇas* spoke the truth, and who spoke falsehood."

Then the Buddha gave them this advice, unique in the history of religions:

"Yes, Kālāmas, it is proper that you have doubt, that you have perplexity, for a doubt has arisen in a matter which is doubtful. Now, look you Kālāmas, do not be led by reports, or tradition, or hearsay. Be not led by the authority of religious texts, nor by mere logic or inference, nor by considering appearances, nor by the delight in speculative opinions, nor by seeming possibilities, nor by the idea: 'this is our teacher'. But, O Kālāmas, when you know for yourselves that certain things are unwholesome (*akusala*), and wrong, and bad, then give them up.... And when you know for yourselves that certain things are wholesome (*kusala*) and good, then accept them and follow them."

The Buddha went even further. He told the bhikkhus that a disciple should examine even the Tathāgata (Buddha) himself, so that he (the disciple) might be fully convinced of the true value of the teacher whom he followed.[6]

We shall revert to a dicussion of the Buddha's and the Buddhist response to the problem after assessing the problem in its modern context.

RELIGIOUS TRUTH CLAIMS IN THE MODERN CONTEXT

The problem, as perceived in the Western philosophy of religion is that if one is confronted with a variety of conflicting truth claims then each undermines the other, paving the way for an all-embracing scepticism. If there are many religions and they make conflicting truth-claims, then "for any particular religion there will always be far more reason for believing it to be false than for believing it to be true. This is the skeptical argument that arises from the conflicting truth claims of the various world faiths."[7]

This argument is an amplification of a point developed by Hume when he claimed that "every miracle, therefore, pretended to have been wrought in any of these religions (and all of them abound in miracles), as its direct scope is to establish the particular religion to which it is attributed; so has it the same force, though more indirectly, to overthrow every other system".[8] Apart from this specific illustration, Hume also presents the more specific argument "that, in matters of religion, whatever is different is contrary; and that it is impossible the religions of ancient Rome, of Turkey, of Siam, and of China should, all of them, be established on any solid foundation".[9]

Buddhism takes a somewhat different view in this matter. First of all, it does not set much store by miracles. In contrast to Hume's claim:

On the whole, the attitude of the Buddhist Church during the first millennium of its existence seems to have been that the occult and the psychic are all right as long as one does not take too much notice of them, and exhibits them as a kind of cheap stunt to the populace. One day the Buddha came across an ascetic who sat by the bank of a river, and who had practised austerities for 25 years. The Buddha asked him what he had got out of all his labour. The ascetic proudly replied that now at last he could cross the river by walking on the water. The Buddha tried to point out that this was little gain for so much labour, since for one penny the ferry would take him across.[10]

Second, Buddhism does not quite concede the point that whatever is different must be contrary in matters of religion. Not only is Buddhism less contentious of other claims, it is less tenacious of its own as becomes evident from the following:

Asked by the young Brahmin to explain the idea of maintaining or protecting truth, the Buddha said: "A man has a faith. If he says 'This is my faith', so far he maintains truth. But by that he cannot proceed to the absolute conclusion: 'This alone is Truth, and everything else is false' ". In other words, a man may believe what he likes, and he may say 'I believe this'. So far he respects truth. But because of his belief or faith, he should not say that what he believes is alone the Truth, and everything else is false.

The Buddha says: 'To be attached to one thing (to a certain view) and to look down upon other things (views) as inferior — this the wise men call a fetter.'

Once the Buddha explained the doctrine of cause and effect to his disciples, and they said that they saw it and understood it clearly. Then the Buddha said:

'O bhikkus, even this view, which is so pure and so clear, if you cling to it, if you fondle it, if you treasure it, if you are attached to it, then you do not understand that the teaching is similar to a raft, which is for crossing over, and not for getting hold of.'[11]

All this does not mean that Buddhism denies the existence of conflicting truth claims, it merely questions their recalcitrance. It faces the issue as other religious or philosophical systems but before we turn to its solution it might be worthwhile reviewing a few suggested solutions from a Buddhist perspective.

W.A. CHRISTIAN'S ANALYSIS

W.A. Christian classified conflicting truth claims into two kinds: those in which "different predicates are affirmed of the same subject" and those in which "different subjects are assigned to the same predicate". The first kind he calls "doctrinal disagreements" as when both Jews and Christians might claim that

Jesus is the Messiah. This might seem to represent an area of agreement till it is realized that what each means by the word Messiah differs sharply. The second kind he calls "basic religious disagreements" as when the goal of life is variously described as the Beatific Vision, *Nirvāṇa, Mokṣa*, etc.

William Christian offers a complex and interesting theory of the relation between basic religious proposals and doctrinal proposals, but we are concerned at the moment only with his demonstration of how disagreements between religions may be located by one's uncovering the presuppositions of statements that might at first seem to have meaning only in the context of a particular religion, and thus not to be candidates for either agreement or disagreement on the part of other religions. We have seen that there are real disagreements concerning religious belief-proposals; that is to say, there are many belief-proposals that are accepted by the adherents of one religion but rejected by those of another.[12]

It is interesting that Buddhism proceeds by accepting Christian's view that adherents of religion may differ about belief-proposals and that "basic religious disagreements" may be a more serious matter than "doctrinal disagreements". For instance, Hinduism and Buddhism doctrinally differ on the issue of rebirth. According to Hinduism it involves a transmigrating soul but it does not do so according to Buddhism.[13] However, this does not cause as much disagreement among the two as the "basic religious disagreement" they have regarding the state of liberation when the wording in the two comparable texts are virtually identical but the subject in one case is theistic and non-theistic in the other.

Some of the final stages of *jhānic* attainment in Buddhism were achieved by Upaniṣadic seers and identified with Brahman, Buddhism points out their inadequacy and the necessity of going beyond. Besides, in some of the Upaniṣads we find a theistic interpretation of the ultimate experience and reality. For example, in the *Śvetāśvatara Upaniṣad*, 6.10 — *Kaṭha*, 2.2.15 — *Muṇḍaka*, 2.2.10 we find the following description:

'The sun shines not there, nor the moon and stars,
These lightnings shine not, much less this (earthly) fire!
After Him, as He shines, doth everything shine,
This whole world is illuminated with His light.'
In the *Udāna* we find a similar passage, which reads as follows:

Where earth, water, fire and air do not penetrate;
There the stars do not glitter, nor the sun shed its light;
The moon too shines not but there is no darkness there.

Here there is no theistic interpretation of the experience and we earlier explained why such an interpretation would be erroneous. Besides, many of the metaphysical ideas about soul (*ātman*) which are rejected in Buddhism are to be found in the Upaniṣads, so that it would be quite misleading to identify the two.[14]

Thus Christian's analysis can be usefully extended to Buddhism in relation to other religions. However, it is possible to identify some other responses from within Buddhism itself, without relating it to other religions such as Hinduism. Thus one such independent Buddhist response to Christian's ideas could be that one should offer not belief-proposals but rather practise-proposals, and only such belief proposals as relate to the latter. Finally, one should not lose sight of the fact that all proposals are finally disposable, to be disposed of like the raft after the other shore is reached, a parable to be cited in full in due course.

W.C. SMITH'S ANALYSIS

Wilfred Cantwell Smith has claimed that the very idea of viewing a religion as true or false is a strangely Western notion and that "it is not appropriate to speak of a religion as being true or false, any more than it is to speak of a civilization as being true or false"[15] on account of the close relation between religion and culture. Moreover, according to him the original insight of the founder and the institutions to which it gives rise often "stand in a questionable relationship".[16] Finally, with the world contracting into a global village each religion is inevitably and inextricably being bound with the other so that a global perspective on the religious tradition of humanity may be more in order. For these three reasons then the issues of conflicting truth claims stand commuted, muted and transmuted.

The Buddhist position on conflicting truth claims is not in opposition to Smith's system on all points but it would insist on retaining the truth question and the value question, without its excesses of fanaticism and self-righteousness. For instance in "the *Sandaka sutta*, Buddhism is contrasted with four types of false religions, and four types of religions which are unsatisfactory though not necessarily false...."[17] Moreover, like Christianity which became identified with one major cultural system, the European, Buddhism also became identified with different cultural systems in the East — with the Southeast Asian as well as the Far-East Asian — and for a time even with its subsystems such as the Sri Lankan, the Thai, the Chinese, or the Japanese. It is thus true that the major religious traditions

... have made their impact upon the stream of human life so as to affect the development of cultures; and what we call Christianity, Islam, Hinduism, Buddhism, are among the resulting historical-cultural phenomena. It is clear, for example, that Christianity has developed through a complex interaction between religious and non-religious factors. Christian ideas have been formed within the intellectual framework provided by Greek philosophy; the Christian church was moulded as an institution by the Roman Empire and its system of laws; the Catholic mind reflects something of the Latin Mediterranean temperament, whereas the Protestant mind reflects something of the northern Germanic temperament, and so on. It is not hard to appreciate the connections between historical Christianity and the continuing life of humanity in the western hemisphere, and of course the same is true, in their own ways, of all the other religions of the world.[18]

This raises the fundamental question between the relationship between *truth* and *temperament*. To explain: liberals and conservatives are found in all religious traditions, to put it at its simplest. Hence the convoluted connection of religion with culture also seems to possess a hidden universal psychological variable. Moreover, while Buddhism has moved into a culture with a spirit of assimilation, it has not given up on its transcultural stand, although it may occasionally appear compromised as in Sri Lankan nationalism or Nichiren's Buddhism. But does this mean that the truth question, which is philosophical, must go unrecognized in cultural camouflage?

Again, on the question of the relationship between the actual institutions of Buddhism and the point that "this development stands in a questionable relationship to that original event or idea",[19] Buddhism will heartily endorse this view but for a pedagogical and not historical reasons. By the very nature of things, and as enshrined in the doctrine of *upāya*, Buddhism may be looked upon as engaged in a perpetual attempt to bridge this gulf between the original vision and the actual institution. In fact, Buddha insists that *his* own teaching stands precisely in such a questionable relationship to his own enlightenment:

Elsewhere the Buddha explains this famous simile in which his teaching is compared to a raft for crossing over, and not for getting hold of and carrying on one's back:

'O bhikkhus, a man is on a journey. He comes to a vast stretch of water. On this side the shore is dangerous, but on the other it is safe and without danger. No boat goes to the other shore which is safe and without danger, nor is there any bridge for crossing over. He says to himself: "This sea of water is vast, and the shore on this side is full of danger; but on the other shore it is safe and without danger. No boat goes to the other side, nor is there a bridge for crossing over. It would be good therefore if I would gather grass, wood, branches and leaves to make a raft, and with the help of the raft cross over safely to the other side, exerting myself with my hands and feet". Then that man, O bhikkhus, gathers grass, wood, branches and leaves and makes a raft, and with the help of that raft crosses over safely to the other side, exerting himself with his hands and feet. Having crossed over and got to the other side, he thinks: "This raft was of great help to me. With its aid I have crossed safely over to this side, exerting myself with my hands and feet. It would be good if I carry this raft on my head or on my back wherever I go".

'What do you think, O bhikkhus, if he acted in this way would that man be acting properly with regard to the raft? "No, Sir." In which way then would he be acting properly with regard to the raft? Having crossed and gone over to the other side, suppose that man should think: "This raft was a great help to me. With its aid I have crossed safely over to this side, exerting myself with my hands and feet. It would be good if I beached this raft on the shore, or moored it and left it afloat, and then went on my way wherever it may be". Acting in this way would that man act properly with regard to that raft.

'In the same manner, O bhikkhus, I have taught a doctrine similar to a raft — it is for crossing over, and not for carrying (lit. 'getting hold of'). You, O bhikkhus, who understand that the teaching is similar to a raft, should give up even good things (*dhamma*) how much more then should you give up evil things (*adhamma*).'[20]

W.C. Smith's analysis, therefore, runs into limitations if an attempt is made to extend it to Buddhism.

A point of some significance in Smith's argument is the claim that there are really no 'religions' in the abstract but people who belong to it in the concrete, that they have interacted throughout history and now that "the world has become a communicational unity we are moving into a new situation in which it becomes both possible and appropriate for religious thinking to transcend these cultural-historical boundaries".[21]

These views have evoked a sharp rejoinder from a Buddhist scholar who regards the changes in usage and understanding suggested by Smith as merely cosmetic. The suggestions of terminological and semantic changes have elicited the following response:

Another subtle attempt has been made by Wilfred Cantwell Smith when he says that there are no religions but only religious people, thereby trying to say that religions should be judged by the moral behavior of the 'religious' people. But this way is really only a way of asking religions to commit suicide in the face of the threat of humanist ethics.[22]

The reaction is perhaps too strong but it does suggest that religious identity may be a stronger factor to contend with than might be apparent at first sight.

JOHN HICK'S ANALYSIS

John H. Hick has provided an attractive model for accommodating the conflicting truth-claims of various religions "as an alternative to total scepticism".[23] He bases his model on the Kantian distinction between "the world as it is in itself" and "the world as it appears to us with our particular cognitive machinery".[24] He argues that the reality as it is in itself is identical but its experience is expressed differently because of the differences in the 'cognitive machinery'. He identifies two basic religious concepts in relation to this cognitive machinery: "One is the concept of God, or of the Real experienced as personal, which presides over the theistic forms of religion. The other is the concept of the Absolute, or of the Real experienced as nonpersonal, which presides over the various non-theistic forms of religion."[25] Thus concepts of Jahweh, Krishna, Shiva, Allah, etc. belong to the first category and concepts of Brahman, *nirvāṇa, śūnyatā, dharma, dharmakāya,* Tao, etc. to the second.[26] Another significant point Hick makes is that when the "divine Reality is experienced and thought within different streams of religious life", there is a dual aspect to this phenomenon. The different manifestations are "partly projections of the divine Reality into human consciousness and partly projections of the human consciousness itself as it has been formed by particular historical cultures".[27]

This model is open to objection from a Buddhist point of view on two counts. Firstly, as we have already seen, Buddhism rejects the theistic concept as inappropriate. This point has been made several times by several scholars.[28] It is worth noting that it even rejects some of the non-theistic concepts such as that of Brahman as false. This is particularly significant because both Buddhist *Nirvāṇa* and Hindu Brahman[29] belong to the non-theistic category. The second criticism, however, is more significant. It rests on the distinction between extrovertive and introvertive cognition of the ultimate Reality. In cases of extrovertive cognitions one may see *different* forms. However, the non-theistic experiences are typically of the introvertive type and here the point is that as images and concepts are cast away in this type of experience, can one say that *different* experiences of the Real are possible? If a room is full, it can be full of different objects; but if it is empty, its emptiness is undifferentiated.

Hick offered his proposal according to which "the great religious traditions of the world represent different perceptions of and response to same infinite divine reality" as "an alternative to total scepticism".[30] This proposal is quite close to the modern Hindu position in this regard[31] and the modern Hindu position is a lineal descendant of an ancient Hindu position. This might provide a clue for identifying a Buddhist response to his proposal.

The practical consequence of John H. Hick's claim seems to be that there are *different ways* of experiencing reality. Yet this position of "many paths" is questioned by the Buddha, at least in the specific context of the *Tevijja Sutta.* The Buddha was told:

Concerning the true path and the false, Gotama. Various Brahmans, Gotama, teach various paths. The Addhariyā Brahmans, the Tittiriyā Brahmans, the Khandokā Brahmans [the Khandavā Brahmans], the

Bavharijā Brahmans. Are all those saving paths? Are they all paths which will lead him, who acts according to them, into a state of union with Brahmā?

Just, Gotama, as near a village or a town there are many and various paths, yet they all meet together in the village — just in that way are all the various paths taught by various Brahmans — the Addhariyā Brahmans, the Tittiriyā Brahmans, the Khandokā Brahmans [the Khandavā Brahmans], the Bavharijā Brahmans. Are all these saving paths? Are they all paths which will lead him, who acts according to them, into a state of union with Brahmā?[32]

K.N. Jayatilleke summarizes the rest of the account as follows:

The Buddha, who, has held this office [of Brahmā] in the past and has verified in the light of his extra-sensory powers of perception the conditions required for attaining fellowship with God or Brahmā, could state that there are not a diversity of paths all leading to such a state *but one and only one path* consisting of acquiring purity of mind, cultivating compassion and being selfless and without possessions.

Modern Buddhists follow the Buddha in this. Thus John H. Hick proposed that both theistic and non-theistic approaches may be placed on par in his philosophical framework but K.N. Jayatilleke unequivocally states that "while some Upanishads hold that 'the world is enveloped by God' (*Iśāvāsyam idaṁ sarvam*), Buddhism held that 'the world was without a refuge and without God' (*Attāno loko anabhissaro*)".[33]

Buddhism, therefore, does not provide a neutral philosophical framework for religious pluralism. It does, however, provide a framework of tolerance in the face of religious pluralism. First of all, it is opposed to attachment, *including* attachment to beliefs of a religious nature (*dhammā-taṇhā*).[34] Second, Buddha is against any *dogmatic* claims that there is only one truth. In the earlier instance, when the Buddha claimed that there is only one path to union with Brahmā, he claimed to be speaking from personal experience. That pragmatic claim is to be distinguished from exclusive dogmatic claims, as the following account indicates:

Once a group of learned and well-known Brahmins went to see the Buddha and had a long discussion with him. One of the group, a Brahmin youth of 16 years of age, named Kāpathika, considered by them all to be an exceptionally brilliant mind, put a question to the Buddha:

"Venerable Gotama, there are the ancient holy scriptures of the Brahmins handed down along the line by unbroken oral tradition of texts. With regard to them, Brahmins come to the absolute conclusion: 'This alone is Truth, and everything else is false'. Now, what does the Venerable Gotama say about this?"

The Buddha inquired: "Among Brahmins is there any one single Brahmin who claims that he personally knows and sees that 'This alone is Truth, and everything else is false'?"

The young man was frank, and said: "No".

"Then, is there any one single teacher, or a teacher of teachers of Brahmins back to the seventh generation, or even any one of those original authors of those scriptures, who claims that he knows and he sees: 'This alone is Truth, and everything else is false'?"

"No."

"Then, it is like a line of blind men, each holding on to the preceding one; the first one does not see, the middle one also does not see, the last one also does not see. Thus, it seems to me that the state of the Brahmins is like that of a line of blind men."

Then the Buddha gave advice of extreme importance to the group of Brahmins: "It is not proper for a wise man who maintains (lit. protects) truth to come to the conclusion: 'This alone is Truth, and everything else is false'."

Asked by the young Brahmin to explain the idea of maintaining or protecting truth, the Buddha said: "A man has a faith. If he says 'This is my faith', so far he maintains truth. But by that he cannot proceed to the absolute conclusion: 'This alone is Truth, and everything else is false'." In other words, a man may believe what he likes, and he may say "I believe this". So far he respects truth. But because of his belief or faith, he should not say that what he believes is alone the Truth, and everything else is false.[35]

Third, Mahāyāna Buddhism more often than not takes a tolerant view of Hindu gods.[36] Fourth, at a practical level Buddhism advocates the Eightfold Path as an objective criterion for both Buddhists and non-Buddhists for judging the acceptability of beliefs and practices, "irrespective of whether or not one understands the theoretical part of the doctrine".[37]

In the course of its history Buddhism has by and large succeeded in preserving its particularity along with an attitude of tolerance towards other religions. "The great Khan Mongka (*c.* 1250) favoured Nestorians, Buddhists and Taoists, in the belief that, as he said to the Franciscan William of Rubrouck, *'all religions are like fingers of one hand'* — although to the

Buddhists he said that Buddhism was like the palm of the hand, the other religions being the fingers."[38] Perhaps it does require a sleight of hand to combine Buddhism's claim to uniqueness with tolerance for other religions — but somehow Buddhism does succeed in performing this feat of ecumenical magic.

THE BUDDHIST VIEW REVISITED

Buddhism is a vast and varied tradition and it has doubtless developed several attitudes to other religions and their truth-claims in the course of its history.[39] David W. Chappel has identified at least six such attitudes; namely, that Buddhism is (1) separate and superior to other religions; (2) compassionately engaged with other religions; (3) other religions are early stages of development; (4) Buddhism and other religions are complementary; (5) all religions are historically relative and limited; and (6) Buddhism and other religions share the same essence.[40]

What is significant about these different attitudes, when extended towards conflicting truth claims, is that they play down the conflict. And the position adopted by the eminent Buddhist leader of Thailand, Buddhadāsa, almost eliminates it. He declares:

The ordinary, ignorant worldling is under the impression that there are many religions and that they are all different to the extent of being hostile and opposed. Thus one considers Christianity, Islam, and Buddhism as incompatible and even bitter enemies. Such is the conception of the common person who speaks according to the impressions held by common people.... If, however, a person has penetrated to the fundamental nature (*dhamma*) of religion, he will regard all religions as essentially similar. Although he may say there is Buddhism, Christianity, Islam, and so on, he will also say that essentially they are all the same. If he should go to a deeper understanding of *dhamma* until finally he realizes the absolute truth, he would discover that there is no such thing called religion — that there is no Buddhism, Christianity, or Islam.[41]

The full significance of Buddhadāsa's statement, with which we intend to conclude, is brought home by applying the metaphor of water to it as David W. Chappell has pointed out:

It is interesting that Buddhadāsa uses the example of water. First there are many kinds of water: rainwater, ditch water, sewer water, which ordinary people can and should distinguish. However, at another level, when the pollutants are removed, fundamentally these waters have the same substance. Nevertheless, there is yet a third level of perception in which water itself disappears when we divide it into hydrogen and oxygen. Based on this simile and his earlier remarks, we can see that there are really three levels outlined by Buddhadāsa; conventional distinctions, shared essence, and voidness. The traditional Buddhist doctrine of emptiness and nonduality eliminates religion, as in Buddhadāsa's third point. What separates Buddhadāsa from those nondualists is the second level that Buddhadāsa proposes, namely, a lower level of dhammic language that moves beyond conventional distinctions, but which is not yet at the highest level that proclaims "No religion!"

It is this intermediate stage between conventional truth and the highest truth that is Buddhadāsa's contribution to our quest for a Buddhist attitude toward other religions. At this level, the distinctions between religions are seen as temporary, partial, and secondary in comparison to the more important understanding of the kinship between different religious people. This provides the most complete approach to other religions ever articulated by a Buddhist, and provides a basis for differentiation, for parity and collaboration, and for transcendence. Accordingly, we who work in the field of interrreligious study and dialogue are deeply indebted to Venerable Bhikku Buddhadāsa for his clear ledership in our new world of religious pluralism. [42]

CHAPTER 9

Human Destiny: Immortality and Resurrection

THE IMMORTALITY OF THE SOUL

The belief in the existence of a soul, or some version of it, is extremely widespread and characterizes almost all the major religious traditions of the world, including the primal. Indeed,

Some kind of distinction between physical body and immaterial or semi-material soul seems to be as old as human culture; the existence of such a distinction has been indicated by the manner of burial of the earliest human skeletons yet discovered. Anthropologists offer various conjectures about the origin of the distinction: perhaps it was first suggested by memories of dead persons, by dreams of them, by the sight of reflections of oneself in water and on other bright surfaces, or by meditation upon the significance of religious rites which grew up spontaneously in face of the fact of death.[1]

Buddhism does not accept this belief in a soul; the question of believing in its immortality, therefore, naturally does not arise. In fact,

Buddhism stands unique in the history of human thought in denying the existence of such a Soul, Self, or Ātman. According to the teaching of the Buddha, the idea of self is an imaginary, false belief which has no corresponding reality, and it produces harmful thoughts of 'me' and 'mine', selfish desire, craving, attachment, hatred, ill-will, conceit, pride, egoism, and other defilements, impurities and problems. It is the source of all the troubles in the world from personal conflicts to wars between nations. In short, to this false view can be traced all the evil in the world.[2]

It should be realized, however, that within the framework of Buddhist thought, it is possible to accept immortality, even without the existence of a soul *if* by immortality is meant the endless continuity of a series. For unless the series which an individual represents is liberated, it will continue to exist, in any of the several realms of existence the Buddhists accept such as divine, demonic, human, animal, ghostly and infernal. One must distinguish clearly here between immortality as meaning, (1) eternal life in the same mode; (2) continued existence in several modes. The term is usually used in the first sense, but if the second sense is conceded, then continuous survival is implied in Buddhism as the process of *saṁsāra* in Buddhism is considered without a natural end for a being,[3] although it could be brought to an end.

The belief in the existence of the soul is an ancient one and acquires philosophical dignity in the thought of Plato (428/7–348/7 BC) "who systematically developed the body–mind dichotomy and first attempted to prove the immortality of the soul".[4] He presented the following vision of the blessedness of the soul.

Plato argues that although the body belongs to the sensible world and shares its changing and impermanent nature, the intellect is related to the unchanging realities of which we are aware when we think not of particular good things but of Goodness itself, not of specific just acts but of Justice itself, and of the other 'universals' or eternal Ideas by participation in which physical things and events have their own specific characteristics. Being related to this higher and abiding realm rather than to the evanescent world of sense, the soul is immortal. Hence, one who devotes one's life to the contemplation of eternal realities rather than to the gratification of the fleeting desires of the body will find at death that whereas one's body turns to dust, one's soul gravitates to the realm of the unchanging, there to live forever. Plato painted an awe-inspiring picture, of haunting beauty and persuasiveness, which has moved and elevated the minds of men and women in many different centuries and lands.[5]

Such a vision calls for at least three comments from a Buddhist point of view. First, there are "no unchanging realities" in Buddhism except *Nirvāṇa* in a very special sense.[6] And the concept of soul is antithetical to *Nirvāṇa* — belief in one precludes the realization of the other.[7] Second, Buddhism does not accept the reality of "universals". They are regarded as merely linguistic conventions. Third, Buddhism presents its own "awe-inspiring picture, of haunting beauty and persuasiveness, which has moved and elevated the minds of men and women in different countries and lands" through its vision of the Pure Land of the Buddhas and the Bodhisattvas, a prominent feature of Mahāyāna Buddhism as it was practised in China and is still practised in Japan. These Pure Lands, however, are ultimately preparation grounds for *Nirvāṇa*, where the divine Bodhisattvas edify the elect by discourses on the "soullessness" of beings and things.

As for the proofs of the existence of a soul, Plato argued for the imperishability of the soul on account of its impartite nature, a doctrine which became standard doctrine in Roman Catholicism. Buddhism, however, reduces the *entire* human "personality to various constituents all of which are in a state of flux. Buddhism does identify a unit called *dharmas* which itself has no constituent parts and is constituent of the universe and individuals therein, but they are ever in motion. They are like flashes of reality," quite different from a soul. Moreover, Buddhism would agree with modern psychology in questioning the

... basic premise that the mind is a simple entity. It seems instead to be a structure of only relative unity, normally fairly stable and tightly integrated but capable under stress of various degrees of division and dissolution. This comment from psychology makes it clear that the assumption that the soul is a simple substance is not an empirical observation but a metaphysical theory. As such, it cannot provide the basis for a general proof of immortality.[8]

If one replaces the body–soul distinction with a body–mind distinction, then Buddhist thought can be brought in further fruitful apposition to modern thought. The relationship between the two in modern thought has tended to take the form of either dualism or identity. Greek dualism persisted through Western thought finding its classical exposition in the Cartesian mind–matter dualism. Descartes' (1596–1650) position, which was "subsequently undermined by trends which, in modern times, have moved in the opposite direction and in what might be called a form of materialism",[9] identified the body and mind so closely as to lead to the claim that,

The words that describe mental characteristics and operations — such as 'intelligent', 'thoughtful', 'carefree', 'happy', 'calculating', and the like — apply in practice to types of human behavior and to behavioral dispositions. They refer to the empirical individual, the observable human being who is born and grows and acts and feels and dies, and not to the shadowy proceedings of a mysterious "ghost in the machine". An individual is thus very much what he or she appears to be — a creature of flesh and blood, who behaves and is capable of behaving in a characteristic range of ways — rather than a nonphysical soul incomprehensibly interacting with a physical body.[10]

The Buddhist position in this respect is an intermediate one for "while Buddhism holds that the person is a psycho-physical unit (*nāmarūpa*), it does not subscribe to the identity hypothesis that the body and mind are one and the same entity or to the dualistic hypothesis that the mind and the body are entirely different".[11]

THE BIBLICAL VIEW OF THE RE-CREATION OF THE PERSON

In an interesting twist in the history of ideas, the virtual identification of body–mind in modern thought has a parallel in ancient Jewish thought in which the body was regarded as the soul in "its outward form".[12] This represented a current of thought which moved in a channel different from the Platonic, a current in which the resurrection of the body rather than the immortality of the soul became the main post-mortem issue.

The religious difference between the Platonic belief in the immortality of the soul, and the Judaic-Christian belief in the resurrection of the body is that the latter postulates a special divine act of recreation. This produces a sense of utter dependence upon God in the hour of death, a feeling that is in accordance with the biblical understanding of the human being as having been formed out of "the dust of the earth", a product (as we say today) of the slow evolution of life from its lowly beginnings in the primeval slime. Hence, in the Jewish and Christian conception, death is something real and fearful. It is not thought to be like walking from one room to another, or like taking off an old coat and putting on a new one. It means sheer unqualified extinction — passing out from the lighted circle of life into "death's dateless night". Only through the sovereign creative love of God can there be a new existence beyond the grave.[13]

The inapplicability of the issue of the immortality of the soul to Buddhist thought has been already indicated earlier. The point at issue from a Buddhist point of view then becomes one of comparing *rebirth* with *resurrection*.[14]

It is interesting that the central point at issue in both the cases turns out to be the same, "that of providing criteria of personal identity". This point is clearly borne out by the three scenarios which are developed around a fictive entity called 'John Smith' by John Hick.

(1) Suppose, first, that someone — John Smith — living in the United States were suddenly and inexplicably to disappear before the eyes of his friends, and that at the same moment an exact replica of him were inexplicably to appear in India. The person who appears in India is exactly similar in both physical and mental characteristics to the person who disappeared in America. There is continuity of memory, complete similarity of bodily features including fingerprints, hair and eye coloration, and stomach contents, and also of beliefs, habits, emotions, and mental dispositions. Further, the 'John Smith' replica thinks of himself as being the John Smith who disappeared in the United States. After all possible tests have been made and have proved positive, the factors leading his friends to accept 'John Smith' as John Smith would surely prevail and would cause them to overlook even his mysterious transference from one continent to another, rather than treat 'John Smith', with all of John Smith's memories and other characteristics, as someone other than John Smith.... (2) Suppose, second, that our John Smith, instead of inexplicably disappearing, dies, but that at the moment of his death a 'John Smith' replica, again complete with memories and all other characteristics, appears in India. Even with the corpse on our hands, we would, I think, still have to accept this 'John Smith' as the John Smith who had died. We would just have to say that he had been miraculously re-created in another place.... (3) Now suppose, third, that on John Smith's death the 'John Smith' replica appears, not in India, but as a resurrection replica in a different world altogether, a resurrection world inhabited only by resurrected persons. This world occupies its own space distinct from that with which we are now familiar. That is to say, an object in the resurrection world is not situated at any distance or in any direction from the objects in our present world, although each object in either world is spatially related to every other object in the same world.[15]

The first supposition represents a case of migration, the second of rebirth and the third of resurrection. The problem of the criterion of personal identity in the Judaic-Christian tradition is in a sense less and in a sense more acute in comparison to Buddhism. In the case of rebirth, the Buddhists admit that the person reborn "is neither the same nor different" from the person who passed away, thereby allowing for more flexibility.[16] The question, which is a thorny one, in Buddhism is: what happens to the Realized One after death, not what happens to the ordinary human being. "The critical question for the Buddhists was not the survival of the individual at death, which they held and defended against the doctrine of annihilation (*ucchedavāda*), but the existence of the individual when the aggregation of the *khandhas* has finally ceased."[17] The intractable nature of the problem is illustrated by the example of the ubiquitous John Smith by Edward Conze thus:

Suppose he wishes to become immortal. Then he has no choice but to deny himself throughout the whole length and breadth of his being. Anything impermanent in himself he has to get rid of. Just try to think of what is left of Mr Smith after he has become immortal. His body would obviously be gone. With the body his instincts would have disappeared — since they are bound up with his glands, with the needs of his tissues, in short with the body. His mind also, as he knows it, would have to be sacrificed. Because this mind of ours is bound up with bodily processes, its operations are based on the data provided by the bodily organs of sense, and it reveals its impermanence by incessantly and restlessly jumping from one thing to another. With the mind would go his sense of logical consistency. As a matter of fact, Mr John Smith, turned immortal, would not recognise himself at all. He would have lost everything that made him recognisable to himself and to others. And he could be born anew only if he had learned to deny all that clutters up the immortal side of his being — which lies, as the Buddhists would put it, outside his five *skandhas* — if he would deny all that constitutes his dear little self. Buddhist training consists, indeed, in systematically weakening our hold on those things in us which keep us from regaining the immortality which we lost when we were born. The body is subdued, the instincts are weakened, the mind is calmed, logical thinking is baffled and exhausted by absurdities, and sensory facts are thought little of, the eye of faith and the eye of wisdom replacing the eyes of the body. It comes really to the same as the precept of John Wesley, when he urged a disciple of his *to kill himself by inches*.[18]

However, if we revert to the case of rebirth and resurrection and leave the case of the Realized One the way Buddha left it — "unexplained", then the following conclusion of K.N. Jayatilleke seems to apply equally well to both the cases as both rebirth and resurrection involve a reconstitution of the "person".

The solution to this problem lies in the criteria that we employ to claim personal identity. In a single human life we normally use two criteria. One is the spatio-temporal continuity of the body. On the basis of this we can claim that so-and-so is a person who as a child went to such-and-such a school, although there may be nothing in common between the two bodies as far as shape and content is concerned. The other criterion is memory, on the basis of which someone may claim that he was such-and-such twenty years ago. When one life is concerned the two criteria normally support each other. In the case of the reborn person or discarnate spirit, it is the memory criterion alone which can establish the identity. In this case, when the body criterion is employed, we have to say that "he is not the same person" but when the memory criterion is employed we would have to say "he is not another person". So according to Buddhism "he is neither the same nor another" (*na ca so na ca añño*) when we give a strictly accurate description, although in common parlance we may say that he is the same person.[19]

HEAVEN AND HELL

Concepts of heaven and hell are found both in Christianity and Buddhism but in different contexts — in relation to resurrection in Christianity and in relaiton to rebirth in Buddhism.

In Christianity, faith in resurrection is based partly on faith in the precedent of Jesus Christ and the promise it embodies but it also "arises as a corollary of faith in the sovereign purpose of God, which is not restricted by death and which holds us in being beyond our natural mortality". The idea of the fellowship of God also required that human creatures do not "pass out of existence when the divine purpose for them still remains largely unfulfilled". Thus it is "this promised fulfilment of God's purpose for the individual in which the full possibilities of human nature will be realized, that constitutes the 'heaven' symbolised in the New Testament as a joyous banquet in which all and sundry rejoice together".[20]

In this context one must distinguish between two Buddhist concepts: heaven with a small h and Heaven with a capital H. The Buddhist heavens (with a small h) are heavens one achieves as a result of beneficial good deeds allowing one to enjoy a happy if temporary existence,[21] or a place from where one moves on towards Realization without having to be reborn in a human realm. This latter case of sanctification in Theravāda Buddhism is called *anāgāmī* or the non-returner.[22] While heavens with a small h suffice to describe the celestial realms in Theravāda Buddhism, this is not the case with Mahāyāna Buddhism which evolved the concept of the Pure Land (*sukhā-vātī*). In Theravāda Buddhism, heavens are really stopping-stations either on the way to *Nirvāṇa* or for returning back into *saṁsāra* as represented by our worldly existence. The beliefs of the Pure Land school come closer to the Christian Heaven.

The Pure Land School takes as its principal text the *Sukhāvatīvyūha* or the *Pure Land Sutra*. This sutra exists in a long and a short version. The former begins with a dialogue between Śākyamuni and Ānanda concerning a monk named Dharmākara, who went to a former Buddha for a description of the ideal Buddha and Buddha land. After having received instructions from that Buddha, Dharmākara then uttered an earnest wish to be reborn as that ideal Buddha presiding over that ideal Buddha land. This earnest wish forms the nucleus of the long *Sukhā-vatīvyūha*.[23]

It was mentioned earlier that the *sutra* exists in two versions: a long one and a short one.

Both the long and short versions of the sutra contain a detailed description of the Pure Land, or the Western Paradise. There is one great difference between the two however. The long version emphasizes that rebirth in the Pure Land comes as the result of meritorious deeds as well as faith and devotion to Amitābha, whereas the short version specifically states that only faith and prayer are necessary.[24]

Perhaps it is significant that the short one gained wider acceptance.[25] Both, however, describe the Pure Land in similar terms:

The Buddha presiding over the Pure Land is designated as Amitābha, meaning Infinite Light, or Amitāyus, Infinite Life. The Pure Land is described as being rich, fertile, comfortable, filled with gods and men but with none of the evil modes of existence, such as animals, ghosts, or denizens of hell. It is adorned with fragrant trees and flowers, especially lotus, and decorated with the most beautiful and precious jewels and gems. Rivers with sweetly scented waters give forth pleasant musical sounds, and are flanked on both banks by scented jewel trees. The heavenly beings sporting in the water can cause it to be hot or cold as they wish. Everywhere they go, they can hear the *dharma* of the Buddha, the teachings of compassion, sympathetic joy, patience, tolerance, equanimity, and so forth. Nowhere do they hear of or meet with anything unpleasant, unwholesome, woeful, or painful. That is why the land is called Sukhāvati, the Pure and Happy Land. Whatever the inhabitants wish, that will they obtain.[26]

This description provides many parallels with the Christian ideas of Heaven. First, the landscape is similar. Second, the role faith plays in this scheme of things is obvious. Third, the Bodhisattva is able to take on himself the sins of others the way Jesus atoned for the sins of others.[27] Fourth, the Pure Lands are connected with a Buddhology involving the "three bodies of the Buddha", just as heaven involves a Christology of three persons.[28] Fifth, the relationship of a Bodhisattva (in this case Avalokiteśvara) to a Buddha (in this case Amitābha) closely resembles that of Jesus to God.[29] There is, however, one major difference. Even in the Pure Lands, the pure beings are still seeking, in a very pleasant environment no doubt, the achievement of Full Enlightenment. It is interesting that the form in which the Buddhas manifest in these realms is called Saṁbhoga-kāya. Though the term has "never been satisfactorily interpreted",[30] it is sometimes translated as the "enjoyment body"[31] and sometimes as the "communal body".[32] It is not impossible to render it as the 'body of communal enjoyment', suggestive of an eschatological banquet!

The Buddhists are somewhat less enthusiastic about hell. It has been pointed out that from a Christian perspective (1) the doctrine of eternal damnation may not possess a "secure New Testament basis" as the Greek word *aionios*, which is usually translated as eternal can also have the more limited meaning of "for an aeon, or age";[33] (2) that the "reconciling of God's goodness and power with the fact of evil"[34] seems to "preclude eternal human misery" and (3) that hell could mean "a continuation of purgatorial suffering often experienced in life".[35]

All of these three points of view find a parallel in Buddhism — but without involving God, whose magisterial role is played by the doctrine of *karma* in Buddhist thought. Thus there is no exclusion from salvation in Buddhism and any such suggestion has quickly invited the charge of heresy.[36] Furthermore, the fact that *karma* combines the punitive and redemptive roles in its operation similarly precludes eternal misery. On the last point, the Buddha is said to have gone even further and to have maintained that hell could be a term for "painful bodily sensation", though he also identified an inhospitable realm similar to the spatial concept of hell in Christianity.[37]

PARAPSYCHOLOGY AND POST-MORTEM EXISTENCE

John Hick has examined the evidence from parapsychology on the question of post-mortem existence in some detail and has demonstrated rather convincingly that cases of apparent contact with the spirits of the dead can be explained through the phenomenon of telepathy. He writes:

> In connection with 'ghosts' in the sense of apparitions of the dead, it has been established that there can be 'meaningful hallucinations', the source of which is almost certainly telepathic. To quote a classic and somewhat dramatic example: a woman sitting by a lake sees the figure of a man running toward the lake and throwing himself in. A few days later a man commits suicide by throwing himself into this same lake. Presumably, the explanation of the vision is that the man's thought while he was contemplating suicide had been telepathically projected onto the scene via the woman's mind.[38]

He goes on to say:

> In many of the cases recorded there is delayed action. The telepathically projected thought lingers in the recipient's unconscious mind until a suitable state of inattention to the outside world enables it to appear to the conscious mind in a dramatized form — for example, by a hallucinatory voice or vision — by means of the same mechanism that operates in dreams.[39] ... [So] if phantoms of the living can be created by previously experienced thoughts and emotions of the person whom they represent, the parallel possibility arises that phantoms of the dead are caused by thoughts and emotions which were experienced by the person represented when he or she was alive. In other words, ghosts may be 'psychic footprints', a kind of mental trace left behind by the dead but not involving the presence or even the

continued existence of those whom they represent.[40]

Buddhism, however, does not establish its case for post-mortem existence on the basis of mediumship or contact with the dead. It establishes it on the basis of clairvoyance. Moreover, the idea of a surviving soul also presents some problems in the case of Buddhism. It has been claimed, for instance, that "the Buddhist theory of survival is a novel theory which is not to be found in pre-Buddhistic literature. It was a doctrine of survival without the concept of a self-identical soul or substance or soul."[41] It would be unwise to connect the denial of a soul too closely with the prospect of non-survival of beings, for after all not only does Buddhism believe in the existence of rebirth, it also believes in the existence of ghosts. The point here, as in the case of a human being, or a stable flame, is that a false sense of permanence is perceived within a world in which everything is in flux. The use of clairvoyance rather than mediumship to establish post-mortem existence is also strikingly Buddhist. It is said that Buddha gained such a clairvoyant insight into his past lives (and that of others) on the night of his enlightenment. The manner in which such a clairvoyant vision might occur is described as follows:

When his mind is thus composed, clear and cleansed, without blemish, free from adventitious defilements, pliant and flexible, steadfast and unperturbed, he turns and directs his mind to the recollection of his former lives, viz. one life, two lives ... ten lives ... a hundred lives ... through evolving aeons, recalling in what place he was born, his name and title, his social status, his environment, experiences and term of life and dying there in what place he was next born and so on up to his present existence, he remembers the varied states of his former lives in all their aspects and details. Just as a man who has travelled from his village to another and from that to yet another, when he returns to his former village by the same route, remembers how he came from that village, where he stayed and rested, what he said and what he did; even so, when the mind is composed.[42]

RESUSCITATION CASES

An impressive body of literature has grown over the past decade documenting the experiences of those who were pronounced clinically dead but were subsequently resuscitated.[43] The experiences of these people naturally have a bearing on the question of the fact and nature of post-mortem existence. However,

Whether or not the resuscitation cases give us reports of the experiences of people who have actually died, and thus provide information about a life to come, it is at present impossible to determine. Do these accounts describe the first phase of another life, or perhaps a transitional stage before the connection between mind and body is finally broken; or do they describe only the last flickers of dream activity before the brain finally loses oxygen? It is to be hoped that further research may find a way to settle this question.[44]

It is nevertheless perhaps a matter of more than passing interest that some of the phenomena described, such as encounter with a bright light, are anticipated in the *Tibetan Book of the Dead*,[45] a point which did not escape the notice of early investigators in the field.[46] There is one point, however, which deserves special notice from a Buddhist point of view. It appears in the book which set the trend in the field of the study of near-death experiences, *Life After Life* by Raymond Moody Jr. In assessing the effect the near-death experiences had on the lives of the people involved, Raymond Moody Jr. was led to the following conclusion:

There is a remarkable agreement in the "lessons", as it were, which have been brought back from these close encounters with death. Almost everyone has stressed the importance in this life of trying to cultivate love for others, a love of a unique and profound kind. One man who met the being of light felt totally loved and accepted, even while his whole life was displayed in a panorama for the being to see. He felt that the "question" that the being was asking him was whether he was able to love others in the same way. He now feels that it is his commission while on earth to try to learn to be able to do so.

In addition, many others have emphasizeed the importance of seeking knowledge. During their experiences, it was intimated to them that the acquisition of knowledge continues even in the after-life. One woman, for example, has taken advantage of every educational opportunity she has had since her "death" experience. Another man offers the advice, "No matter how old you are, don't stop learning. For this is a process, I gather, that goes on for eternity."[47]

The student of Buddhism cannot fail to notice that these "lessons represent the two cardinal virtues the simultaneous cultivation of which is persistently advocated in Buddhism: *karuṇā* (compassion) and *prajñā* (wisdom)".[48]

CHAPTER 10

Human Destiny: Karma and Reincarnation

INTRODUCTION

In one respect at least the East and the West, by and large, operate on very different presuppositions about human destiny. Thus

To nearly everyone formed by our western Atlantic culture it seems self-evident that we came into existence at conception or birth and shall see the last of this world at death: in other words, we are born only once and we die only once. However, to one brought up within the Hindu culture of India it seems self-evident that we have, on the contrary, lived many times before and must live many times again in this world.[1]

The same would hold true for one brought up in Buddhist culture. And the main difficulty which the Buddhist will have with the Western assumption is also the same as that of the Hindu. How does one reconcile the glaring inequalities of life with the existence of a just God if there is only one life? As Queen Mallikā asked the Buddha once:

"Reverend Sir, what is the reason, and what is the cause, when a woman is ugly, of a bad figure, and horrible to look at, and indigent, poor, needy, and low in the social scale?

"Reverend Sir, what is the reason, and what is the cause, when a woman is ugly, of a bad figure, and horrible to look at, and rich, wealthy, affluent, and high in the social scale?

"Reverend Sir, what is the reason, and what is the cause, when a woman is beautiful, attractive, pleasing, and possessed of surpassing loveliness, and indigent, poor, needy, and low in the social scale?

"Reverend Sir, what is the reason, and what is the cause, when a woman is beautiful, attractive, pleasing, and possessed of surpassing loveliness, and rich, wealthy, affluent, and high in the social scale?"[2]

In a theistic context the question acquires a certain sharpness which it lacks as a general query: as is clear from the following text from the Buddhist canon:

If God (Brahmā) is Lord of the whole world and creator of the multitude of beings, then why (1) has he ordained misfortune in the world without making the whole world happy, or (2) for what purpose has he made the world full of injustice, deceit, falsehood, and conceit, or (3) the Lord of creation is evil in that he ordained injustice when there could have been justice.[3]

For if all is the result of God's grace, then "we have all heard the story of John Bradford, who saw a criminal being taken to be hung and said, 'but for the grace of God there goes John Bradford'. The story is edifying insofar as it reminds us of God's grace to John Bradford; but what about God's grace, or lack of grace, to the condemned criminal?"[4]

When in the first century BC a Greek king asked a Buddhist monk, Nāgasena, to account for these inequalities which render theism questionable, he answered by drawing on the doctrine of *karma*:

Said the king, "Bhante Nāgasena, what is the reason that men are not all alike, but some long-lived and some short-lived, some healthy and some sickly, some handsome and some ugly, some powerful and some weak, some rich and some poor, some of high degree and some of low degree, some wise and some foolish?"

Said the elder, "Your majesty, why are not trees all alike, but some sour, some salt, some bitter, some pungent, some astringent, some sweet?"

"I suppose, bhante, because of a difference in the seed."

"In exactly the same way, your majesty, it is through a difference in their *karma* that men are not all alike, but some long-lived and some short-lived, some healthy and some sickly, some handsome and some ugly, some powerful and some weak, some rich and some poor, some of high degree and some of low degree, some wise and some foolish. Moreover, your majesty, The Blessed One has said as follows: 'All beings, O youth, have *karma* as their portion; they are heirs of their *karma*; they are sprung from their *karma*; their *karma* is their kinsman; their *karma* is their refuge; *karma* allots beings to meanness or greatness'."

"You are an able man, bhante Nāgasena."[5]

The remarks of the Buddhist monk would make little sense, however, if the idea of rebirth was not at the back of the mind of both the king and the monk; indeed, if the king did not share that Buddhist assumption he would have perhaps doubted the monk's ability instead of applauding it. John Hick is therefore perfectly justified in connecting *karma* with rebirth in his discussion of human destiny in Indian religions, which work on the "alternative assumption ... that we have all lived before and that the conditions of our present life are the direct consequences of our previous lives".[6]

JOHN HICK'S MODELS

In his discussion of human destiny in terms of *karma* and reincarnation in the context of Hinduism, John H. Hick identifies three models along which the discussion could be carried out; what he calls (1) the popular concept; (2) the Vedantic conception and (3) the demythologized interpretation. If the same models are to do justice to the Buddhist perspective then two modifications need to be carried out before they can be profitably pressed in service.

First of all, a clear distinction must be drawn between reincarnation and rebirth. The idea of reincarnation carries with it the connotation that "our essential self continues from life to life". However, Buddhism, as understood by the Buddhists, does not concede the existence of such an "essential self".[7] In fact, it is claimed that "Buddhism stands unique in the history of human thought in denying the existence of such an essential self".[8] However, while denying that a permanent soul assumes a temporary body — as implied by the term reincarnation — it does *not* deny that living beings are indeed reborn despite the fact that they do not possess a soul. How this is considered possible will be explained later. At this stage, suffice it to say that we would use the word *rebirth* to characterize the Buddhist account of how a living being undergoes the experience of leading several lives in preference to the word *reincarnation*, which may convey implications inconsistent with Buddhist philosophy in this matter.

The second point is as follows. It is clear that the Vedantic conception of reincarnation must by definition be Hindu. One must, therefore, replace it with a Buddhist conception. "This is particularly necessary since the Buddhist doctrine of *karma* is often confused with and assumed to be the same as the Brahmanical one"[9] or the Hindu one. There are, no doubt, some similarities, but there are also vital differences, which may not surface at the popular level of discussion but which cannot be overlooked at a more sophisticated level of discourse.

Now that these clarifications have been made one can embark on a discussion of the Buddhist vision of human destiny in terms of *karma* and rebirth at three levels: at the level of (1) the popular concept; (2) the Buddhist concept in its textual context and (3) the demythologized interpretation.

THE POPULAR CONCEPT

One often hears stories of people recalling their past life, some of which have been carefully investigated.[10] As it is cases of this kind which are involved in the popular concept of rebirth, it might be useful to present at least one such case. Let us, therefore, briefly review the case of Imad Elawar:

Imad was born on 21 December 1958 at Kornayel and talked of a previous life when he was between a year and a half and two years old. He mentioned a considerable number of names of people and some events in this prior life as well as about certain items of property he claimed to have owned. He said he lived in the village of Khriby and had the name Bouhamzy. He had a woman (mistress) called Jamille, who was beautiful and a 'brother' called Amin, who lived at Tripoli, etc.... [The father] discredited the story and scolded Imad for talking about an imaginary past life. Once, it is said, he even recognised a resident (Salim el Aschkar) of Khriby in the presence of his paternal grandmother. The parents attached more importance to Imad's statements after this. But no systematic attempt to verify the authenticity of Imad's statements were made until Dr. Ian Stevenson undertook to investigate the case.... Khriby was situated about twenty-five miles away from Imad's home. The road from Kornayel was an extremely winding mountain road. The items were carefully recorded prior to the investigations at Khriby. It was ultimately revealed that of the fifty-seven items mentioned, fifty-one were correct....[11] Besides the verification of these items of information, there were significant recognitions of persons and places, sixteen of which are listed. For example, we may note the recognition of the place where Ibrahim Bouhamzy (the previous personality) kept his dog and his gun. He also recognised the sister of Ibrahim, namely Huda, and the portrait of Ibrahim's brother Fuad. He was also able, it is said, to recall his last words before death, which his sister, Mrs Huda Bouhamzy, remembered and which were, 'Huda, call Fuad'.[12]

What is one to make of such cases? It has been suggested that,

When we consider the above as well as the similarity in the character traits between the previous and the present personalities, chance — coincidence has to be virtually ruled out. Since neither fraud, self-deception or racial memory could account for the evidence, a para-normal explanation is called for. And of all the different paranormal explanations, such as telepathy-cum-clairvoyance plus personation, spirit-possessions, etc., *rebirth appears to be the most plausible.*[13]

Such instances by no means indubitably establish the case for rebirth. Whether it be the view that we live and die only once or several times "each idea or theory involves its own difficulties", irrespective of whether, as in the case of rebirth, the concept involved is a popular, a textual or a demythologized one.

The content of the popular concept is provided by the kind of the case just presented. As John Hick points out, "One may or may not find cases of this kind to be impressive, if they are considered hard evidence for rebirth. Nevertheless, the fact that supposed recollections of former lives are pointed to as evidence does mark out a particular content for the idea of rebirth."[14] He then proceeds to "formulate a reincarnation hypothesis on the basis of these instances of claimed memories of former lives".[15]

Hick's formulation consists of three crucial elements, what he identifies as "the three strands of continuity that constitute what we normally mean by the identity of a human individual through time".[16] When we say that the person whom we call John Hick today is the same John Hick who was alive, say, forty years ago, we are able to make such a claim because despite the vast difference in time and the unrecognisable transformation in body and mind it involves,

J.H.[60] does have at least one fragmentary memory of an event that was experienced by J.H.[2] He remembers being told when his sister, who is two years younger than himself, was born. Thus there is a tenuous memory link connecting J.H.[60] with J.H.[2] despite all the dissimilarities that we have noted between them; and this fact reminds us that it is possible to speak of memory across the gap of almost any degree of physical and psychological difference.[17]

Memory, then, constitutes the first strand. The second is provided by the body even when viewed as undergoing constant transformation. Thus

a second strand is bodily continuity, an unbroken existence through space and time from the newly born baby to the old man, a continuity stretching thus from the cradle to the grave. It may be that none of the atoms that composed the baby's body are now part of the adult's body. Nonetheless a continuously changing physical organism has existed and has been in principle observable, composed from moment to moment of slightly different populations of atoms, but with sufficient overlap of population and of configuration of population from moment to moment for it to constitute the same organism.[18]

The third strand is provided by "the psychological continuity of a pattern of mental dispositions".[19]

John Hick goes on to argue that in terms of the rebirth hypothesis the second strand is automatically snapped, while so far as the first strand is considered some 99 per cent of people have no memory of previous lives. This leaves us holding the third strand. But general mental dispositions as a basis of establishing identity are so general that

general similarities would never by themselves lead or entitle us to identify the two as the same person. Indeed, to make an identity claim on these grounds — in a case in which there is neither bodily continuity nor any link of memory — would commit us to the principle that all individuals who are not alive at the same time and who exhibit rather similar personality patterns are to be regarded as the same person. But in that case there would be far too many people who qualify under this criterion as being the same person.[20]

John Hick therefore concludes that the popular idea of rebirth "(*though normally without memory of previous lives*) from death in one body to birth in another is beset with conceptual difficulties of the gravest kind".[21]

The Buddhists clearly acknowledge that in cases of rebirth "the memory criterion alone can establish the identity", for Hick himself admits that over the gulf that stretches in a person's life as a child and a man, "the conscious self of the one is very different from the conscious self of the other — so much so that a comparison of the two would never by itself lead us to conclude that they are the same self".[22] Moreover, the general pattern of mental dispositions is problematical in establishing identity even within one life, for "the fact that two individuals exhibit a common character trait, or even a number of such traits, does not lead us to identify them as one person" only because we already know that "they are distinct bodily means".[23]

The burden of proof, therefore, must be borne by memory, especially as

One of the commonest objections against a theory of rebirth, which implies pre-existence, is that we do not remember our past lives. The objection may take three different forms. First, that we do not have any memory of prior lives and that, therefore, there is no evidence of our having lived in the past prior to our present birth. Secondly, that memory is indispensable to the identity of a person. Thirdly, that unless we have memory, rebirth is to no purpose, since no moral or other lesson is learnt in the process.[24]

The second and the third objections seem less serious than the first. As we are concerned with the fact and not the value of rebirth here, the third argument does not apply. Even the second argument possesses only a limited application, for we do not possess a memory of all that we experience even during the course of one life and yet continue to possess a sense of identity. Thus the crux of the matter is the inability to recall past lives. The Buddhist response to this point is twofold: (1) a negative one: "that the lack of memory regarding prior lives is no proof that we have not lived before, any more than the lack of memory regarding the first year of our lives on the part of all or most human beings is no proof that we did not live in the first year of our life";[25] and (2) a positive one: that "quite a few have claimed to have remembered experiences in their alleged prior lives" and one must not dismiss these but ask the question: "How authentic are these memories and what reason have we to believe that they are potentially present in many if not all human beings?"[26]

THE BUDDHIST CONCEPTION

The Buddhist conception of rebirth, first of all, involves the idea that this process of rebirth has no beginning in time. It is not entirely clear whether the Buddha meant that the process has no *absolute* beginning[27] or no *discernible* beginning[28] but the emphasis nevertheless is on its beginninglessness, just as God is considered as not possessing a beginning in theism.[29]

The next crucial point to be recognized in the Buddhist doctrine of rebirth is that it does not involve the passage of a soul from one body to another. The Buddhists give several examples to render this concept plausible — the concept that rebirth is possible without transmigration. Four popular examples progressively clarify the Buddhist position. (1) Let us suppose that our teacher recites a verse in the class and we memorize it. The verse which was in the teacher's mind has now been 'reborn' in our mind. But in doing so, did it leave the mind of the teacher, did it transmigrate from his mind to our mind? If it did, it should no longer be present in the teacher's mind. Hence the correct depiction of the situation is that the verse in the mind of the teacher gave rise to the verse in our mind. This analogy helps one understand how rebirth might be possible without transmigration.[30] (2) A more dynamic example is provided by the case in which the flame of one lamp is used to light the flame in another lamp. The flame in the first lamp is constantly changing, yet its dynamic nature does not prevent it from lighting the wick in the other lamp. However, when the second lamp is lit, can one say that the flame of the first lamp has transmigrated into the other lamp? If that were the case, how could the first lamp still be alight? Here again, then, the correct description of the situation is that the lamp in the first flame gave rise to the flame in the second lamp. Similarly, one psychophysical organism, in ceasing to be, gives rise to another psychophysical organism — there is rebirth without transmigration.

These examples, however, present a problem. The Buddhist view is that one psychophysical organism, *in ceasing to be*, gives rise to another psychophysical organism. However, in our examples, the verse did not disappear from the mind of the teacher; neither did the flame in the first lamp cease to exist in giving rise to the flame in the second lamp. To accommodate these facts other examples are given. (1) On the billiards table it is possible to hit one ball with another in such a way that the first ball, which is in motion, hits the second ball and in doing so comes to a complete stop. Yet, in the process of stopping it can impart all its velocity to the second ball and so on. Similarly, one life, in coming to a complete halt can yet, in that very process, generate a new life. This example is better than the others inasmuch as the stoppage of the first ball is comparable to death and also because it conveys the idea that it is life which goes on — not the same 'living being' as such — just as it is motion which is really transferred from one ball to the other.

But even this example does not do full justice to the Buddhist case. For it leaves behind a trail of static balls, while we see the human body dissolve in real life after death. To clarify the Buddhist position further, therefore, yet another example is given. (2) If one shouts from the precipice of a deep ravine one soon hears the echoes of one's own voice. Notice now how one echo, in ceasing to be, gives rise to the next echo. Nothing is left of the first echo. Similarly the second echo, in giving rise to the third, ceases to be, and yet in the very act of ceasing to be gives rise to the next echoes. Our various lives, therefore, may be compared profitably, from the point of Buddhist philosophy, to a series of echoes down the corridor of time.

The next point to consider is the relation of these various members of the series — A_1, A_2, A_3 etc. What, for instance, is the relationship, to take a more homely example, between John Smith as a child and John Smith as a man. The Western tendency is to regard the two as identical — to regard the two as the same. Buddhists allege, however, that we are here guilty of confusing similarity with sameness, of continuity with identity. They refine the point as follows — the relationship of the child John Smith to the man John Smith is such that they are neither the same nor different. They are not the same inasmuch as John Smith the man is different in shape, size and mental capacity from John Smith the child; yet they are not different inasmuch as the two are part of the same continuum — it was John Smith the child who became John Smith the man.

It might be asked whether, if John Smith is neither the same nor different, is John Smith then karmically responsible for the deeds he commits? The Buddhist answer is that he is, inasmuch as he belongs to the same series. A person who sets fire to a house with a torch cannot claim that he is not guilty of arson because the house-fire is different from the torch-fire. He is still guilty because the torch-fire caused the house-fire, similarly John Smith cannot escape karmic responsibility because John Smith in T_2 is lineally related to John Smith in T_1.[31] Continuity is sufficient to imply responsibility without involving the need for invoking identity.

The question of remembrance of past lives is very important in Buddhism. It should, however, be clearly understood that it is not the person on a substantialist view, but the person in a serial queue who is involved in the process. "When the Buddha says that in a previous birth he was himself Sunetra, a venerable teacher, as he does in the *Saptasūryodaya Sūtra* and in many of the *Jātakas*, this only means that the Buddha-series (*buddha-santāna*) is one — that both Sunetra and Gautama [Buddha] belong to the same continuum."[32]

John Hick sees some problems with this idea of remembrance. He writes:

Now, what exactly does ... [rebirth] mean when it is thus given factual anchorage by a claimed retrospective yogic memory of a series of lives that were not linked by memory while they were being lived? The picture before us is of, say, a hundred distinct empirical selves living their different lives one after another and being as distinct from each other as any other set of a hundred lives; and yet differing from a random series of a hundred lives in that the last member of the series attains a level of consciousness at which he or she is aware of the entire series. Further, she remembers the entire series as lives which she, now in this higher state of awareness, has herself lived. Yet there is something logically odd about such 'remembering', which prompts one to put it in quotation marks. For this higher state of consciousness did not experience those earlier lives and therefore it cannot in any ordinary sense be said to remember them. Rather, it is in a state *as though* it had experienced them, although in fact it did not.[33]

The Buddhist answer to this question could run as follows. Suppose that as of this very moment we remember something we had forgotten — that, say, we had forgotten where we left our keys yesterday and remembered the fact today. It is not a *higher state of awareness* which remembers in this manner but our ordinary awareness in a *higher state of recall*. Though some Buddhist scholars do seem to share the misgivings of John Hick on this point, they are for them more in the nature of questions that remain to be answered than doubts which call the doctrine itself in question. K.N. Jayatilleke begins by pointing out

that according to the Buddhist theory the 'stream of consciousness' has two components without a sharp division between them (*ubhayato abbocchinnaṃ*), the conscious mind and the unconscious, in which accumulate the emotionally charged experiences that we have had going back through childhood and birth into previous lives. Besides, with the expansion and development of consciousness (*vibhūta saññā*), it attains a paranormal state.[34]

But then he also goes on to say:

How much of our memories in the unconscious are associated with the brain? Do they include the memories of prior lives as well? What is the nature of the association between the potentially paranormal mind and the brain? Does the paranormal mind function at its best when the activity of the brain and the body is quiescent (*kāyasaṅkhārā niruddhā*) under its control? The total psyche (*viññāṇa*) of a person comprising the conscious mind, the memories and dispositions in the unconscious and the potentially paranormal mind is said to be "associated with and linked to the body" (*ettha sitaṃ ettha paṭibaddhaṃ*). But it is not clear how close or how loose the association of its several aspects are.[35]

So is it with past lives — only the recall is sustained. John Hick, however, sees other difficulties as well. He writes:

The claim here, then, is that there will in the future exist a supernormal state of consciousness, in which 'memories' of a long succession of different lives occur. However, this leaves open the question of how best to describe such a state of affairs. Let us name the first person in the series A and the last Z. Are we to say that B–Z are a series of reincarnations of A? If we do, we shall be implicitly stipulating the following definition: given two or more non-contemporaneous human lives, if there is a higher consciousness in which they are all 'remembered', then each later individual in the series is defined as being a rebirth of each earlier individual. But rebirth so defined is a concept far removed from the idea that if I am A, then *I* shall be repeatedly reborn as B–Z. Further, there is no conceptual reason why we should even stipulate that the different lives must be non-contemporaneous. If it is possible for a higher consciousness to 'remember' any number of different lives, there seems in principle to be no reason why it should not 'remember' lives that have been going on at the same time as easily as lives that have been going on at different times. Indeed, we can conceive of an unlimited higher consciousness in which 'memories' occur of all human lives that have ever been lived. Then *all* human lives, however different from their own several points of view, would be connected via a higher consciousness in the way postulated by the idea of rebirth. It would then be proper to say of *any* two lives, whether earlier and later, later and earlier, or contemporaneous, that the one individual is a different rebirth of the other. Thus it seems that there are considerable conceptual difficulties in the idea of rebirth in its more subtle form as well as in its more popular form.[36]

It should be borne in mind that what John Hick has *hypothesized* is precisely what the Buddha is said to have *realized* so that the question then really becomes: Does the Buddha continue to be a human being after "enlightenment" and if so in what sense?[37] The significance of the question becomes clear when the bearing of Buddha's experience of "enlightenment" on the rebirth issue is taken into consideration.

The Buddhist theory of survival has its origin in the enlightenment of the Buddha and not in any traditional Indian belief. It is said that it was on the night of his enlightenment that he acquired the capacity to know his prior lives. It was when his mind was composed, clear, cleansed and without blemish, free from adventitious defilements, pliant and flexible, steadfast and unperturbed that he acquired this capacity to recall hundreds and thousands of prior lives and the prehistory of the universe, going back through the immensely long periods of the expansions and contractions of the oscillating universe. This is, in fact, called the first important item of knowledge, which broke through a veil of ignorance (*ayaṁ paṭhamā vijjā*).

As we have seen, the second important item of knowledge (*dutiyā vijjā*) was obtained by the exercise of the faculty of clairvoyance (*dibba-cakkhu*), with which the Buddha was able to see, among other things, the survival of beings in various states of existence, the operations of *karma*, galactic systems, clusters of galactic systems and the vast cosmos.[38]

It is also important to recognize the distinction here between the Hindu and Buddhist contexts. While it is true that *some* Buddhist concepts in *some* versions of Buddhist idealism may be sufficiently comparable to the Vedantic to share the problems John Hick sees in the Vedantic view,[39] typically they differ in two significant ways. As mentioned earlier, the Buddha did not merely recall his own past lives at the time of Enlightenment, but also the past lives of others,[40] so that the type of confusion John Hick visualizes is thereby prevented. Moreover, Buddhism discourages the idea of a higher consciousness as such in the aggregate where all past lives are known; in fact, Buddhism discourages, especially in its Theravāda form, even the abstract notion of consciousness.[41] Hence many of the conceptual difficulties identified by John Hick do not apply in this case.

But one does. This pertains to the fact that the series or the continuum talked about has no identifiable beginning. It was pointed out earlier that whether in fact there is no beginning or that there is no discernible beginning is a debatable point[42] — but for the purposes of this discussion one has to concede that there is no identifiable beginning. Even in the context of the Buddha's vivid recall of past lives the text *never* says that Buddha recalled *all* his past lives.[43] This point has an important bearing on the question of *karma* as an explanation of inequalities.[44] K.N. Jayatilleke doubts whether the concept of *karma* arises in Buddhism as an attempt to rationally explain human inequality[45] but even if it did not arise out of such an attempt it does play that role.[46] The problem such a view presents is that as no first beginning is admitted, a radical explanation of inequality is not offered; it is only "endlessly postponed".[47]

THE DEMYTHOLOGIZED INTERPRETATION

The demythologized interpretation of *karma* is specifically attributed by J.C. Jennings to the Buddha.[48] It is clear from the following two citations that it is the Hindu concept of *karma* which was supposedly demythologized by the Buddha.

Disbelieving in the permanence of the individual soul he [the Buddha] could not accept the Hindu doctrine of *Karma* implying the transmigration of the soul at death to a new body; but believing fully in moral responsibility and the consequences of all acts, words, and thoughts, he fully accepted the doctrine of *Karma* in another sense, implying the transmission of the effects of actions from one generation of men to all succeeding generations....[49]

Assuming the common origin and the fundamental unity of all life and spirit, he [the Buddha] assumed the unity of the force of *Karma* upon the living material of the whole world, and the doctrine of *Karma* taught by him is collective and not individual.[50]

John Hick seems to be in sympathy with this interpretation for he goes on to remark, after citing these lines:

On this view, *karma*, with reincarnation as its mythological expression, is really a moral truth, a teaching of universal human responsibility. All our deeds affect the human future, as the life of each of us has in its turn been affected by those who have lived before us. Instead of individual threads of karmic history there is the universal network of the *karma* of humanity, to which each contributes and by which each is affected. Understood in this manner, the idea of reincarnation is a way of affirming the corporate unity of the human race, and the responsibility of each toward the whole of which he or she is a part. We are not monadic individuals, but mutually interacting parts of the one human world in which the thoughts and acts of each reverberate continually for good or ill through the lives of others.[51]

Such a demythologized interpretation of *karma*, although undeniably attractive, poses extreme difficulties in the context of Buddhism. (1) First of all, it is not at all certain that the Buddha borrowed the idea of *karma* from Hinduism. It may be so,[52] but it is equally plausible that he discovered or, in case the concept was already known, re-discovered it for himself,[53] for it forms part and parcel of that three-fold knowledge "which is crucial for the attainment of enlightenment".[54] (2) Even more important than this historical consideration are the philosophical ones. For instance, if the Buddha had such a communal concept of *karma*, the idea of group *karma* should find an important place in at least early Buddhism. This does not seem to be the case.[55] (3) The Buddha seems to see in *karma* an explanation of the differentia of human beings rather than their solidarity, as seems to be implied by the demythologized version. "Thus when the question is posed in the form: 'What is the reason and the cause for the inequality [....] *among* human beings despite their being human?' The Buddha's reply was as follows: 'Beings inherit their *karma* and it is *karma* which divides beings in terms of their inequalities'."[56] (4) It would follow from the demythologized understanding of *karma* that collective consequences could be both positive or negative. In other words, one person could be the cause of suffering of another, but this is explicitly denied by the Buddha.[57] (5) John Hick suggests that seen as a demythologized doctrine, "*karma* is an ethical doctrine. And both the more popular idea of the transmigration of souls and the more philosophical idea of the continuity of a 'subtle body' from individual to individual in succeeding generations can be seen as mythological expressions of this great moral truth."[58] The preceding discussion, however, makes it clear that Buddhism does not accept the concept of a 'subtle body', despite the difficulties involved in not accepting such a concept.[59]

Buddhism does believe in human solidarity in the sense that it is "the nature of good acts to promote the material and spiritual well-being of mankind",[60] and this understanding may come close to what is implied in the demythologized interpretation of *karma* but Buddhist scholars are critical of attempts to interpret the doctrine of *karma* "to mean the social or biological inheritance of man or both, ignoring altogether and distorting" what they regard as "the authentic teachings of the Buddhist texts".[61]

Notes and References

Introduction

1. John H. Hick, *Philosophy of Religion*, Third Edition. (Englewood Cliffs, New Jersey: Prentice-Hall Inc., 1983), 1.
2. Ibid.
3. Gunapala Dharmasiri, *A Buddhist Critique of the Christian Concept of God* (Antioch, Cal.: Golden Leaves, 1988), 234.
4. Ibid.
5. See Winston L. King, "Religion" in Mircea Eliade, Editor-in-Chief, *The Encyclopedia of Religion*, vol. 12 (New York: Macmillan Publishing Company, 1987), 282-93.
6. John H. Hick, op. cit., 108.
7. See Walpola Sri Rahula, *What the Buddha Taught* (New York: Grove Press Inc., 1974), 2-3.
8. A. Berriedale Keith, *Buddhist Philosophy in India and Ceylon* (Oxford: Clarendon Press, 1923), 33-6.
9. Lama Anagarika Govinda, *The Psychological Attitude of Early Buddhist Philosophy* (London: Rider and Company, 1961), 38.
10. Walpola Sri Rahula, op. cit., 5.
11. K.N. Jayatilleke, *Early Buddhist Theory of Knowledge* (London: George Allen and Unwin Ltd., 1963), 170.
12. Ibid.
13. Ibid., 172.
14. Lama Anagarika Govinda, op. cit., 35.
15. Ibid.
16. Ibid.
17. Ibid., 37-8.
18. Erich Fromm, *Psychoanalysis and Religion* (New Haven: Yale University Press, 1950), 34.
19. Ibid., 38.
20. Ibid., 37.
21. John H. Hick, op. cit., 2.
22. L. Daniel Batson and W. Larry Ventis, *The Religious Experience: A Social-Psychological Perspective* (Oxford: Oxford University Press, 1982), 5.
23. John H. Hick, op. cit., 2.
24. Ibid.
25. Edward J. Thomas, *The History of Buddhist Thought* (New York: Barnes and Noble Inc., 1971; first published 1933), 92.
26. Ibid.
27. John H. Hick, op. cit., 3.
28. The tables can be turned. It has been argued, for instance, that Christian theism is primitive, see Gunapala Dharmasiri, op. cit., 265.

29. John H. Hick, op. cit., 3.
30. Walpola Sri Rahula, op. cit., 11-12.

CHAPTER 1

The Concept of God

1. John H. Hick, op. cit., 6. For proof text, see Deuteronomy 6:4-5.
2. Exodus 20:1-5.
3. Edward Conze, *Buddhism: Its Essence and Development* (New York: Harper and Brothers, 1959), 42.
4. John H. Hick, op. cit., 7.
5. William James, *The Varieties of Religious Experience* (New York: Longmans, Green and Co., 1928), 131.
6. Edward Conze, op. cit., 42.
7. John H. Hick, op. cit., 7.
8. Edward Conze, op. cit., 41.
9. K.N. Jayatilleke, *The Message of the Buddha*, edited by Ninian Smart (London: George Allen and Unwin, 1975), 99.
10. Ibid., 60.
11. Ibid.
12. Ibid., 111.
13. Ibid., 97-8.
14. A.L. Basham, *The Wonder That Was India* (London: Sigewick and Jackson, 1967), 270. Kenneth K.S. Ch'en carries the ball forward: "If, as the Buddhists say, everything is a becoming, without beginning or end, then one would very naturally raise the question, just how did the universe originate? Although the Buddha discouraged speculation on the origins of the universe, there is a theory of evolution found in the Buddhist scriptures. In the limitless expanse of space, the Buddhists conceive of an infinite number of world systems coming into existence and passing away through beginningless and endless time. The process of evolving and devolving each of these world systems requires immense periods of time called *kalpas*, or aeons. Once the Buddha was asked how long a *kalpa* was, and he replied with the following simile. Suppose there were a mighty mountain crag, four leagues in dimensions all around, one solid mass of rock without any crack. Suppose also a man should come at the end of every century, and wipe that crag with a fine piece of cloth. That mighty mountain would be worn away and ended, sooner than would the aeon." In *Buddhism: The Light of Asia* (Woodbury, New York: Barron's Educational Series, Inc., 1968), 42.
15. Walpola Sri Rahula, op. cit., 58.
16. Edward Conze, "Buddhism: The Mahāyāna" in R.C. Zaehner, ed., *The Concise Encyclopedia of Living Faiths* (Boston: Beacon Press, 1959), 301.
17. Ibid., 301.
18. Walpola Sri Rahula, op. cit., 26-7. Emphasis added.
19. Edward Conze, *Buddhism: Its Essence and Development*, op. cit., 39.

20. Ibid., 43.
21. K.N. Jayatilleke, *The Message of the Buddha*, op. cit., 105.
22. Ibid., 115.
23. Ibid.
24. Ibid., 63.
25. John H. Hick, op. cit., 10-11.
26. Edward Conze, *Buddhism, Its Essence and Development*, op. cit., 39.
27. K.N. Jayatilleke, *The Message of the Buddha*, op. cit., 115.
28. Edward Conze, "Buddhism: The Mahāyāna", op. cit., 305.
29. Edward Conze, *Buddhist Thought in India: Three Phases of Buddhist Philosophy* (Ann Arbor: University of Michigan Press, 1967), 232.
30. Edward Conze, "Buddhism: The Mahāyāna", op. cit., 301.
31. Richard H. Robinson, *The Buddhist Religion: A Historical Introduction* (Belmont, California: Dickenson Publishing Company, Inc., 1970), 59. Emphasis added. Also see Edward Conze, "Buddhism: The Mahāyāna", op. cit., 302.
32. Edward Conze, *Buddhism: Its Essence and Development*, op. cit., 40.
33. Ibid., 300. Also see Walpola Sri Rahula, op. cit., 46.
34. Edward Conze, *Buddhism: Its Essence and Development*, op. cit., 40.
35. John H. Hick, op. cit., 12.
36. Ibid.
37. Cited by Edward Conze, "Buddhism: The Mahāyāna", op. cit., 301.
38. Ibid.
39. Ibid.
40. A.L. Basham, op. cit., 275.
41. Edward Conze, "Buddhism: The Mahāyāna", op. cit., 304.
42. K.N. Jayatilleke, *The Message of the Buddha*, op. cit., 115.
43. Ibid., 116. Emphasis added.
44. Michael Pye, "Upāya" in Mircea Eliade, Editor-in-Chief, *The Encyclopedia of Religion*, vol. 15 (New York: Macmillan, 1987), 153.
45. John H. Hick, op. cit., 13.
46. Ibid., 12-13.
47. Edward Conze, *Buddhism: Its Essence and Development*, op. cit., 173.
48. John H. Hick, op. cit., 13.
49. Ibid.
50. Ibid., 14.
51. I.B. Horner, "Buddhism: The Theravāda" in R.C. Zaehner, ed., *The Concise Encyclopedia of Living Faiths* (Boston: Beacon Press, 1959), 289.
52. Bimala Churn Law, *Concepts of Buddhism* (Leiden: Kern Institute, 1937), 97-8.

CHAPTER 2

Grounds for Belief in God

1. K.N. Jayatilleke, *The Message of the Buddha*, edited by Ninian Smart (London: George Allen & Unwin Ltd., 1975), 104-5.

2. See William L. Rowe and William J. Wainwright, eds., *Philosophy of Religion: Selected Readings* (New York: Harcourt, Brace, Jovanovich Inc., 1973), 103-5.
3. K.N. Jayatilleke, *The Message of the Buddha*, op. cit., 111.
4. S. Radhakrishnan, *Indian Philosophy*, vol. 1 (New York: The Macmillan Company, 1962), 457.
5. John H. Hick, *The Philosophy of Religion*, third edition (Englewood Cliffs, New Jersey: Prentice-Hall Inc., 1983), 19.
6. Lama Anagarika Govinda, *The Psychological Attitude of Early Buddhist Philosophy* (New York: Samuel Weiser, 1974), 42-3; K.N. Jayatilleke, *Early Buddhist Theory of Knowledge* (London: George Allen and Unwin, 1963), 243.
7. The Buddhist critique of God's inconceivability is not without interest though. It is found in the *Bodhicaryāvatāra* of Śāntideva (7th/8th century) in the following form: "If, as theists say, God is too great for man to be able to comprehend him, then it follows that his qualities also surpass our range of thought, and that we neither know him nor attribute to him the quality of a creator". See K.N. Jayatilleke, *The Message of the Buddha*, op. cit., 112.
8. William L. Rowe and William J. Wainwright, eds., op. cit., 117ff.
9. John H. Hick, op. cit., 20.
10. Chandradhar Sharma, *A Critical Survey of Indian Philosophy* (London: Rider and Company, 1960), 139.
11. John H. Hick, op. cit., 20-1.
12. Ibid., 20.
13. Ibid., 21.
14. See Walpola Sri Rahula, *What the Buddha Taught* (New York: Grove Press, Inc., 1974), 27.
15. Kenneth K.S. Ch'en, *Buddhism: The Light of Asia* (Woodbury, New York: Barron's Educational Series, Inc., 1968), 42-4.
16. I.B. Horner, "Buddhism: The Theravāda" in R.C. Zaehner, ed., *The Concise Encyclopedia of Living Faiths* (Boston: Beacon Press, 1959), 285.
17. S. Radhakrishnan, op. cit., vol. 1, 455.
18. Buddhists in general avoided discussing cosmic origins, hence issues of creator, creation and first cause. The one exception, noted earlier, was that of the Ādibuddha. "The traditions about the Adi-Buddha were considered as a particularly secret part of the teaching, and we are at present not in a position to distinguish clearly between the different schools of thought. Many schools seem to have singled out one of the five Jinas, usually Vairocana, as the chief. Others introduced a sixth person to preside over them. This person bears the name sometimes of Mahavairocana, sometimes of Vajradhara, and sometimes he is simply called the Adi-Buddha.
    It is at this point that Buddhism at last deviates completely from its original teachings, and prepares the way for its own extinction. It is quite clear that this kind of teaching must tend in the direction of Henotheism. As we saw before, it has always been a basic conviction of the Buddhist tradition that the object of thinking about the world was escape from it, and not explanation of its origin. As far as the origin of the appearance of this universe around us was concerned, one was content to put it down to ignorance and not to God. The Yogacarins were the first to build up an extremely complicated and involved system which was designed to deduce

the appearance of a world of external objects from ignorance as the cause, and from the 'Store-consciousness' as the basis of the universe. 500 years later, about 950, some Tantric scholars, who lived near the Jaxartes, came to regard a near-monotheistic cosmogony as the very centre of the Buddhist doctrine. Up to then the Tathagata had been the one who delivers the true teaching about the cause of the universe. Now the Tathagata himself becomes the cause. In the *Kalacakra Tantra*, and in some Chinese systems, the Buddha acts as a kind of creator. As *Lords of the Yogis*, the Buddhas were transformed into magicians, who created this world by means of their meditation. All things are their magical creations. Everything that exists, they see in their creative meditation. And what they see in their meditation, must be real because, except for this meditation, nothing at all exists, and everything, as it is, is really Thought. It had been usual for many centuries, in Yogacara circles, to describe ultimate reality as the '*Womb of the Tathagatas*'. It is now from this Womb of the Tathagatas that the world is said to issue. The elaboration of this cosmogony was the last creative act of Buddhist thought. Once it had reached this stage of development it could do no more than merge into the monotheistic religions around it." In Edward Conze, *Buddhism: Its Essence and Development* (New York: Harper and Row, 1959), 190-1.

19. John H. Hick, op. cit., 21.
20. Ibid.
21. Ibid. Emphasis added.
22. K.N. Jayatilleke, *Early Buddhist Theory of Knowledge*, op. cit., 187.
23. S. Radhakrishnan, op. cit., vol. 1, 453.
24. K.N. Jayatilleke, *The Message of the Buddha*, op. cit., 108.
25. K.N. Jayatilleke, *The Message of the Buddha*, op. cit., 111. S. Radhakrishnan remarks that to the Buddha "the cosmological argument had no force. Enough if we know how things happen, we need not go behind the order of the world. Though an explanation by antecedent conditions is no final truth, still to man nothing more is open. A first cause which is itself uncaused seems to be self-contradictory. The necessity of conceiving every cause as effect which has its cause in a preceding one makes the conception of an uncaused cause absolutely unthinkable." Op. cit., vol. 1, 455-6.
26. John H. Hick, op. cit., 21-22.
27. Ibid.
28. Ibid., 22.
29. Walpola Sri Rahula, op. cit., 51.
30. G.P. Malalasekera, ed., *Encyclopedia of Buddhism*, vol. 1 (Government of Ceylon, 1961), 573-4.
31. Chandradhar Sharma, op. cit., 139.
32. Ibid., 137-8.
33. John H. Hick, op. cit., 23.
34. William L. Rowe and William J. Wainwright, eds., op. cit., 119.
35. K.N. Jayatilleke, *The Message of the Buddha*, op. cit., 59.
36. Ibid., 110.
37. John H. Hick, op. cit., 24.
38. Ibid., 23-4.

39. Ibid., 24.
40. S. Radhakrishnan, op. cit., vol. 1, 455.
41. Chandradhar Sharma, op. cit., 139.
42. S. Radhakrishnan, op. cit., vol. 1, 455.
43. K.N. Jayatilleke, *The Message of the Buddha*, op. cit., 111. K.N. Jayatilleke formulates his position more cautiously elsewhere (*Early Buddhist Theory of Knowledge*, 260-1. Emphasis added): "*Issara* — in the sense of God as the creator is known in the *Nikāyas*. At D. III.28, the theory that the origin of the universe is to be traced to creation by Issara is mentioned as a theory put forward by one of the current schools of thought (*santi eke samaṇabrāhmaṇā Issarakuttaṃ ... aggaññaṃ paññapenti*, i.e. there are some recluses and brahmins who propose the theory that the origin of the world is (to be traced to) creation on the part of *Issara*). Elsewhere, we find that 'pleasure and pain may be due to creation by Issara (=Skr. *Īśvara*)' stated as one of the current theories (*sattā Issaranimmāṇahetu sukhadukkhaṃ paṭisaṃvedenti*, M. II.222, A. I.273). In the *śvetāśvatara Upaniṣad* we find that *Īśvara*, who is the 'highest God of the gods' (*īśvarāṇāṃ paramam maheśvaram*, 6.7) is considered the ultimate 'cause' (*kāraṇam*, 6.9). In the Jain texts, the theory that *Īśvara* is the cause of the world (*loë*), souls (*jīvā*) as well as of pleasure and pain (*sukhadukkhā*) is expressly stated: *Īsarena kaḍe loë ... jivājivasamaütte sukhadukkha samannië*, i.e. the world has been created by *Īśvara* ... endowed with souls and non-souls, pleasure and pain, *Sū.* 1.1.3.6). Here Śīlāṅka mentions the argument from *design* as the argument put forward by the Theists. The argument as stated by Śīlāṅka takes as its major premiss the proposition that 'whatever is characterized by design is seen to be preceded by an intelligent cause' (*yadyatsaṃsthānaviśeṣṣavattattadbuddhimatkāra (ṇa) pūrvakam*, op. cit., vol. 1. fol. 42 on *Sū.* 1.1.3.6); the things in the world, it is said, are characterized by design and (considering the nature of the design) 'the author of the whole universe cannot be an ordinary person but must be *Īśvara* himself' (*yaśca samastasyāṣya jagataḥ kartā sa sāmānyapuruṣṣo na bhavatītyasāvīśvara iti*, loc. cit.). It is an inductive argument with a metaphysical conclusion, an argument from empirical facts to transcendent reality which, the positivist school of Materialists argued, does not come within the sphere of inference proper (*v. supra*, 94). *There is no direct evidence that the argument was known to the Pali Nikāyas, but the argument from evil against the possibility of a creator* (*v. infra*, *698*), which is an extension of the argument from design, showing that if God exists evil must be part of the design, may have been intended to counter an argument of the above sort."
44. S. Radhakrishnan, op. cit., vol. 1, 456.
45. John H. Hick, op. cit., 29.
46. Ibid.
47. K.N. Jayatilleke, *The Message of the Buddha*, op. cit., 115.
48. Ibid., 114.
49. John H. Hick, op. cit., 30.
50. Ibid.
51. K.N. Jayatilleke, *The Message of the Buddha*, op. cit., 63. Emphasis added.

52. T.W. Rhys Davids, tr., *Dialogues of the Buddha*, part 1 (London: Luzac and Company, Ltd., 1956), 304.
53. Edward Conze, *Buddhism: Its Essence and Development*, op. cit., 81.

CHAPTER 3

Grounds for Disbelief in God

1. K.N. Jayatilleke, *The Message of the Buddha*, op. cit., 105.
2. John H. Hick, *Philosophy of Religion*, op. cit., 31.
3. S.G.F. Brandon, general editor, *A Dictionary of Comparative Religion* (New York: Macmillan Publishing Company, 1970), 85.
4. Ibid., 583.
5. A.L. Basham, *The Wonder that was India*, op. cit., 82.
6. Ibid.
7. Wm. Theodore de Bary et al., *Sources of Indian Tradition* (New York: Columbia University Press, 1958), 41.
8. S.G.F. Brandon, op. cit., 583-4.
9. Sukumar Dutt, *Early Buddhist Monachism* (New York: Asia Publishing House, 1960), 11-12.
10. See Kenneth K.S. Ch'en, *Buddhism: The Light of Asia*, chapter 5, op. cit.
11. John H. Hick, *Philosophy of Religion*, op. cit., 34.
12. Ibid.
13. Ibid.
14. Ibid.
15. Ibid.
16. Ibid., 35.
17. Erich Fromm, *Psychoanalysis and Religion* (New Haven: Yale University Press, 1950), 11.
18. Ibid., 11-12.
19. Walpola Sri Rahula, *What the Buddha Taught*, op. cit., 51.
20. Edward Conze, "Buddhism: The Mahāyāna", op. cit., 302.
21. Kenneth K.S. Ch'en, op. cit., 101-2.
22. Ibid., 101.
23. Nyanatiloka, *Buddhist Dictionary* (Colombo: Frewin and Co. 1950), 148.
24. Edward Conze, *Buddhist Scriptures* (Harmondsworth: Penguin Books, 1959), 231.
25. James P. McDermott, "Karma and Rebirth in Early Buddhism" in Wendy Doniger O'Flaherty, ed., *Karma and Rebirth in Classical Indian Traditions* (Berkeley: University of California Press, 1980), 171-2.
26. T.W. Rhys Davids, tr., *Dialogues of the Buddha*, vol. 1 (Oxford University Press, 1899; 1923 reprint), 114-5.
27. Ibid., 307-8.
28. K.N. Jayatilleke, *The Message of the Buddha*, op. cit., 172.
29. Ibid. Also see Erich Fromm, *Psychoanalysis and Religion*, op. cit., 12, note 1.
30. K.N. Jayatilleke, *The Message of the Buddha*, op. cit., 34.
31. Ibid.

32. The latest citation of it I have come across is in Peter Harvey, "Consciousness Mysticism in the Discourses of the Buddha" in Karl Werner, ed., *The Yogi and the Mystic* (London: Curzon Press, 1989), 82-3, which is followed by an interesting discussion.

33. John H. Hick, *Philosophy of Religion*, op. cit., 37.

34. Paul Demieville, "Foreword" to Walpola Sri Rahula, *What the Buddha Taught*, op. cit., x.

35. Edward Conze, *Buddhist Thought in India* (Ann Arbor: The University of Michigan Press, 1967), 29.

36. Kenneth K.S. Ch'en, *Buddhism: The Light of Asia*, op. cit., 274-5.

37. Ibid., 274. Also see Erich Fromm, *Psychoanalysis and Religion*, op. cit., 38ff. But Buddha's unquestioning belief in parapsychology may raise a few eyebrows, see K.N. Jayatilleke, *Early Buddhist Theory of Knowledge*, op. cit., 437ff.

38. But occult and supernatural aspects of Buddhism cannot be totally ignored; see Heinrich Zimmer, *Philosophies of India*, edited by Joseph Campbell (New York: Parthenon Books, 1951), 161-2, 167, etc.; Melford E. Spiro, *Buddhism and Society: A Great Tradition and its Burmese Vicissitudes* (Berkeley: University of California Press, 1982).

39. The attitude of the Buddhists, however, towards the Buddha is sometimes at variance with that of the Buddha himself. The Divyāvadāna declares: "The sky will fall with moon and stars, earth with its mountains and forests will ascend, oceans will be dried up, but the Buddhas speak not wrongly". See S. Radhakrishnan, *Indian Philosophy*, vol. 1, op. cit., 611, note 1.

40. This argument occupies a prominent place in demonstrating Buddhism's ability to match the findings of modern science. See K.N. Jayatilleke, *The Message of the Buddha*, chapter 7 op. cit.; Huston Smith, "Foreword" to Philip Kapleau, ed., *The Three Pillars of Zen* (New York: Harper and Row, 1966), xii.

41. Kenneth K.S. Ch'en, *Buddhism: The Light of Asia*, op. cit., 275-6, summarizes the position thus: "In the minds of some modern scholars, however, the scientific nature of Buddhism has been exaggerated. Such people contend that instead of being open-minded and tolerant, the Buddha is authoritarian, for he claims to be omniscient and infallible, and that his path is the only path leading to salvation. Nor can the Buddha be said to be scientific when he consciously excludes from his field of inquiry the whole range of the indeterminate questions, and when he fails to give precise definition to such fundamental concepts as *nirvana* and *sunyata* or emptiness. The Mahayana Buddhists especially claim that enlightenment consists of an intuitive awakening, and there is nothing scientific about this. Science is interested in acquiring knowledge for the sake of knowledge, but Buddhism is interested in acquiring knowledge for the sake of salvation. In motive and method, therefore, Buddhism is not scientific."

42. John H. Hick, op. cit., 39.

43. T.W. Rhys Davids, tr., *The Questions of King Milinda*, Part 1 (Delhi: Motilal Banarsidass, 1965, reprint), 146-7.

44. Ibid., 150-1.

CHAPTER 4

The Problem of Evil

1. John H. Hick, *Philosophy of Religion*, op. cit., 40.
2. K.N. Jayatilleke, *The Message of the Buddha*, op. cit., 243.
3. John H. Hick, *Philosophy of Religion*, op. cit., 40-1.
4. Ibid., 257.
5. John H. Hick, ibid., 40: "Rather than attempt to define 'evil' in terms of some theological theory (for example, as 'that which is contrary to God's will'), it seems better to define it ostensively, by indicating that to which the word refers. It refers to physical pain, mental suffering, and moral wickedness. The last is one of the causes of the first two, for an enormous amount of human pain arises from mankind's inhumanity. This pain includes such major scourges as poverty, oppression and persecution, war, and all the injustice, indignity, and inequity that occur in human societies. Even disease is fostered, to an extent that has not yet been precisely determined by psychosomatic medicine, by emotional and moral factors seated both in the individual and in his or her social environment. However, although a great deal of pain and suffering are caused by human action, there is much more that arises from such natural causes as bacteria and earthquakes, storm, fire, lightning, flood, and drought."
6. Buddhists believe that this was entirely due to natural causes. See T.W. Rhys Davids, tr., *The Questions of King Milinda*, vol. 1 (Oxford: Oxford University Press, 1890; Indian reprint 1965), 190-5.
7. Arvind Sharma, *Spokes of the Wheel*, Chapter 3 (New Delhi: Books, 1985).
8. K.N. Jayatilleke, *The Message of the Buddha*, op. cit., 253.
9. John H. Hick, *Philosophy of Religion*, op. cit., 41.
10. Henry Clarke Warren, tr., *Buddhism in Translations* (Cambridge, Mass.: The Harvard University Press, 1915), 56-7.
11. Huston Smith, *The Religions of Man* (New York: Harper and Brother Publishers, 1958), 100.
12. It should be noted, however, that in Mahāyāna Buddhism, of the four noble truths that of the existence of suffering etc. belong to the conventional level and *Nirvāṇa* alone to the absolute.
13. John H. Hick, *Philosophy of Religion*, op. cit., 41.
14. K.N. Jayatilleke, *Early Buddhist Theory of Knowledge*, op. cit., 411.
15. Quoted, ibid., 42.
16. Ibid.
17. See K.N. Jayatilleke, *The Message of the Buddha*, op. cit., 106.
18. A.L. Basham, "The Background of Jainism and Buddhism" in Wm. Theodore De Bary, ed., *Sources of Indian Tradition* (New York: Columbia University Press, 1958), 42-3.
19. K.N. Jayatilleke *The Message of the Buddha*, op. cit., 107.
20. See David J. Kalupahana, *Buddhist Philosophy: A Historical Analysis*, Appendix 1 (Honolulu: The University Press of Hawaii, 1976).
21. K.N. Jayatilleke, *The Message of the Buddha*, op. cit., 149.

22. John H. Hick, *Philosophy of Religion*, op. cit., 41.
23. Gunapala Dharmasiri, *A Buddhist Critique of the Christian Concept of God*, op. cit., 42-3.
24. Ibid., 42.
25. Ibid.
26. Ibid., 43.
27. Ibid., 44.
28. John H. Hick, *Philosophy of Religion*, op. cit., 43.
29. Cited, ibid.
30. Ibid., 43-5.
31. Ibid., 45.
32. Walpola Sri Rahula, *What the Buddha Taught*, op. cit., 92.
33. Lama Angarika Govinda, *The Psychological Attitude of Early Buddhist Philosophy*, op. cit., 47-8.
34. Gunapala Dharmasiri, *A Buddhist Critique of the Christian Concept of God*, op. cit., 7. Emphasis and exclamation added.
35. Lama Anagarika Govinda, *The Psychological Attitude of Early Buddhist Philosophy*, op. cit., 101.
36. John H. Hick, *Philosophy of Religion*, op. cit., 45.
37. Ibid., 49.
38. Kenneth K.S. Ch'en, *Buddhism: the Light of Asia*, op. cit., 42-4.
39. A.L. Basham, *The Wonder That Was India* (London: Sidgwick & Jackson, 1988; first published 1954), 272.
40. Ibid., 273.
41. Gunapala Dharmasiri, *A Buddhist Critique of the Christian Concept of God*, op. cit., 50.
42. Hans Wolfgang Schumann, *Buddhism* (Wheaton, Ill.: The Theosophical Publishing House, 1973), 169.
43. K.N. Jayatilleke, *The Message of the Buddha*, op. cit., 131.
44. John H. Hick, op. cit., p. 50. John H. Hick goes on to point out that "In some passages, indeed, Whitehead seems to say that the ultimate metaphysical principles were initially established by a primordial divine decision. However, Griffin follows Charles Hartshorne, another leading process thinker, in holding that those ultimate principles are eternal necessities, not matters of divine fiat." ibid. David Griffin is credited with developing a full-fledged process theodicy in his *God, Power and Evil: A Process Theodicy*.
45. Ibid.
46. K.N. Jayatilleke, *The Message of the Buddha*, op. cit., 63.
47. Ibid., 114.
48. Ibid.
49. A.L. Basham, *The Wonder That Was India*, op. cit., 272.
50. Walpola Sri Rahula, *What the Buddha Taught*, op. cit., 31.
51. Ibid., 42.
52. Gunapala Dharmasiri, *The Buddhist Critique of the Christian Concept of God*, op. cit., 19.
53. Ibid.
54. Ibid., 19-20.

55. John H. Hick, *Philosophy of Religion*, op. cit., 54.
56. Ibid., 55.
57. Ibid., 56.
58. Ibid., 53.
59. Ibid., 55.
60. Gunapala Dharmasiri, *The Buddhist Critique of the Christian Concept of God*, op. cit., 259. Also see 98, 100, 110-11.
61. John H. Hick, *Philosophy of Religion*, op. cit., 46.
62. Ibid., 49.
63. Ibid., 47.
64. Ibid., 47-8.
65. K.N. Jayatilleke, *The Message of the Buddha*, op. cit., 253.
66. Lama Anagarika Govinda, *The Psychological Attitude of Early Buddhist Philosophy*, op. cit., 111; also see T.W. Rhys Davids, tr., op. cit., part 2, 75-8.
67. K.N. Jayatilleke, *The Message of the Buddha*, op. cit., 254. S = *Saṃyatta Nikāya*.
68. Ibid., 254-5.
69. Ibid.
70. Ibid., 255.
71. Ibid.
72. Ibid.
73. John B. Cobb Jr., *A Christian Natural Theology* (London: Butterworth Press, 1966), 94.
74. A.L. Basham, "Hinduism", in R.C. Zaehner, ed., *The Concise Encyclopedia of Living Faiths* (Boston: Beacon Press, 1959), 225.
75. G.P. Malasekera, ed., *Encyclopedia of Buddhism*, vol. 1 (Government of Ceylon, 1961), 668-9.
76. Ibid., 669.
77. See Philip Kapleau, ed., *The Three Pillars of Zen* (New York: Harper and Row, 1966), 71-82.
78. G.P. Malasekera, ed., *Encyclopedia of Buddhism*, vol. 1, op. cit., 670.
79. Antony Flew, quoted by K.N. Jayatilleke, *The Message of the Buddha*, op. cit., 111.
80. John H. Hick, *Philosophy of Religion*, chapter four, op. cit.
81. As cited in K.N. Jayatilleke, *The Message of the Buddha*, op. cit., 111; Gunapala Dharmasiri, *A Buddhist Critique of the Christian Concept of God*, op. cit., 46.
82. Ibid., 110-11.
83. Gunapala Dharmasiri, *A Buddhist Critique of the Christian Concept of God*, op. cit., 45-6. He goes on to add: "It is not contradictory to think of such an alternative world. The relevant objection, here, that without moral evil free will becomes meaningless, loses much of its justificatory value when one thinks of the enormous evils such a freedom can lead to. That is why some, like McCloskey and Flew, have gone so far as to prefer a world with no evil to a world with free will."
84. Ibid., 46-7.
85. Walpola Sri Rahula, *What the Buddha Taught*, op. cit., 55.
86. John H. Hick, *Philosophy of Religion*, op. cit., 40.

CHAPTER 5

Revelation and Faith

1. John H. Hick, *Philosophy of Religion*, op. cit., 57.
2. Ibid.
3. Edward Conze, *Buddhist Thought in India* (Ann Arbor: The University of Michigan Press, 1967), 41.
4. See Richard P. Hayes, "Principled Atheism in the Buddhist Scholastic Tradition", *Journal of Indian Philosophy* 16 (1988), 5-28.
5. Edward Conze, *Buddhist Thought in India*, op. cit., 27.
6. Ibid., 227; Edward Conze, *Buddhism: Its Essence and Development*, op. cit., 39-40.
7. Gunapala Dharmasiri, *A Buddhist Critique of the Christian Concept of God*, op. cit., xix.
8. K.N. Jayatilleke, *The Message of the Buddha*, op. cit., 114.
9. K.N. Jayatilleke, *Early Buddhist Theory of Knowledge*, op. cit., 454.
10. Ibid., 447.
11. John H. Hick, *Philosophy of Religion*, op. cit., 27.
12. Ibid., 57.
13. K.N. Jayatilleke, *The Message of the Buddha*, op. cit., 124.
14. Ibid., 124-5.
15. Ibid.
16. Walpola Sri Rahula, *What the Buddha Taught*, op. cit., 43.
17. K.N. Jayatilleke, *The Message of the Buddha*, op. cit., 126.
18. Ibid., 127.
19. Ibid.
20. John H. Hick, *Philosophy of Religion*, op. cit., 120-1.
21. Ibid., 57-8.
22. K.N. Jayatilleke, *Early Buddhist Theories of Knowledge*, op. cit., 405.
23. Ibid., 403.
24. Ibid., 403-4. Pali text omitted from citation.
25. Walpola Sri Rahula, *What the Buddha Taught*, op. cit., 26. Emphasis added.
26. K.N. Jayatilleke, *Early Buddhist Theories of Knowledge*, op. cit., 463-4.
27. John H. Hick, *Philosophy of Religion*, op. cit., 59-60: "This empiricist reasoning is in agreement with the unformulated epistemological assumptions of the Bible. Philosophers of the rationalist tradition, holding that to know means to be able to prove, have been shocked to find that in the Bible, which is the basis of western religion, there is no attempt whatever to demonstrate the existence of God. Instead of professing to establish the reality of God by philosophical reasoning, the Bible takes God's reality for granted. Indeed, to the biblical writers it would have seemed absurd to try to prove by logical argument that God exists, for they were convinced that they were already having to do with God, and God with them, in all the affairs of their lives. God was known to them as a dynamic will interacting with their own wills — a sheer given reality, as inescapably to be reckoned with as destructive storm and life-giving sunshine, or the hatred of their enemies and the friendship of their neighbors. They thought of God as an

experienced reality rather than as an inferred entity. The biblical writers were (sometimes, though doubtless not at all times) as vividly conscious of being in God's presence as they were of living in a material environment. It is impossible to read their writings with any degree of sensitivity without realizing that to these people God was not a proposition completing a syllogism, or an abstract idea accepted by the mind, but the reality that gave meaning to their lives. Their pages resound and vibrate with the sense of God's presence as a building might resound and vibrate from the tread of some great being walking through it. It would be as sensible for a husband to desire a philosophical proof of the existence of the wife and family who contribute so much to the meaning in his life as for the person of faith to seek a proof of the existence of the God within whose purpose one is conscious that one lives and moves and has one's being."

28. K.N. Jayatilleke, *Early Buddhist Theories of Knowledge,* op. cit., 464. Emphasis added. Also see Wayne Proudfoot, *Religious Experience* (Berkeley: University of California Press, 1985), *passim.*

29. Edward Conze, *Buddhist Thought in India,* op. cit., 266. He observes later (p. 267): "If it were taken at its face value, the thesis that sense-perception and inference are the only sources of valid knowledge should endear these later logicians to our present generation of philosophers and prove utterly destructive of all spiritual teaching. In fact the candour of Dharmakirti and Dharmottara is only apparent, and the intuition of the saints and the revelations of the Buddhas are smuggled in through the back door."

30. John H. Hick, *Philosophy of Religion,* op. cit., 58.

31. T.R.V. Murty, *The Central Philosophy of Buddhism* (London: George Allen and Unwin, 1955), 97.

32. Kenneth K.S. Ch'en, *Buddhism: The Light of Asia,* op. cit., 79.

33. John H. Hick, *Philosophy of Religion,* op. cit., 58.

34. M. Hiriyanna, *Outlines of Indian Philosophy* (London: George Allen and Unwin, 1932), 200.

35. John H. Hick, *Philosophy of Religion,* op. cit., 59.

36. Ibid.

37. Edward Conze, *Buddhist Thought in India,* op. cit., 267-8.

38. John H. Hick, *Philosophy of Religion,* op. cit., 60.

39. Cited, ibid., 61.

40. Ibid.

41. Gunapala Dharmasiri, *A Buddhist Critique of the Christian Concept of God,* op. cit., 138.

42. Cited in John H. Hick, *Philosophy of Religion,* op. cit., 61.

43. Kenneth K.S. Ch'en, *Buddhism: The Light of Asia,* op. cit., 62.

44. Walpola Sri Rahula, *What the Buddha Taught,* op. cit., 19.

45. Ibid., 19-20.

46. Ibid., 20 ff.

47. Edward Conze, *Buddhist Thought in India,* op. cit., 36-9.

48. Ibid., 122 ff.

49. Gunapala Dharmasiri, *A Buddhist Critique of the Christian Concept of God,* op. cit., 245-6.

50. Ibid., 246.

51. Ibid.
52. Nalinaksha Dutt, *Early Monastic Buddhism* (Calcutta: Calcutta Oriental Book Agency, 1960), 254 ff.
53. Beni Madhab Barua, "Some Aspects of Early Buddhism", in Haridas Bhattacharya, ed., *The Cultural Heritage of India*, Vol. 1 (Calcutta: The Ramakrishna Mission Institute of Culture, 1958), 445-6.
54. K.N. Jayatilleke, *The Message of the Buddha*, op. cit., 58.
55. Gunapala Dharmasiri, *A Buddhist Critique of the Christian Concept of God*, op. cit., 251.
56. See Walpola Sri Rahula, *What the Buddha Taught*, op. cit., 138.
57. Ibid.
58. Gunapala Dharmasiri, *A Buddhist Critique of the Christian Concept of God*, op. cit., 251.
59. John H. Hick, *Philosophy of Religion*, op. cit., 63.
60. Ibid.
61. Ibid.
62. K.N. Jayatilleke, *Early Buddhist Theory of Knowledge*, op. cit., 104-6.
63. Ibid., 406.
64. Ibid.
65. Cited in John H. Hick, *Philosophy of Religion*, op. cit., 63-4.
66. Ibid., 64.
67. Ibid.
68. Ibid., 64, 65.
69. Walpola Sri Rahula, *What the Buddha Taught*, op. cit., 6-7.
70. Gunapala Dharmasiri, *A Buddhist Critique of the Christian Concept of God*, op. cit., 249-50.
71. Walpola Sri Rahula, *What the Buddha Taught*, op. cit., 7-8.
72. Cited in John H. Hick, *Philosophy of Religion*, op. cit., 65.
73. Ibid.
74. Ibid., 66.
75. Ibid., 66-7.
76. Cited, ibid., 66.
77. Ibid.
78. Cited by John H. Hick, *Philosophy of Religion*, op. cit., 66.
79. Ibid., 66-67.
80. I.B. Horner, "Buddhism: The Theravāda", in R.C. Zaehner, ed., *The Concise Encyclopedia of Living Faiths*, op. cit., 289. Also see Walpola Sri Rahula, *What the Buddha Taught*, op. cit., 40-1.
81. John H. Hick, *Philosophy of Religion*, op. cit., 67.
82. Lama Anagarika Govinda, *The Psychological Attitude of Early Buddhist Philosophy*, op. cit., 42.
83. Walpola Sri Rahula, *What the Buddha Taught*, op. cit., 37.
84. John H. Hick, *Philosophy of Religion*, op. cit., 67.
85. T.W. Rhys Davids, tr., *The Questions of King Milinda*, Part 1, (Oxford: Oxford University Press, 1890; 1965 Reprint) 150-1.
86. Edward Conze, *Buddhism: Its Essence and Development*, op. cit., 81.
87. John H. Hick, op. cit., 67.
88. Edward Conze, *Buddhism: Its Essence and Development*, op. cit., 42.

89. Hans Wolfgang Schumann, *Buddhism: An Outline of its Teachings and Schools*, op. cit., 163.
90. Edward Conze, *Buddhism : Its Essence and Development*, op. cit., 190.
91. Ibid., 149.
92. Ibid., 188-9.
93. Kenneth K.S. Ch'en, *Buddhism: The Light of Asia*, op. cit., 72-3.
94. John H. Hick, *Philosophy of Religion*, op. cit., 68.
95. Ibid., 68.
96. Cited in John H. Hick, *Philosophy of Religion*, op. cit., 73.
97. Ibid., 68.
98. Ibid.
99. Ibid., 72.
100. D.T. Suzuki, *An Introduction to Zen Buddhism* (New York: The Philosophical Library, 1949), 76, 78.
101. Edward Conze, *Buddhism: Its Essence and Development*, op. cit., 34.
102. Henry Clarke Warren, tr., *Buddhism in Translations*, op. cit., xiv.
103. John H. Hick, *Philosophy of Religion*, op. cit., 68-9.
104. Ibid., 69.
105. K.N. Jayatilleke, *Early Buddhist Theory of Knowledge*, op. cit., 445, 446, 469.
106. Edward J. Thomas, *The Life of the Buddha as Legend and History* (New York: Barnes and Noble Inc., 1956), 98.
107. Ibid., 112-3.
108. Nalinaksha Dutt, *Early Buddhist Monasticism*, op.cit., 124.
109. Richard Robinson, *The Buddhist Religion: A Historical Introduction* (Belmont, California: Dickenson Publishing Company, Inc., 1970), 25.
110. John H. Hick, *Philosophy of Religion*, op. cit., 74.
111. Gunapala Dharmasiri, *A Buddhist Critique of the Christian Concept of God*, op. cit., 268.
112. Ibid., 244.
113. John H. Hick, *Philosophy of Religion*, op. cit., 74.
114. Bimala Churn Law, *Concepts of Buddhism* (Leiden: Kern Institute, 1937), 77.
115. Ibid., 76.
116. K.N. Jayatilleke, *Early Buddhist Theory of Knowledge*, op. cit., 276.
117. Ibid., 409 ff.
118. Ibid., 405 ff.
119. Ibid., 409.
120. Ibid., 393-4. Also see Richard Robinson, *The Buddhist Religion: A Historical Introduction*, op. cit., 27: "Faith in the Buddha as revealer of the *Dharma* is a first step on the path. Faith is not a substitute for knowledge but is the seed which grows into confirmatory realization. It is willingness to take statements provisionally on trust, confidence in the integrity of a witness, and determination to practice according to instructions. It is not a mental state of boiling zeal but rather of serenity and lucidity. Śāriputra, one of the great disciples, explained that the confidence, like that of a lion, with which he proclaimed the Doctrine, came, not from his own superknowledge but from the faith inspired in him as he heard Gautama teach. 'I, understanding that *Dharma*, perfected the quality of faith in the Teacher. And I confessed in my heart: The Blessed One is supremely awakened; the *Dharma* is well

proclaimed by him; the *Saṅgha* has followed it well'."
121. K.N. Jayatilleke, *Early Buddhist Theory of Knowledge*, op. cit., 394.
122. Gunapala Dharmasiri, *A Buddhist Critique of the Christian Concept of God*, op. cit., 256-7.
123. Ibid., 257.
124. Quoted, ibid., 236-7.
125. Ibid., 237.
126. Personal communication, Richard P. Hayes.
127. Gunapala Dharmasiri, *A Buddhist Critique of the Christian Concept of God*, op. cit., 244-245.
128. Ibid., 257.

CHAPTER 6

Problems of Religious Language

1. John H. Hick, *Philosophy of Religion*, op. cit., 76.
2. Ibid.
3. Ibid.
4. Ibid., 77.
5. Ibid.
6. Ibid.
7. Gunapala Dharmasiri, *A Buddhist Critique of the Christian Concept of God*, op. cit., 196.
8. On the possibility of using God in Buddhist discourse, see Edward Conze, *Buddhism: Its essence and Development*, op. cit., 39-40.
9. Ibid., 40.
10. In Gunapala Dharmasiri, *A Buddhist Critique of the Christian Concept of God*, op. cit., 192.
11. See K.N Jayatilleke, *Early Buddhist Theory of Knowledge*, op. cit., 362.
12. Gunapala Dharmasiri, *A Buddhist Critique of the Christian Concept of God*, op. cit., 38.
13. Edward Conze, *Buddhism: Its Essence and Development*, op. cit., 152-3.
14. Edward Conze, "Buddhism: The Mahāyāna", in R.C. Zaehner, ed., *The Concise Encyclopedia of Living Faiths*, op. cit., 304.
15. Walpola Sri Rahula, *What the Buddha Taught*, op. cit., 43.
16. Ibid.
17. John H. Hick, *Philosophy of Religion*, op. cit., 77.
18. Ibid., 78-9.
19. Ibid., 78.
20. Ibid., 79.
21. Gunapala Dharmasiri, *A Buddhist Critique of the Christian Concept of God*, op. cit., 190.
22. Ibid., 190-1.
23. Cited in K.N. Jayatilleke, *Early Buddhist Theory of Knowledge*, op. cit., 361.
24. Ibid., 362.
25. Ibid., 363.

26. Ibid.
27. Ibid., 364.
28. Ibid., 366.
29. Cited in T.R.V. Murti, *The Central Philosophy of Buddha*, op. cit., 243-4.
30. Ibid., 245.
31. K.N. Jayatilleke, *The Message of the Buddha*, op. cit., 52.
32. Cited in John H. Hick, *Philosophy of Religion*, op. cit., 80.
33. Cited, ibid.
34. Ibid.
35. Cited, ibid.
36. Walpola Sri Rahula, *What the Buddha Taught*, op. cit., 35.
37. Ibid., 39-40.
38. Ibid., 40.
39. Ibid., 66.
40. Kenneth K.S. Ch'en, *Buddhism: The Light of Asia*, op. cit., 72.
41. Ibid.
42. John H. Hick, *Philosophy of Religion*, op. cit., 81.
43. Ibid., 31.
44. Alan W. Watts, *The Way of Zen* (New York: Random House, 1957), 179.
45. Daisetsu T. Suzuki, *The Essentials of Zen Buddhism*, edited by Bernard Phillips (New York: E.P. Dutton and Co. Inc. 1962), 433.
46. John H. Hick, *Philosophy of Religion*, op. cit., 82.
47. Cited, ibid.
48. Kenneth K.S. Ch'en, *Buddhism: The Light of Asia*, op. cit., 63. But also see K.N. Jayatilleke, *The Message of the Buddha*, op. cit., 59.
49. Ibid., 66. Also see Edward Conze, "Buddhism: The Mahāyāna" in R.C. Zaehner, ed., *The Concise Encyclopedia of Living Faiths*, op. cit., 306.
50. Hermann Oldenberg, *Buddha: His Life, His Doctrine, His Order*, tr. William Hoey (London: Williams and Novgate, 1822), 279-80.
51. I.B. Horner, "Buddhism: The Theravāda" in R.C. Zaehner, ed., *The Concise Encyclopedia of Living Faiths*, op. cit., 282.
52. Ibid.
53. Hans Wolfgang Schumann, *Buddhism: An Outline of its Teachings and Schools*, op. cit., 102-4.
54. Edward Conze, "Buddhism: The Mahāyāna", in R.C. Zaehner, ed., *The Concise Encyclopedia of Living Faiths*, op. cit., 301.
55. Henry Clarke Warren, *Buddhism in Translations*, op. cit., 126-8.
56. Harvey Cox, "Christianity", in Arvind Sharma, ed., *Our Religions* (New York: Harper Collins Publishers, 1993) p. 368.
57 John H. Hick, *Philosophy of Religion*, op. cit., 83.
58. Ibid.
59. Ibid., 84.
60. Ibid.
61. Ibid.
62. J.H. Randall, Jr., cited ibid., 84-5.
63. Hans Wolfgang Schumann, *Buddhism: An Outline of its Teachings and Schools*, op. cit., 160.
64. John H. Hick, *Philosophy of Religion*, op. cit., 87.

65. Gunapala Dharmasiri, *A Buddhist Critique of the Christian Concept of God*, op. cit., 83.

66. Robert Lawson Slater, *World Religions and World Community* (New York: Columbia Press, 1963), 90.

67. R.B. Braithwaite, 'An Empiricist's View of the Nature of Religious Belief', in John H. Hick, ed. *The Existence of God* (New York: Macmillan, 1964), 64.

68. Gunapala Dharmasiri, *A Buddhist Critique of the Christian Concept of God*, op. cit., 83.

69. Ibid., 83-4.

70. K.N. Jayatilleke, *The Message of the Buddha*, op. cit., 112.

71. Gunapala Dharmasiri, *A Buddhist Critique of the Christian Concept of God*, op. cit., 206.

72. Ibid.

73. Ibid.

74. Ibid.

75. Ibid., 207.

76. Ibid.

77. John H. Hick, *Philosophy of Religion*, op. cit., 91.

78. Ibid.

79. Ibid.

80. Cited, ibid., 92.

81. Cited, ibid., 92.

82. Walpola Sri Rahula, *What the Buddha Taught*, op. cit., 51-2.

83. Cited in Gunapala Dharmasiri, *A Buddhist Critique of the Christian Concept of God*, op. cit., 210.

84. Ibid., 211.

85. Ibid.

86. Ibid., 222.

87. John H. Hick, *Philosophy of Religion*, op. cit., 92-3.

88. K.N. Jayatilleke, *The Message of the Buddha*, op. cit., 45-6.

89. Ibid., 46.

CHAPTER 7

The Problem of Verification

1. John H. Hick, *Philosophy of Religion*, op. cit., 94.

2. Ibid., 95.

3. Cited ibid., 96.

4. Ibid., 96. Gunapala Dharmasiri regards John Wisdom's position along with those of several others as attitudinal rather than factual in nature. He writes (*A Buddhist Critique of the Christian Concept of God*, 212): "John Wisdom, in his article on 'Gods', enunciates the fundamental principle that lies behind these attitudinal theories of religion. He says: 'The difference as to whether a God exists involves our feelings more than most scientific disputes and in this respect is more like a difference as to whether there is

beauty in a thing.' J.L. Stocks illuminates us more on the nature of this perspectival approach. He believes in 'the religious truth emerging in the religious act as the vision of the ordering principle of the whole.' He further illuminates us as to the slender nature of the existence of the God that is implied in this type of perspectival approach. 'The proof of the existence of poetry is in the poetical act, performed by the maker or reader or hearer of the poem. And there are in fact in this world many people who, if they were sufficiently honest and clear-minded, would deny the existence of poetry as well as the existence of God, and on the same grounds, viz., because of the absence of extreme poverty of the appropriate activity in their personal experience.' Bertocci is an exemplary instance of how these thinkers try to suggest a doctrine of the nature and existence of God as based on this perspectival or attitudinal theory of religion: '... when the personalist says that God is a unity-in-continuity of knowing–willing–caring, he is asserting that the essential constitution of the world and the essential constitution of man are such that the highest good of man is realized in that kind of community in which persons respect and care for each other's growth.' 'In knowing-loving he enters into a fuller relationship with a universe that responds to him in his growth as inspired by truth and love. Why not then conceive of the Unity-Continuity of the Cosmic-Knower as a lodging Person?' "

5. Ibid.
6. Cited, ibid., 211-12.
7. K.N. Jayatilleke, *Early Buddhist Theory of Knowledge*, op. cit., 352.
8. K.N. Jayatilleke, *The Message of the Buddha*, op. cit., 46.
9. Ibid., 45.
10. John H. Hick, *Philosophy of Religion*, op. cit., 95.
11. Gunapala Dharmasiri, *A Buddhist Critique of the Christian Concept of God*, op. cit., 195.
12. Ibid., 195-6.
13. John H. Hick, *Philosophy of Religion*, op. cit., 97.
14. Cited, ibid.
15. See K.N. Jayatilleke, *The Message of the Buddha*, op. cit., 108-9; Gunapala Dharmasiri, *A Buddhist Critique of the Christian Concept of God*, op. cit., 197.
16. John H. Hick, *Philosophy of Religion*, op. cit., 97.
17. Ibid.
18. Cited, ibid., 98.
19. Ibid., 98-9.
20. Edward J. Thomas, *The History of Buddhist Thought* (New York: Barnes and Noble, Inc., 1971), 191.
21. K.N. Jayatilleke, *The Message of the Buddha*, op. cit., 115.
22. John H. Hick, *Philosophy of Religion*, op. cit., 99.
23. Ibid.
24. K.N. Jayatilleke, *The Message of the Buddha*, op. cit., 47.
25. John H. Hick, op. cit., 101. He goes on to say: "During the course of the journey, the issue between them is not an experimental one. That is to say, they do not entertain different expectations about the coming details of the road, but only about its ultimate destination. Yet, when they turn the last

corner, it will be apparent that one of them has been right all the time and the other wrong. Thus, although the issue between them has not been experimental, it has nevertheless been a real issue. They have not merely felt differently about the road, for one was feeling appropriately and the other inappropriately in relation to the actual state of affairs. Their opposed interpretations of the situation have constituted genuinely rival assertions, whose assertion-status has the peculiar characteristic of being guaranteed retrospectively by a future crux."

26. Ibid., 101-2.
27. Ibid., 100-1.
28. Gunapala Dharmasiri, *A Buddhist Critique of the Christian Concept of God*, op. cit., 228-9.
29. Walpola Sri Rahula, *What the Buddha Taught*, op. cit., 9.
30. John H. Hick, *Philosophy of Religion*, op. cit., 103.

CHAPTER 8

The Conflicting Truth Claims of Different Religions

1. John H. Hick, *Philosophy of Religion*, third edition (Englewood Cliffs, New Jersey: Prentice Hall, 1983), 107-8.
2. Heinrich Zimmer, *Philosophies of India*, edited by Joseph Campbell (New York: Pantheon Books, 1951), 1.
3. A.L. Basham, "The Background of Jainism and Buddhism", in Wm. Theodore de Bary, ed., *Sources of Indian Tradition* (New York: Columbia University Press, 1958), 39. For a more detailed account see Nalinaksha Dutt, *Early Monastic Buddhism* (Calcutta: Calcutta Oriental Book Agency, 1960); K.N. Jayatilleke, *Early Buddhist Theory of Knowledge*, etc.
4. Nalinaksha Dutt, *Early Monastic Buddhism*, op. cit., 36.
5. K.N. Jayatilleke, *Early Buddhist Theory of Knowledge*, op. cit., 121.
6. Walpola Sri Rahula, *What the Buddha Taught*, op. cit., 2-3.
7. John H. Hick, *Philosophy of Religion*, op. cit., 108.
8. Ibid.
9. Ibid.
10. Edward Conze, *Buddhism: Its Essence and Development* (New York: Harper and Row, 1959), 104-5.
11. Walpola Sri Rahula, *What the Buddha Taught*, op. cit., 10-11.
12. John H. Hick, *Philosophy of Religion*, op. cit., 111.
13. K.N. Jayatilleke, *The Message of the Buddha*, op. cit., Chapter 12.
14. Ibid., 127.
15. John H. Hick, *Philosophy of Religion*, op. cit., 113.
16. Ibid.
17. K.N. Jayatilleke, *The Message of the Buddha*, op. cit., 57.
18. John H. Hick, *Philosophy of Religion*, op. cit., 113.
19. Ibid., 113.
20. Walpola Sri Rahula, *What the Buddha Taught*, op. cit., 11-12.
21. John H. Hick, *Philosophy of Religion*, op. cit., 113.

22. Gunapala Dharmasiri, *A Buddhist Critique of the Christian Concept of God*, op. cit., 149.
23. John H. Hick, *Philosophy of Religion*, op. cit., 121.
24. Ibid.
25. Ibid.
26. Ibid.
27. Ibid.
28. Walpola Sri Rahula, *What the Buddha Taught*, op. cit., 51 ff; K.N. Jayatilleke, *The Message of the Buddha*, op. cit., 126-7.
29. Walpola Sri Rahula, *What the Buddha Taught*, op. cit., 51.
30. John H. Hick, *Philosophy of Religion*, op. cit., 129.
31. Arvind Sharma, *A Hindu Perspective on the Philosophy of Religion* (London: Macmillan, 1990), 162-3.
32. T.W. Rhys Davids, tr., *Dialogues of the Buddha*, Part 1 (London: Luzac and Company, 1956), 303.
33. K.N. Jayatilleke, *The Message of the Buddha*, op. cit., 111.
34. See Walpola Sri Rahula, *What the Buddha Taught*, op. cit., 30: "Here the term 'thirst' includes not only desire for, and attachment to, sense-pleasures, wealth and power, but also desire for, and attachment to, ideas and ideals, views, opinions, theories, conceptions and beliefs (*dhamma-taṇhā*). According to the Buddha's analysis, all the troubles and strife in the world, from little personal quarrels in families to great wars between nations and countries, arise out of this selfish 'thirst'. From this point of view, all economic, political and social problems are rooted in this selfish 'thirst'. Great statesmen who try to settle international disputes and talk of war and peace only in economic and political terms touch the superficialities, and never go deep into the real root of the problem. As the Buddha told Raṭṭapāla: 'The world lacks and hankers, and is enslaved to 'thirst' (*taṇhādāso*)'."
35. Ibid., 9-10.
36. Edward J. Thomas, *The History of Buddhist Thought*, op. cit., 190-1.
37. H. Wolfgang Schumann, *Buddhism: An Outline of its Teachings and Schools*, op. cit., 172.
38. Edward Conze, *Buddhism: Its Essence and Development*, op. cit., 73.
39. David W. Chappell, "Six Buddhist Attitudes Towards Other Religions", in Sulak Sivaraksha et al., eds., *Radical Conservatism. Buddhism in the Contemporary World* (Bangkok: Thai Inter-Religious Commission for Development, 1990).
40. Ibid.
41. Cited by David W. Chappell from Donald Swearer, ed., *Me and Mine: Selected Essays of Bhikku Buddhadāsa* (Albany, N.Y.: SUNY Press, 1989), 146.
42. David W. Chappell, "Six Buddhist Attitudes Towards Other Religions", op. cit., p. 551-2.

CHAPTER 9

Human Destiny: Immortality and Resurrection

1. John H. Hick, *Philosophy of Religion*, op. cit., 122.
2. Walpola Sri Rahula, *What the Buddha Taught*, op. cit., 51. The idea that Buddhism rejects the reality of a soul has met with resistance and scholars are sometimes reluctant to accept it. However there seems to be little doubt that such might well be the case: See Walpola Sri Rahula, *What the Buddha Taught*, op. cit., Chapter 6; T.R.V. Murti, *The Central Philosophy of Buddhism*, op. cit., 20-35. G.P. Malasekera, ed., *Encyclopedia of Buddhism*, vol. 1, op. cit., 567-76. As to the question of how Buddhism can accept rebirth without believing in a soul see next chapter; briefly "Buddha *replaced* the soul by the theory of a mind-continuum, by a series of psychical states rigorously conditioned as to their nature by the causal law governing them (*dharma-sanketa*). According to him this alone provides for progress (change, efficacy) and continuity (responsibility), as each succeeding state (good or bad) is the result of the previous state", T.R.V. Murti, *The Central Philosophy of Buddhism*, op. cit., 32. It may be worth adding that after "Buddhism was introduced, the Chinese had difficulty understanding the fundamental doctrine of no-soul or no-self (*anatta*). They could not comprehend the idea of successive rebirths without some abiding spirit or soul that connects the different rebirths, and to resolve their difficulty, they created the concept of an entity called *shen*, spirit or soul, that transmigrated from one life to the next", Kenneth K.S. Ch'en, *Buddhism: The Light of Asia*, op. cit., 142-3.
3. In this respect the Buddha differed from his contemporary Makkhali Gosāla who believed that every being was predestined to liberation in due course.
4. John H. Hick, *Philosophy of Religion*, op. cit., 122.
5. Ibid., 123.
6. Bimala Churn Law, *Concepts of Buddhism*, 78.
7. T.R.V. Murti, *The Central Philosophy of Buddhism*, op. cit., 10.
8. John H. Hick, *Philosophy of Religion*, op. cit., 123.
9. For an Indian parallel see M. Hiriyanna, *Outlines of Indian Philosophy* (London: George Allen and Unwin, 1932), 192.
10. John H. Hick, *Philosophy of Religion,*op. cit., 124.
11. K.N. Jayatilleke, *The Message of the Buddha*, op. cit., 165.
12. Buddhism attaches considerable significance to the body while it dispenses with the soul, see Edward Conze, *Buddhism: Its Essence and Development*, op. cit., 197-8.
13. John H. Hick, *Philosophy of Religion*, op. cit., 125. For Buddhism in relation to death and evil see T.O. Ling, *Buddhism and the Mythology of Evil* (London: George Allen and Unwin Ltd., 1962).
14. This, of course, would also hold for the Indic religious tradition in general, see R.C. Zaehner, ed., *The Concise Encyclopedia of Living Faiths*, op. cit., 416.
15. John H. Hick, *Philosophy of Religion*, op. cit., 123-4. It should be noted that in the third case "the element of the strange and the mysterious has been reduced to a minimum by one's following the view of some of the early

Church Fathers that the resurrection body has the same shape as the physical body, and ignoring Paul's own hint that it may be as unlike the physical body as a full grain of wheat differs from the wheat seed." Ibid., 126.

16. See Henry Clarke Warren, tr., *Buddhism in Translations*, op. cit., 148-50.
17. Edward J. Thomas, *The History of Buddhist Thought* (New York: Barnes and Noble, Inc., 1971), 106.
18. Edward Conze, *Buddhism: Its Essence and Development*, op. cit., 24.
19. K.N. Jayatilleke, *The Message of the Buddha*, op. cit., 137-8.
20. John H. Hick, *Philosophy of Religion*, op. cit., 126.
21. Edward J. Thomas, *The History of Buddhist Thought*, op. cit., 110-11.
22. Ibid., 118.
23. Kenneth K.S. Ch'en, *Buddhism in China: A Historical Survey*, op. cit., 338.
24. Ibid.
25. Ibid., 339.
26. Ibid.
27. Ibid., 339-40. Also see A.L. Basham, *The Wonder That Was India*, op. cit., 275-6.
28. The doctrine is technically known as the *trikāya* (three-body) doctrine and invites comparison with the Trinity.
29. From a Buddhist perspective Jesus Christ could be felicitously accommodated in the category of a Bodhisattva, the last of whose ten stations is strikingly called *abhiṣeka* (anointment)!
30. Hans Wolfgang Schumann, *Buddhism: An Outline of its Teachings and Schools*, op. cit., 104.
31. Edward Conze, *Buddhism: Its Essence and Development*, op. cit., 171.
32. Edward Conze, "Buddhism: The Mahāyāna", in R.C. Zaehner, ed., *The Concise Encyclopedia of Living Faiths*, op. cit., 306.
33. John H. Hick, *Philosophy of Religion*, op. cit., 127.
34. Ibid.
35. Ibid.
36. Edward Conze, "Buddhism: The Mahāyāna", in R.C. Zaehner, ed., *The Concise Encyclopedia of Living Faiths*, op. cit., 299.
37. K.N. Jayatilleke, *The Message of the Buddha*, op. cit., 251. Also see Daigan and Alicia Matsunaga, *The Buddhist Concept of Hell* (New York: Philosophical Library, 1972).
38. John H. Hick, *Philosophy of Religion*, op. cit., 129.
39. Ibid.
40. Ibid.
41. K.N. Jayatilleke *The Message of the Buddha*, op. cit., 153.
42. Ibid.
43. John H. Hick, *Philosophy of Religion*, op. cit., 131 n. 22.
44. Ibid., 132.
45. W.Y. Evans-Wentz, ed., *The Tibetan Book of the Dead* (New York: Oxford University Press, 1960), 89 ff.
46. Raymond A. Moody, Jr., *Life after Life* (New York: Bantam Books, 1975), 119-22.
47. Ibid., 92-3.

48. Walpola Sri Rahula, *What the Buddha Taught*, op. cit., 46; Edward Conze, "Buddhism: the Mahāyāna", in R.C. Zaehner, ed., *The Concise Encyclopedia of Living Faiths*, op. cit., 299.

CHAPTER 10

Human Destiny: Karma and Reincarnation

1. John H. Hick, *Philosophy of Religion*, op. cit., 133.
2. Henry Clarke Warren, *Buddhism in Translations*, op. cit., 228-9.
3. K.N. Jayatilleke, *The Message of the Buddha*, op. cit., 110.
4. John H. Hick, *Philosophy of Religion*, op. cit., 133-4.
5. Henry Clarke Warren, *Buddhism in Translations*, op. cit., 214-5.
6. John H. Hick, *Philosophy of Religion*, op. cit., 134.
7. Walpola Sri Rahula, *What the Buddha Taught*, chapter 6, op. cit.
8. Ibid., 51.
9. K.N. Jayatilleke, *The Message of the Buddha*, op. cit., 139.
10. "There is an extensive literature reporting and discussing such cases. The most scientifically valuable are those of Professor Ian Stevenson: *Twenty Cases Suggestive of Reincarnation*, 2nd ed. (Charlottesville, University of Virginia Press, 1974); *Cases of the Reincarnation Type*, vol. 1: *Ten Cases in India*; vol. 2: *Ten Cases in Sri Lanka*; and vol. 3: *Twelve Cases in Lebanon and Turkey* (Charlottesville: University of Virginia Press, 1975-9)." In John H. Hick, *Philosophy of Religion*, op. cit., 134 n. 1.
11. K.N. Jayatilleke, *The Message of the Buddha*, op. cit., 191-2.
12. Ibid., 192.
13. Ibid., 192-3. Emphasis added.
14. John H. Hick, *Philosophy of Religion*, op. cit., 134.
15. Ibid.
16. Ibid., 136.
17. Ibid., 135.
18. Ibid., 136.
19. Ibid.
20. Ibid., 137.
21. Ibid., 137. Emphasis added.
22. Ibid., 135.
23. Ibid., 136.
24. K. N. Jayatilleke, *The Message of the Buddha*, op. cit., p. 167.
25. The Buddhists concede, however, that "this is an argument from silence. In the case of our present life, we have another criterion to go on, namely the criterion of bodily continuity, and other people can testify to the fact that we existed in the first year of our lives and lived through certain experiences. But in the case of rebirth we have no evidence at all if we do not have actual or potential memories. Memory is, therefore, very relevant to the problem of rebirth." Ibid., 168.
26. Ibid., 170-1.
27. Walpola Sri Rahula, *What the Buddha Taught*, op. cit., 27.

28. Ibid.
29. Ibid.
30. Some Buddhist scholars are not satisfied with the explanation Buddhism provides of how rebirth is possible without a soul, see Edward Conze, *Buddhism: Its Essence and Development*, op. cit., 169-70.
31. For more interesting illustrations of this point see Henry Clarke Warren, *Buddhism in Translations* (Cambridge, Massachusetts: The Harvard University Press, 1915), 234-8. Also see Walpola Sri Rahula, *What the Buddha Taught*, op. cit., 34, "As there is no permanent, unchanging substance, nothing passes from one moment to the next. So quite obviously, nothing permanent or unchanging can pass or transmigrate from one life to the next. It is a series that continues unbroken, but changes every moment. The series is, really speaking, nothing but movement. It is like a flame that burns through the night: it is not the same flame nor is it another. A child grows up to be a man of sixty. Certainly, the man of sixty is not the same as the child of sixty years ago, nor is he another person. Similarly, a person who dies here and is reborn elsewhere is neither the same person, nor another (*na ca so na ca añño*). It is the continuity of the same series. The difference between death and birth is only a thought-moment: the last thought-moment in this life conditions the first thought-moment in the so-called next life, which, in fact, is the continuity of the same series. During this life itself, too, one thought-moment conditions the next thought-moment. So from the Buddhist point of view, the question of life after death is not a great mystery, and a Buddhist is never worried about this problem."
32. T.R.V. Murti, *The Central Philosophy of Buddhism*, op. cit., 33.
33. John H. Hick, *Philosophy of Religion*, op. cit., 141.
34. K.N. Jayatilleke, *The Message of the Buddha*, op. cit., 165-6.
35. Ibid., 166.
36. John H. Hick, *Philosophy of Religion*, op. cit., 141. The word reincarnation has been substituted by the word rebirth in the passage for reasons mentioned earlier.
37. K.N. Jayatilleke, *The Message of the Buddha*, op. cit., 59.
38. Ibid., 134-5.
39. M. Hiriyanna, *Outlines of Indian Philosophy* (London: George Allen and Unwin, 1932), 219-20.
40. K.N. Jayatilleke, *The Message of the Buddha*, op. cit., 143-4.
41. Walpola Sri Rahula, *What the Buddha Taught*, op. cit., 23-5.
42. See J.B. Horner, "Buddhism: The Theravāda", in R.C. Zaehner, ed., *The Concise Encyclopedia of Living Faiths*, op. cit., 285.
43. See K.N. Jayatilleke *Early Buddhist Theories of Knowledge*, op. cit., 468-9.
44. Ibid., 404.
45. Ibid.
46. Ibid., 404-5, 460-3; Henry Clarke Warren, *Buddhism in Translations*, op. cit., 214-15, 228-31.
47. John H. Hick, *Philosophy of Religion*, op. cit., 142.
48. J.C. Jennings, *The Vedāntic Buddhism of the Buddha* (London: Oxford University Press, 1948).

206   *The Philosophy of Religion: A Buddhist Perspective*

49. Ibid., xxvii.
50. Ibid., xxv.
51. John H. Hick, *Philosophy of Religion*, 143.
52. Edward J. Thomas, *The History of Buddhist Thought*, op. cit., 110-11.
53. K.N. Jayatilleke, *The Message of the Buddha*, op. cit., 134-5.
54. Ibid.
55. James P. McDermott, 'Is there Group Karma in Theravāda Buddhism?', *Numen* 23:67-80.
56. K.N. Jayatilleke, *The Message of the Buddha*, op. cit., 141-2.
57. David J. Kaluphana, *Buddhist Philosophy: A Historical Analysis* (Honolulu: The University Press of Hawaii, 1976), 153-4.
58. John Hick, *Philosophy of Religion*, op. cit., 143.
59. See Edward Conze, *Buddhism: Its Essence and Development* (New York: Harper and Row, 1959), 169-70; also see T.R.V. Murti, *The Central Philosophy of Buddhism*, op. cit., 20-4.
60. K.N. Jayatilleke, *The Message of the Buddha*, op. cit., 147.
61. Ibid., 140.

Index